Contents

PART I

England: Southern Counties

PART 2

England: Western Counties
South Wales

The National Trust and The National Trust for Scotland

COMPLETE IN TEXT AND PICTURES

by

PETER RYAN

J. M. DENT & SONS LTD

LONDON

Made in Great Britain
at the
Aldine Press · Letchworth · Herts
for
J. M. DENT & SONS LTD
Aldine House · Bedford Street · London
First published 1969

SBN: 460 03869 9

PART 3

England: Midland Counties and East Anglia

PART 4

England: Northern Counties
North Wales
Northern Ireland
Isle of Man (Appendix)

PART 5

Scotland

Illustrations

BLACK-AND-WHITE ILLUSTRATIONS

England: Southern Counties

England: Western Counties
South Wales

England: Midland Counties and East Anglia

England: Northern Counties
North Wales
Northern Ireland

Scotland

COLOUR PLATES

MAPS

Author's Note

In pictures or text, or both, this book, in a single volume covering the whole of Britain or in five separate area parts, complete to the end of March 1969, deals with every property of the National Trust in some degree, from a full entry down to a listing by name. Each illustration is accompanied by a description of the property illustrated, and also, in some cases, by notes on other properties near to or associated with it. Thus the text accompanying an illustration of a bay or headland may include notes on several properties in the district from which the illustration is taken. Other properties, which are not illustrated and are not mentioned in the texts which accompany illustrations, are referred to in the appendix covering the relevant area.

When writing the texts which accompany the photographs, I set myself the following guidelines. I would say what in my opinion are the most notable things about the property; give a brief factual account of what the visitor sees there; and give a report on any aspects of its history or of the history of people associated with it that may help the visitor to understand the interest of the place.

I apologize to architects, botanists, art historians, archaeologists, ornithologists and the many other specialists whose studies can be enjoyably pursued on Trust property, if I have failed to bring forward what are to each the most significant points. Please treat these notes as a menu, which even in the best of restaurants can provide no more than an indication of what is available. To be proved and enjoyed, the pudding must be eaten.

Names italicized in the texts are of features not already referred to in the heading to the text, that are (1) illustrated in the accompanying pictures, or (2) illustrated elsewhere in that or another area part, or (3) referred to in the relevant appendix.

I am indebted to Mr Philip Sked, publicity officer of the National Trust for Scotland. He placed his knowledge of their properties at my disposal, and his enthusiasm and love for them encouraged and helped me in a most agreeable task. Although he has generously volunteered to accept blame for any deficiencies or errors in the Scottish part of the book, they should in fairness be charged to my Sassenach pen.

1969 PETER RYAN

Publisher's Note

The author and publishers are grateful to the National Trusts, the publishers and the photographers acknowledged, for their indispensable aid in the preparation of this book.

As an aid to visitors, an approximate location is given at the head of each entry and on the maps provided. It is assumed that the intending visitor will be equipped with his own road maps, also with the National Trust publications *National Trust Properties* and *The National Trust for Scotland Year Book*, which give more precise locations. The present book is intended not as a guide-book but as a complement to a guide-book.

Unless otherwise indicated with the description of the property, or unless it is obviously closed (e.g. where it is leased to a private body), the property is open to the public at certain seasons, days and times.

Using the Trust publications, *National Trust Properties Annual Opening Arrangements* and *The National Trust for Scotland Year Book*, intending visitors should always check opening times in advance, since they frequently change. This is the reason why opening times are not given in this book.

A small number of properties that appear in the appendices will not be found on the maps: they are recent accessions, obtained by the Trusts too late for inclusion in the maps. Approximate locations are given in the appendices.

Introduction

THE NATIONAL TRUST which operates in England, Wales and Northern Ireland has been in existence since 1895, and the National Trust for Scotland since 1931.

Both work on the same lines, and their object is to preserve places of historic interest or natural beauty. They are independent charities; that is to say, they are not under government control and have the legal status of charities. They are run by their own members, subject to the requirement, contained in the National Trust Acts, that half the members of their councils must be nominated by other bodies. The present lists of nominating bodies include museums, universities, the Royal Institute of British Architects, scientific societies, the County Councils Association and the Youth Hostels Association.

Service on the councils and on the committees which run the Trusts' affairs is voluntary. Each Trust employs a paid staff which deals with day-to-day property management and accounting, and includes specialists in matters with which the Trusts are much concerned: gardens, for example.

The Trusts are dependent financially on voluntary support which they receive in the form of donations, legacies and members' annual subscriptions, membership being open to all.

The National Trust was founded at a time when, although both the Society for the Protection of Ancient Buildings and the Commons Preservation Society had been established for a number of years, public interest in preservation was far less widespread than it is now. Also, there were, then, no Town and County Planning Acts as we have them today. Sir Robert Hunter, Octavia Hill and Canon Hardwicke Rawnsley, who were effectively the founders of the National Trust, had been active in campaigns to prevent unsuitable development, notably on Wimbledon Common and in the Lake District. They decided that the time had come to form a society which could act as a holding body, in appropriate cases, for buildings and lands which rank for permanent preservation. In framing the constitution of the society and defining its objects they were remarkably far-sighted. The National Trust was registered under the Companies Act in 1895 as a non-profit-making company. In 1907, when it had grown in public confidence to the extent that Parliament recognized the importance of its work by passing the National Trust Act of 1907, the constitution of the 1895 Society needed no amendment. Nor has it since been altered, subsequent legislation affecting the Trust having been designed to facilitate its work, not to amend its constitution or powers. When the National Trust for Scotland was incorporated by statute (in 1935) the Confirming Act followed closely the provisions of the National Trust Act of 1907.

The history of the Trust's work in furthering the aims so clearly established by its founders is a record of growth. This growth has not followed any recognizable pattern, but it has been a continuous process. The first acquisition—by the gift of $4\frac{1}{2}$ acres of cliff-land at Dinas Oleu above Barmouth in Merioneth, overlooking Cardigan Bay—was made in 1895. By 1967 the total acreage in the Trust's ownership had grown to nearly 400,000 acres (approximately the equivalent in area of the county of Hertfordshire). The figure for the National Trust for Scotland was 74,000 acres on the mainland. In the same year the list of buildings, gardens and other places which are opened to the public at stated times and on payment of an admission fee contained 257 entries, and that for the National Trust for Scotland, thirty-two.

Some properties have been acquired after public appeal for funds for their purchase. Gifts of property have been made not only by private individuals and some commercial and industrial firms, but also by local authorities, many of whom in addition help the Trusts by making grants towards the upkeep of Trust properties. Since 1946 there has been a further important factor in this growth. In that year the Treasury was empowered, when accepting buildings or lands in payment of death duty, to transfer them, with the Trust's agreement, to the ownership of one of the Trusts. Among the well-known places acquired by the Trusts in this way are Hardwick Hall, Brodick Castle and Brownsea Island.

Membership of the Trust, which in 1968 was 160,000 (that for the National Trust for Scotland being 37,000), has grown mainly in the years since 1945. Before the 1914–18 war and during the 1920's and 1930's, although numbers increased each year, the rate of increase was very small and total membership of the National Trust in 1939 was under 10,000.

As property owners the Trusts have one unique privilege—they are empowered by the National Trust Act of 1907 and later legislation to declare land inalienable. Such a declaration having been made, the property is protected against compulsory purchase by local authority or by a ministry; it can only be taken from either Trust by special will of Parliament.

From their beginnings the Trusts have regarded themselves as trustees for the nation, and for that reason adopted the name 'National Trust'. For that same reason the public have access to Trust properties; it is not restricted to Trust members. At many properties a charge is made for admission and the proceeds put towards upkeep. Access to open spaces is usually free but is always subject to the needs of farming, forestry and the protection of nature.

In deciding what should interest them, i.e. what constitutes 'historic interest or natural beauty', the Trusts take a very broad view. As this volume shows, the properties which they have accepted for protection include industrial monuments, nature reserves and prehistoric sites as well as historic buildings of interest and beautiful countryside.

RESTRICTIVE COVENANTS AND RESTRICTIVE AGREEMENTS

In addition to being a property owner, the National Trust has been given or has bought restrictive covenants over some properties which are not in its ownership. These covenants are legal agreements which provide, for example, that alterations to the exterior of a building may not be made without the Trust's consent. The covenant continues despite changes in ownership. Thus it affords a useful measure of protection for the appearance of the property under covenant.

There is, however, an important difference between the legal position of land owned by the Trust and that of land under covenant. Under the National Trust Act of 1907 the Trust has, as explained above, the power to declare its land inalienable. Land under covenant is not eligible for this unique protection.

There is also an important difference in regard to public access. Subject to the needs of farming, forestry and nature protection, there is access to all properties *owned* by the Trust. But covenants do not include any provision for access, and visitors are not usually admitted to covenanted land.

In Scotland the term 'restrictive covenant' is not used, but the term 'restrictive agreement' covers very similar arrangements. The National Trust for Scotland is party to a number of such agreements.

1

ENGLAND
Southern Counties

Key to Maps

SOUTHERN COUNTIES

1 Afton Down
2 Alfriston Priest's House
3 Ascott
4 Ashdown House
5 Ashridge Estate
6 Batemans
7 Bembridge Windmill
8 Berg Cottage
9 Blake's Wood
10 Boarstall Tower
11 Bodiam Castle
12 Borthwood Copse
13 Bosham
14 Bourne Mill
15 Bradenham
16 Bramber Castle
17 Bramshaw Commons
18 Buscot
19 Chantry Chapel, Buckingham
20 Chichester Harbour
21 Cissbury Ring
22 City Mill, Winchester
23 Claydon House
24 Coldrum Long Barrow
25 Coleshill
26 Compton Down
27 Coombe Hill
28 Crowlink
29 Danbury Common
30 Dedham
31 Ditchling Beacon
32 Drovers
33 Exceat Saltings
34 Fairlight
35 Falkland Memorial
36 Golden Hill, Harbledown
37 Gover Hill
38 Great Coxwell Tithe Barn
39 Hale Purlieu
40 Hamble River
41 Hanover Point
42 Hatfield Forest
43 Highdown Hill
44 Hightown Common
45 Hogback Wood
46 Hudnall Common
47 Hughenden Manor
48 Ivinghoe, Pitstone Windmill
49 King's Head, The, Aylesbury
50 Knole
51 Lake Meadow, Battle
52 Lamb House
53 Lardon Chase
54 Little Heath
55 Long Crendon Courthouse
56 Manor House, Princes Risborough
57 Morven
58 Mottisfont Abbey
59 Nap Wood
60 Newtimber Hill
61 Newtown
62 Newtown Common
63 Oldbury Hill
64 Old Soar Manor
65 One Tree Hill
66 Owletts
67 Pangbourne Meadow
68 Paycockes
69 Priory Cottages, Steventon
70 Rainham Hall
71 Rayleigh Mount
72 Royal Military Canal
73 Ruskin Reserve
74 St Boniface Down
75 St Catherine's Point
76 St Helen's Common
77 St John's Jerusalem
78 Sandham Memorial Chapel
79 Shaw's Corner
80 Shoreham Gap
81 Sissinghurst Castle
82 Slindon
83 Smallhythe Place
84 Sole Street
85 Sparsholt
86 Stockbridge Down
87 Stoneacre
88 Sullington Warren
89 Sun Inn, Saffron Walden
90 Telscombe
91 Tennyson Down
92 Uppark
93 Vyne, The
94 Waddesdon Manor
95 Warren Hill
96 Waterend Moor
97 West Wycombe Park and Village
98 Whiteleaf Fields
99 Wool House, Loose
100 Woolton Hill
101 Wrotham Water

LONDON AREA

1 Abinger Roughs
2 Ambarrow Hill
3 Black Down
4 Blackheath
5 Blewcoat School
6 Bookham Common
7 Box Hill
8 Brockham, The Big Field
9 Carlyle's House
10 Cedar House, Church Cobham
11 Chartwell
12 97–100 Cheyne Walk
13 Chiddingstone
14 Clandon Park
15 Claremont Woods
16 Cliveden
17 Cookham Dean Common
18 Cookham Moor
19 Coopers Hill
20 Crockham Grange Farms and Mariners Hill
21 Dorney Wood
22 Durford Heath
23 Eashing Bridges
24 Eastbury House
25 East Sheen Common
26 Fenton House
27 Finchampstead Ridges
28 Frensham
29 Gatton
30 George Inn, Southwark
31 Goswells, The, Windsor
32 Gray's Monument
33 Hackhurst Down
34 Hambledon
35 Ham House
36 Harewoods
37 Hatch Furlong
38 Hatchlands
39 Headley Heath
40 Hindhead
41 Holmwood Common
42 Hydon's Ball
43 Ide Hill
44 33 Kensington Square
45 Lavington Common
46 Leith Hill
47 Lodge Farm, Medmenham
48 Ludshott
49 Maidenhead Thicket
50 Marley
51 Morden Hall
52 Netley Park
53 North Town Moor
54 Nymans
55 Ockford Road, Godalming
56 Osterley Park
57 Park Downs
58 Parson's Marsh
59 Petts Wood
60 Petworth
61 Polesden Lacey
62 Quebec House
63 Queen Anne's Gate
64 Ranmore Common
65 Reigate
66 River Wey Navigation ($15\frac{1}{2}$ miles)
67 Roman Bath
68 Runnymede
69 Sandhills Common
70 Scord's Wood
71 Selborne
72 Selsdon Wood
73 Selsfield Common
74 Shalford Mill
75 Sheffield Park Gardens
76 Six Brothers Field
77 South Hawke
78 Squire's Mount
79 Stony Jump
80 Sutton House
81 Swan Barn Farm
82 Terwick
83 Thursley
84 Toys Hill and Emmetts
85 Wakehurst Place
86 Wandle
87 Watermeads
88 West Green House
89 West Humble Chapel
90 Widbrook Common
91 Winkworth Arboretum
92 Winter Hill
93 Witley
94 Woolbeding
95 Wych Cross

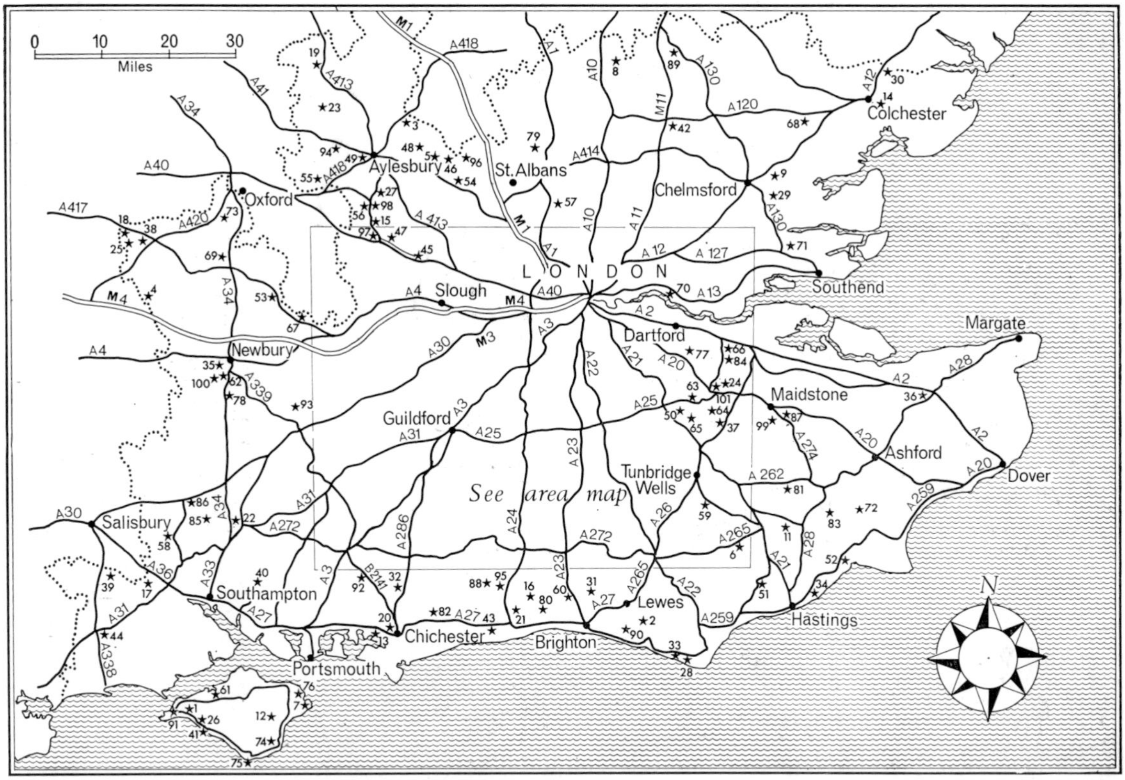
0 10 20 30
Miles
N
Oxford
Aylesbury
St. Albans
Chelmsford
Colchester
Southend
L O N D O N
Slough
Newbury
Dartford
Margate
Maidstone
Guildford
Ashford
Dover
Tunbridge Wells
See area map
Salisbury
Southampton
Chichester
Brighton
Lewes
Hastings
Portsmouth
M1
M4
M3
A418
A413
A41
A34
A40
A417
A420
A4
A1
A10
M11
A130
A120
A12
A414
A11
A127
A13
A2
A3
A22
A21
A20
A28
A25
A31
A30
A339
A23
A24
A26
A262
A274
A259
A272
A265
A286
A36
A33
A27
A338
B2141

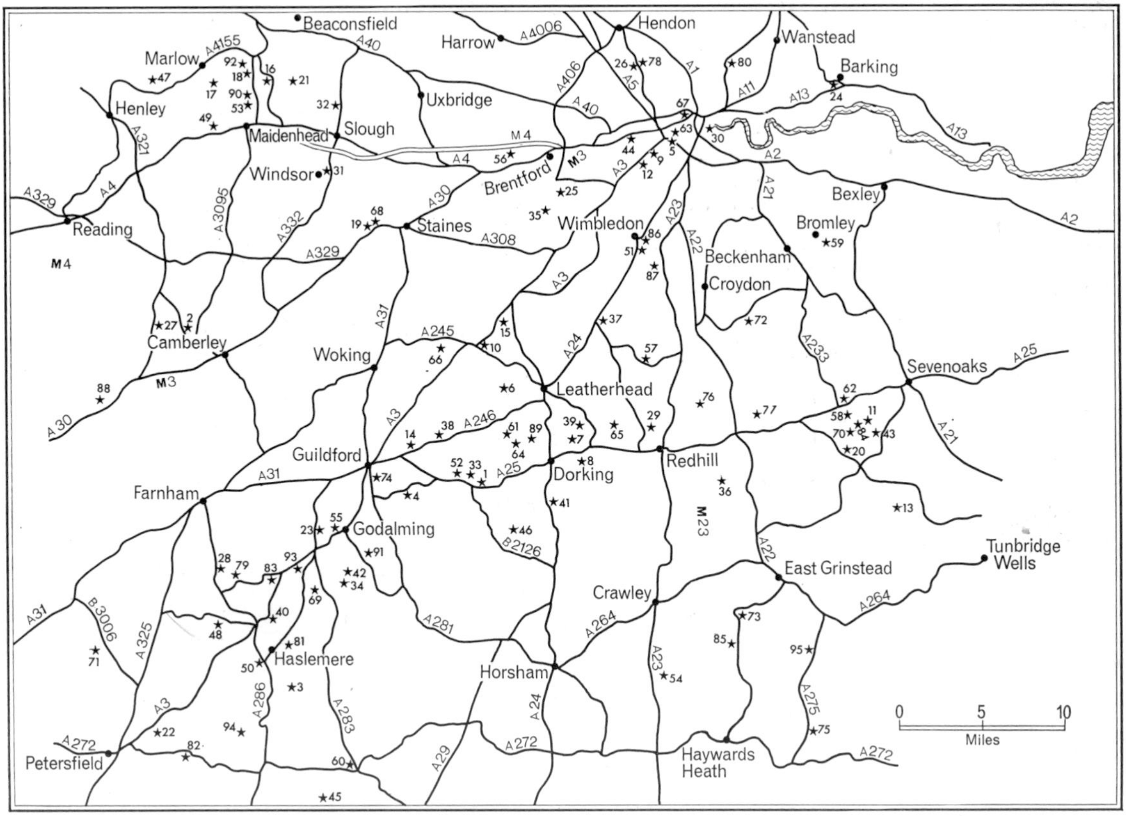
Beaconsfield
Harrow
Hendon
Wanstead
Barking
Marlow
Henley
Uxbridge
Maidenhead
Slough
Windsor
Brentford
Reading
Staines
Wimbledon
Bexley
Bromley
Beckenham
Croydon
Camberley
Woking
Leatherhead
Sevenoaks
Guildford
Dorking
Redhill
Farnham
Godalming
East Grinstead
Tunbridge Wells
Crawley
Haslemere
Horsham
Petersfield
Haywards Heath
0 5 10
Miles
M4
M3
M23
A4155
A40
A4006
A406
A5
A1
A11
A13
A2
A321
A4
A329
A3095
A332
A30
A308
A3
A23
A22
A21
A233
A25
A31
A245
A246
A24
B2126
A281
A264
A325
B3006
A286
A283
A29
A272
A275

Hatfield Forest, Essex: the lake.

Hatfield Forest

ESSEX

three miles east of Bishop's Stortford

The Trust's Hatfield Forest property, near Bishop's Stortford, measures roughly a mile by a mile and a half and covers just over a thousand acres of woodland and open chases (the wide grass rides between coppices). There is also a *lake* which provides boating and fishing.

Hatfield was a part of the Royal Forest of Essex from King Harold's time and during the Middle Ages was subject to the Forest Laws. A map of Essex made in 1594 shows Hallingbury and Hatfield Forests as one, and as about the same size as now. It was in private hands during the eighteenth and nineteenth centuries. The lake was made about 1760 and deep drains, which still exist, were laid in the forest in the 1850's. Some ornamental planting was carried out, as witness a group of horse chestnuts near the lake.

Although there was felling of older trees in the 1920's, there are some particularly fine old hornbeams and coppices of oak, hornbeam and other trees. Since 1961 the Trust has been able to adopt a programme of replanting. There are fallow deer, but the red deer were killed off during the 1914–18 war. The bird population includes nightingales and many green woodpeckers. The main part of the property was given to the Trust in 1924 by Mr E. North Buxton, gifts of additional land being made at later dates by his sons and by other donors.

Paycockes

ESSEX

in Coggeshall on the south side of West Street

Paycockes is a two-storey half-timbered house, a fine example of its period and much enriched inside with carving. It was built about 1500 and named for the man who had it built, John Paycocke. His will, which describes him as a butcher, also reveals that in addition to Paycockes he had two other houses, in one of which he himself lived. It has been suggested that in addition

Paycockes, Essex, looking from the dining-room to the hall.

to being a butcher, or grazier, he had prospered as a clothier—Coggeshall, Colchester and other neighbouring towns having at that time a flourishing cloth trade—and that he built Paycockes for one of his sons.

During the seventeenth century and until 1746 the house belonged to the Buxton family, and there is some evidence that they—who certainly were concerned with the cloth trade—may have set up looms in the back of the premises. Their descendant, Lord Noel-Buxton, bought the house back in 1904, made some necessary renovations and gave it to the Trust in 1924.

The house is now furnished with seventeenth- and sixteenth-century oak furniture from the Grigsby Collection from West Drayton. The table in the illustration above is part of this collection.

Ashridge Estate, Hertfordshire: a woodland view.

Ashridge Estate

HERTFORDSHIRE

three miles north of Berkhamsted between A 41 and B 489 and astride B 4586

This estate covers about six square miles along the main ridge of the Chiltern Hills. It includes five commons, woodlands (page 7) and the hills up to Ivinghoe Beacon (700 feet), where there is a direction dial to point out the landmarks. The Bridgewater Monument (172 steps), which was built in 1832 in memory of the canal-building Duke of Bridgewater, also provides a splendid viewpoint.

Pitstone Windmill (built 1627), close to the village of Ivinghoe on the road from Tring, is an historic landmark.

The Trust's Ashridge Committee produced an interesting leaflet for visitors in 1967, giving notes on natural history and other aspects of the estate.

Ashridge House itself and parts of the park do not belong to the Trust. The Trust's Ashridge property was acquired partly after public appeals in the 1920's and later, and partly by gifts from Dr G. M. Trevelyan, Miss S. R. Courtauld and other donors.

Shaw's Corner

AYOT ST LAWRENCE, HERTFORDSHIRE

at the south-west end of the village, three miles north-west of Welwyn

Shaw's Corner is a twentieth-century house and was known as The New Rectory until Shaw bought and renamed it in 1906. He lived there until his death in 1950 and his ashes were scattered in the garden. In addition to the *study*, illustrated opposite, he had another writing place in a summer-house in the garden. He gave the house to the Trust in 1944 and the contents were acquired under his will.

He was fifty when he went to Shaw's Corner. *Pygmalion* and *Saint Joan* are among the works which date from his time there. The study and summer-

Shaw's Corner, Ayot St Lawrence, Hertfordshire: George Bernard Shaw's study.

house are arranged exactly as he had them. In the hall are his hats and sticks and the piano which he used. In the drawing-room are bronzes by Rodin and Troubetskoy, including busts of Shaw.

Claydon House

BUCKINGHAMSHIRE

thirteen miles north-west of Aylesbury

Claydon House (pages 10 and 11) contains what the Trust's guide-book describes as 'the most astounding rococo suite of rooms in Great Britain'—and for good measure a quite exceptionally fine staircase.

It is part of what was intended to be a very much larger house. It is complete in itself, a delightful two-storey building of 1768 agreeably sited in its own parkland and having a great wealth of interest inside.

The builder was the second Lord Verney. He came of a family which had owned land in Claydon since the fifteenth century. One of his ancestors was

Claydon House, Buckinghamshire.

Edmund Verney, the Royalist standard-bearer killed in the battle of Edgehill. Another—his grandfather—made a fortune after the Restoration trading with eastern countries. It was this grandfather's fortune which enabled Lord Verney to embark on, among other things, some ambitious building projects.

He built a brick stable block to the east of the present house and altered the old manor-house (which was further altered in 1860) to the south of it. Then he got down to his major plan for a 250-foot west wing that included a ballroom and a hall with an observatory over it. He ran out of money before he had finished. Some of what he built was pulled down by his niece when she inherited his unfinished mansion. What remains is one block: the delightful house one sees today.

He employed as architect for the whole plan Thomas Robinson of Rokeby Hall, in Yorkshire. But from correspondence in the Claydon papers it seems that the surviving part of the building may have been designed by a carpenter-

Claydon House, Buckinghamshire: the north wall of the north hall.

contractor called Lightfoot, who certainly contributed much of the interior decoration. The correspondence reveals Lightfoot as extremely eccentric. Nothing else at all is known about him; but the wood carving at Claydon is of amazing delicacy and richness of detail. In addition to the carving there is beautiful plasterwork in the saloon, library and stairwell, most if not all of it by the famous stuccoist Joseph Rose. The staircase has an ironwork balustrade with a continuous garland of ears of corn so delicately wrought that they rustle when somebody walks upstairs. The stairs themselves are in mahogany with holly, ebony and ivory parquetry.

The house remained in the Verney family until they gave it to the Trust in 1956.

Florence Nightingale frequently stayed at Claydon after her sister married Sir Henry Verney in 1858, and many objects associated with her have been preserved in the house.

Cliveden

BUCKINGHAMSHIRE

three miles upstream from Maidenhead

Cliveden was built in 1850 by Sir Charles Barry for the Duke of Sutherland on the wide terraces which had been constructed for an earlier house. This earlier house was built in about 1670 by William Winde for the Duke of Buckingham, the Zimori of Dryden's *Absalom and Achitophel.* It was very seriously damaged by fire in 1795 and remained derelict for thirty years; it was then rebuilt, but in 1849 was again burned down.

In preparing his design for the impressive building in the classic style which stands there today, Barry fitted it most skilfully to the terraces of the earlier building. Mr Gladstone thought highly of Barry's design and recorded his approval in a sentence in Latin which the Duke of Sutherland had inscribed on the house. Rendered into English this reads: 'Built with the skill and devotion of Charles Barry.' The Clock Tower and Stable Block were built a little later, to designs of Henry Clutton. The interior is not as Barry intended it, having been altered in the 1870's and again in the 1890's when J. L. Pearson redesigned the hall and staircase.

The gardens, like the house, command sweeping views of the Thames below, and they are flanked by magnificent woodlands. Various owners have introduced buildings and statuary of beauty and interest. These include an octagonal temple (now a chapel) designed here for Lord Orkney in 1735 by Giacomo Leoni; and a balustrade brought from gardens in Rome by Lord Astor.

The then Cliveden House was let from 1739 to 1751 to Frederick Prince of Wales, father of George III, and during his tenancy Cliveden heard the first performance of *Rule, Britannia!* This was part of the music composed by Dr Arne for a *Masque of Alfred* which was given its first performance in the Rustic Theatre in the woods below the gardens.

The Cliveden estate was bought in 1893 by William Waldorf Astor—the first Viscount Astor. After the 1914–18 war his son, the second Viscount Astor, entertained British and foreign politicians, journalists and men of affairs at Cliveden—hence references in memoirs and histories of the 1930's to 'the Cliveden Set'. In 1942 he gave the property to the Trust with the expressed wish that, should it cease to be used as a private residence, it should be used 'as my wife and I have tried to use it, to bring about a better understanding between the English-speaking world and between various groups or sections of people of this and other countries'.

Cliveden, Buckinghamshire.

Waddesdon Manor, Buckinghamshire: the red drawing-room.

Waddesdon Manor, Buckinghamshire: the south front.

Waddesdon Manor

BUCKINGHAMSHIRE

six miles north-west of Aylesbury

The superb contents of Waddesdon come from three collections. Baron Ferdinand de Rothschild, who built the manor to house his collections, had a great knowledge of French eighteenth-century art. His sister Miss Alice de Rothschild lived there after him and added to the collections, particularly much of the Sèvres china. She left Waddesdon to her great-nephew, Mr James de Rothschild, who brought over from France the pictures, furniture and china which he inherited from his father Baron Edmond de Rothschild of Paris. When he died in 1957 he left Waddesdon and these three remarkable collections to the Trust.

They include paintings of the French eighteenth-century school, Dutch seventeenth-century paintings, and portraits by Reynolds and Gainsborough; Sèvres and Dresden china; Savonnerie carpets and some of the magnificent eighteenth-century French furniture made for the French royal palaces.

Baron Ferdinand had the house built between 1874 and 1889, employing a French architect to design a building in French Renaissance style. He also had the grounds laid out, planting the bare hillside with full-grown trees. He was active in local affairs, as J.P. and as Member of Parliament for the local constituency, and received many notable visitors at his new house, Queen Victoria, Lord Rosebery and de Maupassant among them.

Hughenden Manor

BUCKINGHAMSHIRE

one and a half miles north of High Wycombe

Hughenden was the house of Disraeli's choice and in large measure of his making. When he bought it in 1847 it was a very plain late Georgian house outside as well as in. He and Mrs Disraeli added the ornamental parapet and other decorative detail which gave the house, as he wrote, 'a new form and character'. It has not been altered since his time, except for the addition of the west wing. The interior is decorated and furnished in the style that they adopted and many of the rooms, including his *study*, contain the furniture which belonged to them.

Disraeli got great pleasure from Hughenden, which he used, from 1848 until his death in 1881, whenever parliamentary duties did not tie him to London. He enjoyed the surroundings as well as the house itself. Describing how he spent his time there he wrote: 'When I come down to Hughenden I pass the first week in sauntering about my park and examining all the trees, and then I saunter in the library and survey the books.'

There are many portraits of Disraeli's family, political colleagues and others with whom he was associated. There is a bronze of Queen Victoria which she presented to him and an inscribed copy of her *Leaves from the*

Hughenden Manor, Buckinghamshire: Disraeli's study.

Journal of Our Life in the Highlands, the publication which allowed him to say to her: 'We authors, ma'am.' The Queen also planted a tree in the grounds, but this has not survived. In the drawing-room, which has a delightful view of the garden and was in Disraeli's time the library, there is a charming miniature of his wife, Mary Anne Disraeli. A great many items connected with his career, which have been gathered there in recent years, are also on view in the house.

After Disraeli's death Hughenden was lived in first by a nephew and then by a niece, until the latter sold it in 1937 to Mr W. H. Abbey, who vested it in a special trust. It was given to the National Trust in 1947, the Disraelian Society contributing funds for decorating and adapting the house.

West Wycombe Park, Buckinghamshire: the south front.

West Wycombe Park, Buckinghamshire: the dining-room.

West Wycombe Park

BUCKINGHAMSHIRE

at the west end of West Wycombe

Wycombe sets one wondering—how many cooks is *too* many? No less than six people had a hand in the designing of the house and park: three architects, two landscape architects—and Sir Francis Dashwood, who owned the property. Yet so far from spoiling the broth they produced an unusual, handsome mansion set in one of the best of eighteenth-century landscaped parks.

It took them from around 1740 till about 1800 to transform an earlier house. Sir Francis Dashwood (later Lord le Despencer) was, among other things, a founder of the Dilettante Society, and from his travels and study well versed in architectural styles. At different times he commissioned Robert Adam and Nicolas Revett to produce designs, and the garden buildings and various parts of the house are attributable to them. He also employed John Donowell, who designed the *south front* (page 18), and Thomas Cook, who laid out the grounds about 1760. Twenty years after Francis Dashwood's death his successors employed Humphrey Repton to make improvements in the gardens.

The exterior of the house is on neo-classical lines with a double colonnade along the south front and porticoes at both the east and west sides of the house. The interior is handsomely decorated and has some splendid ceiling paintings. These are copies of pictures by Raphael and others which were executed by an artist brought by Sir Francis from Italy, Giuseppe Borgnis. There are beautiful marble fireplaces and a staircase of mahogany, satinwood and walnut. The contents of the house, which belong to the present Sir Francis Dashwood, include some fine eighteenth-century English furniture and portraits of his ancestor of the same name who built the house.

The house and grounds were given to the Trust in 1943 by the late Sir John Dashwood, who also gave (in 1935) Church Hill, which looks on to the grounds from the other side of West Wycombe village. It was on this hill that Francis Dashwood had built a mausoleum for members of the Hell Fire Club, of which he was a founder. The mausoleum remains. It is not Trust property. Most of *West Wycombe village* belongs to the Trust (illustration on page 21).

West Wycombe Village

BUCKINGHAMSHIRE

west of High Wycombe on A 40

At West Wycombe, as at *Lacock* (in Wiltshire), the Trust own virtually the whole village. The buildings are let as private dwellings or shops and are not open to visitors. The Trust as landlords are concerned to preserve the attractive appearance of the village, which has an agreeable mixture of

West Wycombe village, Buckinghamshire.

architectural styles from the fifteenth century onwards. The illustration above shows several rather conspicuous television aerials. The Trust aim at substituting for these one communal aerial inconspicuously sited outside the village, and an appeal was made in 1967 for help in doing this. A similar tidying-up operation carried out at Lacock had the additional advantage of improving reception.

Most of the cottages were bought and modernized by the Royal Society of Arts and sold to the Trust about 1930. Church Hill was given by Sir John Dashwood.

Ashdown House, Berkshire.

Ashdown House

BERKSHIRE

three and a half miles north of Lambourn on the west side of B 4000

Ashdown House, as the photograph on this page shows, is unusually tall and narrow for a country house. It is also unusual in being built of chalk—chalk blocks with stone quoins.

It was built about 1665 by the first Earl of Craven, but it is not known for certain who was his architect. Lord Craven dedicated it to James I's daughter Elizabeth, Queen of Bohemia. He devoted himself to her service throughout her life and spent much of his considerable wealth in supporting her interests. Unfortunately she did not live to see Ashdown finished.

The rooms are well proportioned, but very little of any original decoration remains. The staircase occupies about a quarter of the floor space in the house and rises to the attic. The roof is a good viewing point.

Ashdown was given to the Trust in 1956 by Cornelia, Countess of Craven.

Great Coxwell Tithe Barn

BERKSHIRE

about one and a half miles south-west of Faringdon

This is a stone-built barn with stone tiled roof that dates from the early thirteenth century. The Trust carried out extensive repairs in the 1960's. Professor Walter Horn of the University of California, in a long report on his study of the barn, quotes William Morris's description of it as 'the finest piece of architecture in England'. He also makes his own comment on the interior: that it displays 'one of the most magnificent medieval frames of roof supporting timber'. The barn is 152 feet long by 43 feet wide and at the ridge is 48 feet high.

It was acquired by the Trust in 1956 under the will of Mr E. E. Cook. The Trust owns nine other tithe barns distributed over Cornwall, Devon, Gloucestershire, Somerset, Wiltshire, Worcester and Yorkshire.

Great Coxwell Tithe Barn, Berkshire.

Osterley Park, Middlesex: the portico on the south front.

Osterley Park

MIDDLESEX

just north of Osterley station

Osterley is almost entirely the work of Robert Adam outside and in: from the great *portico* to the furniture in the rooms and the design of the elegant gilt brass door handles. But he did not start with an empty field. His task was to remodel an Elizabethan house, and he retained from this the corner towers with their cupolas.

Adam was at work on Osterley between 1766 and 1777. Horace

Osterley Park, Middlesex: the library.

Walpole visited the house twice, and his letters describe the principal rooms almost exactly as they are seen by today's visitor. The decoration of the rooms and the inset paintings are as Adam had them. Much of the furniture which he designed for the house is in place.

The Elizabethan house at Osterley was built for Sir Thomas Gresham about 1570. It was described as 'a faire and stately building of bricke', and Queen Elizabeth visited Sir Thomas there. Although it changed hands several times during the seventeenth century none of the various owners made any major alterations. In 1711 it was bought by Francis Child (of Child's Bank) and his grandsons employed Adam to design and decorate the present house. The property passed by marriage in 1804 to the Earl of Jersey. It was given to the Trust in 1949 by the ninth Earl of Jersey. The contents belong to the Victoria and Albert Museum, which manages the house for the Trust.

Carlyle's House, London: the drawing-room.

Carlyle's House

LONDON

24 Cheyne Row, Chelsea

Thomas and Jane Carlyle lived at 24 Cheyne Row from 1834 till her death in 1866; he continued to live there until he died in 1881. It is very fully supplied with their furniture, books, papers and personal relics. The house was given to the Trust in 1936 by the Carlyle's House Memorial Trust which had cared for it during the previous forty years. At the same time the Memorial Trust handed over Carlyle's birthplace, the *Arched House* at Ecclefechan, to the National Trust for Scotland.

24 Cheyne Row (numbered 5 in Carlyle's time) is a plain, commodious terrace house built in about 1708. Jane Carlyle wrote in a letter soon after moving in: 'We have got an excellent lodgement . . . quite to our humour . . . all wainscotted, carved and queer looking, roomy, substantial, commodious, with closets to satisfy any Bluebeard . . .' Carlyle found the small garden at the back, which he cultivated himself, an excellent place to smoke in.

But it seems not to have been quite commodious enough. In 1852 they took a new, repairing lease and enlarged the library or *drawing-room* on the first floor. And shortly after that they had constructed under Carlyle's own direction the attic study as a soundproof room at the top of the house, with double roof and doors and special ventilation. This was an improvement but not an unqualified success. It cut off the noise of the immediate neighbourhood—the pianos, dogs and parrots that he had found intolerable; but it brought in distant noises, such as train whistles.

Pianos and parrots notwithstanding, it was at 24 Cheyne Row that Carlyle did much of his writing. And during the years of their residence the Carlyles received in the house a great many of the distinguished literary figures of their time: Leigh Hunt, John Stuart Mill, Erasmus Darwin, Emerson, Charles Kingsley, and Tennyson, who once came at two p.m. and stayed till eleven.

Fenton House

LONDON

Hampstead, on the west side of The Grove

Fenton House (page 28) stands in about an acre and a half three hundred yards from Hampstead underground railway station. It is a square brick house with a steeply pitched roof, two storeys and an attic floor, which was built about 1693. Who built Fenton and who was his architect is not known. It changed hands and also names several times during the eighteenth century, being first Ostend House and then Clock House. Finally it became Fenton House after Mr F. I. Fenton, a Riga merchant who bought it in 1793.

The main rooms, which retain their original panelling, are now used to display two collections, one of porcelain and the other of keyboard musical

Fenton House, London.

instruments. The porcelain was collected by Lady Binning, who bought Fenton House in 1936 and left both house and collection to the Trust in her will. She died in 1952. Some fine Meissen Italian Comedy figures and groups form the feature of the collection. There is also a representative collection of English porcelain.

The musical instruments now at Fenton House were given to the Trust in 1937 by the late Major Benton Fletcher. There are harpsichords by the leading London and continental makers of the seventeenth and eighteenth centuries, and some spinets. They are in playing order and used by students, as Major Benton Fletcher intended that they should be when he made the collection.

Box Hill

SURREY

a mile north of Dorking

The Trust has been accumulating bits of Box Hill since 1914 when the late Mr L. Salomons, who then lived at Norbury Park near by, made a gift of 230 acres, including the summit. A number of other donors have made gifts at various dates since, and in 1967 the Trust owned 840 acres of the down and woodland of the hill and held protective covenants over another 280. (See note in Introduction.)

It is a fine picnic place and much used as such—so much used, in fact, that after a sunny week-end there may be several tons of litter for the Trust to clear. It is also of great interest to students of natural history, partly because it is an area of chalk down where the plant life is not affected by agricultural

Box Hill, Surrey.

activities. Juniper Hall (on the westward slope of the hill near Mickleham) is let to the Council for the Promotion of Field Studies.

There has been some speculation as to when box trees first grew on the hill. It was at least as early as 1655, which is the date of a note about them in John Evelyn's diary. The wooded western flank, where on the most steeply sloping parts only box and yew can maintain a hold, is exceptionally beautiful. Seventy acres of Mickleham Downs, adjoining the Box Hill property, were given by Lord Beaverbrook in 1938; and West Humble Chapel, a ruined twelfth-century chapel near Box Hill station, was given in the same year by Cubitt Estates.

Clandon Park

SURREY

at West Clandon, three miles east of Guildford

Clandon was built about 1730 in the Palladian style by the Venetian architect Leoni for the second Baron Onslow. It is constructed in red brick, the west front faced in stone. The only change made to the exterior since it was built was the addition in 1876 of a porch to the front door. The interior of the house, too, remains basically unaltered. The original magnificent plasterwork, for which Clandon is famous, decorates the ceilings of the two-storey *entrance hall* and of other rooms. Changes were made in the decoration of some of the rooms in the latter part of the eighteenth century, during the period when the Adam style was in fashion, gilt mirrors, cut-glass chandeliers and flock wallpapers being introduced.

The rooms contain fine eighteenth-century furniture, French and English, Mortlake tapestry and some interesting portraits. Among these are portraits of three members of the Onslow family who have been Speakers of the House of Commons. In the morning-room there is a seventeenth-century painting of the Elizabethan house which was pulled down when the present Clandon was built.

The Lord Onslow who employed Leoni to build the present house had married a wealthy heiress, the daughter of a well-known Jamaica family. It was her money which helped her husband to carry out his building plans. A full-length portrait of her hangs in the Palladio Room.

Clandon was given to the Trust in 1956 by the Countess of Iveagh, daughter of the fourth Earl of Onslow.

Clandon Park, Surrey: the entrance hall.

Ham House, Surrey: the door on the north front.

Ham House

SURREY

near Richmond, on the south bank of the Thames opposite Twickenham

Ham House shows us how a rich and influential couple planned, decorated and furnished a grand house in the Restoration period. Some of their decoration has become dulled with time; but it has not been altered and a great deal of their furniture remains. Only their much admired garden has not survived.

Ham House, Surrey: the staircase.

The property belonged in 1672 to Elizabeth, Countess of Dysart in her own right. In that year she married (her second marriage) John Maitland who, as Duke of Lauderdale, was the 'L' in Charles II's Cabal Ministry. They enlarged the relatively modest house of 1610, which she had inherited, by enclosing the space between the wings on the south side, thus doubling the depth of the central block, and building extensions to each side. On the exterior they expended much careful planning as well as a great deal of money. The rooms are surprisingly small but lavishly decorated and furnished. Chimney-pieces, ceilings, woodwork, and parquetry floors were designed and executed with an eye to their whole effect, and tapestry and other hangings and furniture chosen or made to accord with it. Much of this work was done by Dutch joiners and cabinet makers, and many of the decorative paintings were commissioned from foreign artists. There are a number of portraits in the house, including eight by the most fashionable portrait painter of the time, Sir Peter Lely.

When Elizabeth died Ham was inherited by Lionel Tollemache, Earl of Dysart, her son by her first marriage. It remained in the possession of the Tollemache family until 1948, when they gave the house to the Trust. At the same time Parliament bought the contents and put them in the care of the Victoria and Albert Museum, which now administers Ham on behalf of the Trust.

Hatchlands

SURREY

east of East Clandon, north of the Guildford–Leatherhead road

Hatchlands is a mid-Georgian house, and its interior decoration is among the earliest work known to have been done by Robert Adam after his return from Italy. His *drawings* for this, dated 1759 and entitled *Designs for Admiral the Hon. E. Boscawen*, are in the Soane Museum.

There is no record of who designed the building. But it is known from their correspondence that the admiral and his wife had been making plans for some years to build a house at Hatchlands. It had a very unusual internal plan. The main block was divided partly into two storeys, partly into three and partly into four, with staircases arranged to make this multiplicity of floors a workable proposition. Perhaps the late Mr Goodhart-Rendel was right when he described this plan in the Trust guide-book as '. . . a very ingenious piece of packing which I like to think was the work of the admiral himself, aided by his talented and adorable wife'. The admiral used his prize-money for building the house, and it is described in the epitaph his wife wrote as 'a seat he had just finished at the expense of the enemies of his country'. But the admiral did not live long to enjoy his new house, dying

Hatchlands, Surrey: Robert Adam's drawing for one of the chimney-pieces.

there of fever in 1761. His widow sold the property some years later and it changed hands again in the nineteenth century. Internal and external alterations have been made at various dates. Robert Adam's work remains in the drawing-room, library and morning-room.

Hatchlands was given to the Trust by the late Mr Goodhart-Rendel in 1945.

Headley Heath

SURREY

four miles south of Epsom and three and a half miles south-east of Leatherhead

Headley Heath is close to the north-east side of *Box Hill*, on the north downs; an open space of nearly five hundred acres with wide-ranging views. There are rides as well as footpaths. Here, as in many other parts of the country, the Trust get much welcome help in maintenance from volunteers. The photograph below was taken when Surrey Scouts and Rangers, in conjunction with the Council for Nature's Conservation Corps, were making a carefully planned assault on the birch scrub which has become a threat to the heath.

The heath was given to the Trust, with some wayside strips in Headley village and Heath Plantation, twenty-three acres to the south, between 1946 and 1952.

Headley Heath, Surrey: Surrey Scouts and Rangers clearing birch scrub.

Hindhead, Surrey: looking north from Gibbet Hill.

Hindhead

SURREY

twelve miles south-west of Guildford

Gibbet Hill, from which the photograph shown above was taken, is to the east of Hindhead village. It is nearly nine hundred feet high and a good viewpoint.

The Trust own a thousand acres of connected common, heath and woodland in this area east of Hindhead. The greater part of it was given in 1906 by the Hindhead Preservation Committee, other donors adding further land at later dates.

Polesden Lacey, Surrey: from the east.

Polesden Lacey

SURREY

three miles north-west of Dorking

Polesden Lacey stands in the beautiful surroundings of its own lawns, trees and garden with views of the fine woods on Ranmore.

From 1906 until she died in 1942 the house belonged to the Hon. Mrs Ronald Greville, who entertained many distinguished guests there. She completely redecorated the interior of the house and furnished it with fine collections of pictures and furniture, some of which she had inherited from

Polesden Lacey, Surrey: the drawing-room.

her father but most of which she collected herself while at Polesden. There is much variety in the style of decoration chosen for the different rooms. The *drawing-room* sparkles with a gilded ceiling brought from an Italian *palazzo*; the corridor around the central courtyard is panelled in Jacobean style; the library is neo-Grecian. The contents of the rooms, too, are varied. They include interesting pieces of French furniture of the Louis XV and Louis XVI periods, Flemish and Italian seventeenth-century chairs, Chippendale chairs, Dresden and Fürstenberg china, Chinese seventeenth- and eighteenth-century porcelain and pictures of English, Dutch and Italian schools. In sum, the gardens, house and collections at Polesden fulfil completely the wish that Mrs Greville expressed when she bequeathed the property to the Trust, namely that the grounds should be open to the public and that the house should become a museum and picture gallery.

The house which Mrs Greville acquired in 1906 had been built in

Runnymede, Surrey: the lily pond with Cooper's Hill in the background.

1824 on the site of an earlier house destroyed by fire. The main part of the south front, with its fine colonnade, remains as in 1824. But the entrance front was altered and given its cupola later in the century.

For a few years around 1800 Richard Brinsley Sheridan lived at Polesden in the house that was later burned. He made an important contribution to the charms of the present Polesden by completing and lengthening the long terraced walk from which there are views to Ranmore woods.

Runnymede

SURREY

half a mile above Runnymede Bridge, on the south side of A 308

At Runnymede the Trust own practically the whole of the meadows where Magna Carta was sealed, a hundred acres on *Cooper's Hill* slopes overlooking the meadows and the *lily pond* pictured opposite. The Kennedy Memorial is on land adjoining the Trust property.

The meadows were given by Lady Fairhaven and her sons in memory of her husband in 1931, and the Cooper's Hill Slopes by Egham Urban District Council in 1963.

The River Wey Navigation, Surrey: a view near Send.

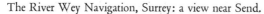

The River Wey Navigation

SURREY

from Guildford to Weybridge

This 15½-mile stretch of the Wey (page 41) was made navigable by Richard Weston (grandson of the builder of Sutton Place, on the river) and others, who opened it in 1653. The necessary cutting and deepening and the provision of twelve locks is said to have cost them £15,000. There were teething troubles. For one thing the builders failed to compensate all the landowners through whose property they cut, and the landowners retaliated by damaging locks and breaking down banks. Also, the operators quarrelled about sharing the profits. But these troubles were overcome and a substantial barge traffic was established. The owners were in trouble again during the eighteenth century, this time with the water mill owners, who interfered with barge traffic. But an agreement was finally achieved, and by 1831 more than 30,000 tons of freight were carried in one year from the Thames into the Wey. Loads included corn, coal, slate and hemp. For return trips there were flour, malt, hay, cheese, and gunpowder from Chilworth. Barge traffic continued to be quite substantial until the end of the First World War. Today this has virtually disappeared, but the navigation is much used by pleasure craft, which have many delightful stretches on which to ply.

The property was given to the Trust in 1964 by Mr Harry W. Stevens. His family had bought control in 1902 and he himself had been for twenty-four years sole proprietor from 1940.

Selborne

HAMPSHIRE

four miles south of Alton

About 240 acres of the common where Gilbert White made some of the observations for *The Natural History of Selborne* were given to the Trust by Magdalen College in 1932. In 1962 another donor gave part of the long and short lythes—the hanging beech woods overlooking Selborne stream.

Selborne, Hampshire.

The Vyne, Hampshire: the staircase.

The Vyne, Hampshire.

The Vyne

HAMPSHIRE

four miles north of Basingstoke

The Vyne has been happy in its architectural history. It was built, in a pleasing red brick, in the early sixteenth century (1500–20). In 1654 the northern side was given a *portico* (page 45), the first occasion on which such a feature was used on an English country house. About the middle of the eighteenth century the stone hall and staircase of the Tudor building were ingeniously replaced by a very fine classical *staircase* (page 44) and hall. The Tudor chapel, substantially unchanged, has carved stalls and quite exceptionally fine stained glass.

Eighteenth-century accounts and inventories of the contents of the house list much of the furniture which still remains in the principal rooms.

The Vyne was built by William Sandys, later Lord Sandys of the Vyne, who held important offices under Henry VIII. His descendant sold it in 1653 to Chaloner Chute, lawyer, M.P. and briefly in 1659 Speaker of the House of Commons. It remained in the possession of the Chute family until Sir Charles Chute, who died in 1956, bequeathed it to the Trust.

It was Chaloner Chute who added the portico, his architect being, almost certainly, John Webb. His grandson, John Chute, who made the eighteenth-century alterations to the interior, was his own architect.

Newtown

ISLE OF WIGHT

midway between Newport and Yarmouth

The Trust was helped in 1965 by local societies and individuals to buy the mooring and harbour rights in the estuary of the *Newtown river* (page 48), together with a mile of the Solent and Newtown and Shalfleet quays. In the days of active coastal trade Newtown was a busy port, but there is no commercial traffic today. It was also a 'rotten borough'. The *Old Town Hall* (page 48) contains copies of documents and of the mace of the borough.

Bembridge Windmill, Isle of Wight.

Bembridge Windmill

ISLE OF WIGHT

half a mile south of Bembridge

This is a stone tower mill built about 1700, last used in 1913 but still retaining most of its original, wooden machinery, which is of unique interest.

It is the last remaining windmill on the island.

It was given to the Trust in 1961, and restored by funds raised by the Trust's Isle of Wight Committee.

Newtown river,
Isle of Wight.

Newtown, Isle of Wight:
the Old Town Hall.

Alfriston Priest's House

SUSSEX

four miles north-east of Seaford just east of B 2108

The Alfriston priest's house was bought in 1896, and was the first building to be acquired by the Trust. (The first property acquired by the Trust was *Dinas Oleu*, a piece of cliff-land in Merionethshire above Barmouth with views over Cardigan Bay, which was given in 1895.)

The priest's house dates from about 1350. It is half-timbered and thatched.

Alfriston, Sussex: the priest's house.

Batemans

SUSSEX

half a mile south of Burwash on A 265

Batemans was more than 260 years old when Kipling came there on a house-hunting expedition and fell in love with the place at first sight. That was in 1902, and he lived there until he died in 1936. During those years he made his mark physically in the garden, where he planted the yew hedges, created the rose garden, for which he made a delightfully amateurish sketch plan, and made the pond with a concrete bottom for his children and their friends to bathe and boat in.

Inside the house he wrote in the first ten years of his residence *Traffics and Discoveries*, *Puck of Pook's Hill* and *Rewards and Fairies*. Pook's Hill can be seen from the garden, and it needs very little imagination indeed to see how much of the surroundings of Batemans went into the stories.

Mrs Kipling left the house to the Trust when she died in 1939, and with it the books, pictures and furniture which he had known there. His study is exactly as he left it. A number of his manuscripts, unpublished early verse, letters and first editions are displayed in another room.

In addition to the appeal of its Kipling associations, Batemans is of interest as a fine example of the country building of the first half of the seventeenth century. It is a stone-built house with brick chimneys and has a gable porch over the front door. It was built at a time when the Sussex iron industry was still flourishing, probably for the owner of the forge which then stood by the stream a quarter of a mile away.

Bodiam Castle

SUSSEX

three miles south of Hawkhurst

The walls and towers of Bodiam (page 52) remain almost intact; from across the moat it looks every inch a castle. It is a large rectangular building about 50 yards long and 40 yards wide with 40-foot-high walls and 60-foot-

Batemans, Sussex.

high towers. Within the six-foot-thick walls it is largely in ruins, but enough remains to show the layout of the hall, chapel, kitchens, staterooms and living quarters.

So far as is known it has never stood siege; but the building of it, in 1385, was no idle fancy. A few years earlier the French had sacked first Rye and then Winchelsea. The River Rother was navigable up to Bodiam and Sir Edward Dalyngrigge was given royal licence to fortify his manor house at

Bodiam Castle, Sussex.

Bodiam 'in defence of the adjacent countryside and for resistance against our enemies'. Sir Edward was an experienced soldier who had campaigned in Normandy and Brittany.

Bodiam has changed owners a number of times. It is referred to in accounts of the Wars of the Roses, Richard III issuing instructions for its seizure, but there is no evidence of what ensued. It was lived in during the fifteenth and sixteenth centuries. It may have received internal damage during the Civil War, but here again there is insufficient evidence to say clearly what happened.

Lord Curzon bought the castle in 1917, carried out repairs, made some excavations to explore its history and wrote a book about it. He left the castle to the Trust in his will.

Chichester Harbour

SUSSEX

The photograph reproduced on this page was taken on a spit of land on the east side of Chichester Harbour entrance. In 1966 the West Sussex County Council gave the Trust fifty acres of the sand dunes and twenty acres of sandy beach here—a mile-and-a-quarter stretch of the coast. This was a contribution to Enterprise Neptune, the Trust's coastal preservation appeal.

To the west of Chichester, at Bosham between the church and the creek, the Trust has an acre of land. Here Harold Godwinsson embarked for Normandy in 1064.

Chichester Harbour, Sussex: East Head, inner side of sandbank looking north.

Petworth House, Sussex: the west front.

Petworth House

SUSSEX

five and a half miles east of Midhurst

Petworth has a whole string of claims to fame—its pictures, its Grinling Gibbons carving, its long succession of splendid staterooms, its magnificent *west front* and the beautiful park which the west front overlooks.

The making of Petworth has been a long process. The Earls of Northumberland had a house here at least from the thirteenth century onwards and the chapel which they built for it, altered and finely decorated in the late seventeenth century, is still the chapel today.

Everything else was swept away about 1690 when the Duke of Somerset

Petworth House, Sussex: the Grinling Gibbons room.

(who had married a Percy heiress) did a grand rebuilding which included the present splendid west front.

The house is sited on the very edge of the park with its back to the town. On that side there are the stables, lodge and offices. From the park the west front is in view, and quite evidently a triumph of architectural design. The design is a combination of French and English elements. The architect is unknown, although his identity has been the subject of much ingenious speculation by writers on architectural history.

Some of the decoration of the interior was carried out when the house was built and some has been introduced since. Grinling Gibbons worked there while the house was building, putting into the *room* which is named after him a wealth of carving that is widely accepted as being the best he ever did. The staircase had to be repaired after a fire early in the eighteenth century, and is now decorated with murals which are attributed to Louis Laguerre. The North Gallery was made later in the eighteenth century by the third Lord Egremont to contain his almost unique collection of pictures and the antique sculptures acquired earlier in the century by his predecessors. The Square Dining-room was redecorated early in the nineteenth century and contains carving by Jonathan Ritson, a local man.

In this room are hung some Van Dyck portraits which were transferred from the older house. The Red Room is given over to the paintings of Turner, who was a frequent visitor to Petworth. In the Beauty Room are the contemporary portraits of beauties of the court of Queen Anne which gave the room its name.

The house and park were given to the Trust in 1947 by the third Lord Leconfield. The greater part of the pictures and furniture are on loan to the Trust from the Treasury.

Sheffield Park Gardens

SUSSEX

midway between East Grinstead and Lewes

Sheffield Park Gardens are not far from the busy motor roads which take Londoners to and from the south coast. But inside the gardens, beside the water or among the tall trees, the visitor is at all times immersed in a great peacefulness.

The layout is on the spacious eighteenth-century scale, covering nearly 100 acres and including five lakes. Basically this is the work of 'Capability' Brown, who designed a garden here in 1775 for the first Lord Sheffield. Brown's layout was extended and the trees and shrubs of the present garden planted between 1909 and 1934 by Mr Arthur G. Soames, who bought the estate in 1909.

When Mr Soames began his planting he was able to do so against a background of fine mature oaks and sweet chestnuts. He introduced a great variety of trees and shrubs, giving colour and interest to the gardens at all seasons. They reach their peak in October and November when maples and tupelo trees add brilliance to the autumn tints of the native trees and, for good measure, autumn gentians and cyclamens are in bloom. The lakes in spring reflect the azaleas and rhododendrons in flower and in summer carry water lilies.

The Trust bought Sheffield Park Gardens in 1954 with money from the Penfold and Gordon Daviot Funds, a public subscription and grants from local authorities. The house at Sheffield Park (built at the time when Brown laid out the gardens) does not belong to the Trust.

Sheffield Park Gardens, Sussex: the middle lake.

Nymans

SUSSEX

four and a half miles south of Crawley on the south-east edge of Handcross

The garden (page 58) at Nymans extends to about thirty acres and consists of a series of small, linked gardens which not only show a variety of plants but also are delightfully varied in design. The charm of the whole garden is enhanced by the beauty of the surrounding woodlands. Its seasons of special interest are spring and autumn, when its rare trees and shrubs make their displays.

Nymans, Sussex: in the walled garden.

Nymans was the creation of Mr Ludwig Messel, who bought the property in the 1880's, and his son, Lt-Col. L. C. R. Messel, who bequeathed it to the Trust when he died in 1954. Mr Messel's granddaughter, the Countess of Rosse, writing in the Trust's guide-book to the gardens, records his appreciation of the encouragement that he received in the early years from Miss Jekyll, Mr Robinson and others of the famous gardeners of the time.

Uppark

SUSSEX

five miles south of Petersfield

Uppark (page 60) was built about 1690 by one of the then most successful country house architects, William Talman. From the outside it is a charming Wren-style country house. But inside it is all eighteenth century, an unusually complete preservation of an eighteenth-century interior. The house was completely redecorated and refurnished in 1750–60 by people with taste and the money to indulge it. Their work has been very little touched since then, so that not only their furniture but even some of their fabrics and wall-papers remain in place.

Apart from the intrinsic charms of the house and its contents and their remarkable preservation, there are a number of points of interest in its associations. The builder of the house (Forde Lord Grey of Tankerton and later Earl of Tankerville) had an adventurous career, being involved in the Rye House Plot and in Monmouth's Rebellion, but contriving to finish up as Lord Privy Seal under William III. There is no record of his building activities except that he employed Talman as architect. But Sir Mathew Fetherstonhaugh, who bought the house in 1747, kept detailed accounts. These deal with the changes he and his wife made when transforming the interior in 1750–60, and identify furniture and china to be seen there today.

Sir Harry Fetherstonhaugh, who succeeded to the estate in 1774, brought the young Emma Hamilton from London to Uppark, and she lived there for a year in 1780–1. He entertained lavishly for a time. The Prince Regent was frequently a guest between 1785 and 1810, and in the Red Drawing-room there is the Carlton House writing-table which he gave to his host. About 1813 Sir Harry had a change of heart or perhaps wished to economize, and withdrew from society. At this point the Duke of Wellington appears briefly on the scene. It was proposed in 1816 that he should be

Uppark, Sussex.

presented with a country house and Uppark was among those offered for his consideration. But when he came to inspect the house and saw that it was up a steep hill, he decided that to live there would entail the expense of frequent replacements of carriage horses, and so withdrew.

During his retirement Sir Harry married his dairymaid. They had no children and after his death (in 1846 at the age of ninety-two) she lived on at Uppark with her sister, carefully preserving all the contents. Her sister lived there till 1895 and employed H. G. Wells's mother as housekeeper. Wells's boyhood recollections of Uppark are given in his autobiography.

Uppark was given to the Trust in 1954 by the late Admiral the Hon. Sir Herbert Meade-Fetherstonhaugh and his son. In the last forty years a great deal has been done to ensure the continued preservation of the fabrics by Lady Meade-Fetherstonhaugh. Her rediscovery of the value of the Saponaria plant has helped this work.

Telscombe, Sussex: looking across Telscombe village towards the sea.

Telscombe

SUSSEX

three miles north-west of Newhaven and one and a half miles north of Peacehaven

At Telscombe the Trust is owner of about sixty acres of agricultural land and of the manor-house and its garden. These properties were the gift of Mr Ernest Thornton-Smith in 1959.

In addition to this gift of property the Trust was also given, by the owners of neighbouring farms, protective covenants over about 800 acres of the agricultural land surrounding the village. (See note in Introduction.)

Woolbeding Common, Sussex: a view on the common looking towards Telegraph Hill.

Woolbeding Common

SUSSEX

two miles north-west of Midhurst

The 400-acre common at Woolbeding forms part of a thousand-acre estate which was accepted by the Treasury in payment of death duty and given to the Trust in 1958.

There is public access to some of the woodlands as well as to the common.

Chartwell, Kent: the view from Chartwell.

Chartwell

KENT

one and a half miles south of Westerham

The *view* from Chartwell was one of the things that made Winston Churchill love his house. It stands on the side of a hill with wide-ranging, far-searching views of the weald of Kent and the south downs. Churchill bought it in 1922 and made extensive alterations and additions. Except during the war years he lived there until his death. At Chartwell he wrote and painted, built the brick wall round his kitchen garden and enjoyed the company of his family and friends.

In 1946 a group of his friends bought the house and gave it to the Trust on the understanding that it would eventually be preserved as a memorial to him.

The main rooms today are furnished as they were in the 1930's, except for some pictures and objects which were added after the war. Two bedrooms have been converted for the display of trophies and objects presented to him and of some of his uniforms. His study is furnished and arranged as he last used it. A number of his paintings hang in the house. As the garden and grounds now receive very large numbers of visitors, it has not been practicable to maintain them precisely as they were arranged when Chartwell was a family home. But Lady Churchill's preferences in flowers and colours continue to be observed; and there remain unchanged the pool where Sir Winston fed the Golden Orfe, the island he made in the lake and the little brick cottage he built for his younger daughters.

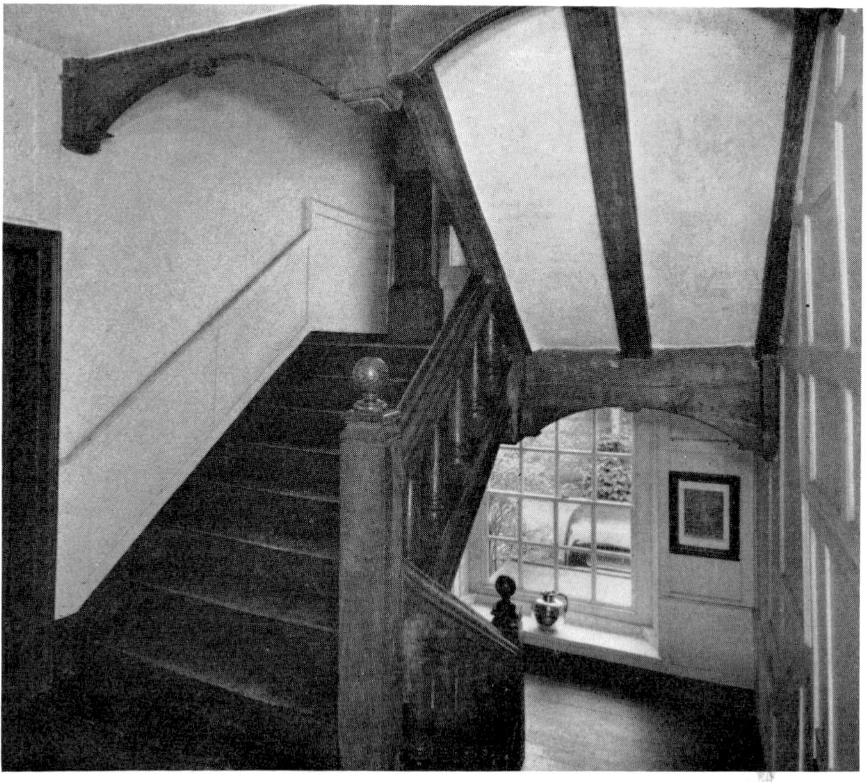

Quebec House, Kent: the seventeenth-century staircase.

Quebec House

KENT

Westerham

Quebec House (formerly named Spiers) stands at the foot of the hill in Westerham village, now bedevilled by the motor traffic of the A 25. It is a square-looking three-storey house of brick and Kent ragstone. Inside, the downstairs rooms are panelled and there is a pleasing seventeenth-century *staircase*. Since various early nineteenth-century alterations were done away with it must look, apart from the walls round the garden, almost exactly as it did when Colonel Edward Wolfe took a lease of it in 1726. The following year James Wolfe was born in the rectory close by, his mother having gone to stay there while her husband was on service. Spiers was James Wolfe's home until he was eleven, and his younger brother was born there.

Today Spiers has become Quebec House and is dedicated to the memory of General James Wolfe. In the principal rooms paintings, books, letters and objects connected with his career are displayed. These include portraits and busts of the general, his snuff-box and the travelling canteen which he had made for the Quebec campaign.

The house was given to the Trust in 1918 by Mrs J. B. Learmont of Montreal.

Knole

KENT

at the Tonbridge end of Sevenoaks

Knole (pages 66 and 67)—called 'a whole that is as unforgettable as it is indescribable'—was given its great size and its internal splendour by stages. There was first a medieval house, and its towers remain as reminder of the fact. Then in 1456 this building was enlarged and altered to be an archbishop's palace. Next Henry VIII, although Cranmer tried to persuade him that it was too small for the King's convenience, took it over and spent money on it without, it seems, ever actually living there. Queen Elizabeth

Knole, Kent.

gave it to Thomas Sackville, first Earl of Dorset, and in 1607 and the following years he made extensive alterations and additions, transforming the interior. He introduced the panelling and plasterwork in the Great Hall and other principal rooms, and installed the Great Staircase. At the same time he laid the foundations of the unique collection of Jacobean furniture which is one of the great distinctions of Knole to this day. The contents of

Knole, Kent: the spangled bedroom. The bed dates from James I's time, and its hangings were sewn with glittering metallic spangles.

the house, which belong to Lord Sackville, include seventeenth- and eighteenth-century rugs and tapestries and a large collection of family pictures, among them paintings by Van Dyck, Kneller, Lely and Reynolds.

Knole continued in the possession of the Sackville family (as the surrounding park still does) until 1946 when the house was given by the fourth Lord Sackville to the Trust.

St John's Jerusalem

KENT

three miles south of Dartford on the east side of A 225

St John's Jerusalem was, in the thirteenth century, one of the Commanderies of the Knights Hospitallers of the Order of St John of Jerusalem, and the chapel of their building survives. The rest was probably pulled down when the order was dissolved in 1540.

Abraham Hill, one of the founders of the Royal Society, bought the property in 1665 and lived there till 1721. He rebuilt the house substantially as it is now, though alterations were made in the second half of the eighteenth century when the rooms were decorated with plasterwork.

It was given to the Trust in 1943 by the late Sir Stephen Tallents and Lady Tallents.

Sissinghurst Castle

KENT

about eleven miles east of Tunbridge Wells and one and three-quarter miles north-east of Cranbrook

The very beautiful garden at Sissinghurst (page 70) was created by the late V. Sackville-West and her husband Sir Harold Nicolson. It is a post-1930 creation, not a restoration or embellishment of an earlier work. Her own description of their starting-point allows that there were Tudor brick walls to provide the anatomy of a garden, remains of a moat for quiet water and a top spit of quite good soil. But for the rest, the place had been in the market for some years, and the surroundings of the castle used as a dump for old bedsteads and tins which lay in a tangle of weeds.

The general plan of the garden was to make long walks leading to grouped trees or statues; to have small gardens opening off these walks; and in the planting of these small gardens to have an eye to the seasons so that a spring garden is followed by summer gardens, and they in turn by an autumn garden. V. Sackville-West was a poet and brought her gift of poetry to the

St John's Jerusalem, Kent.

making of the garden. To this she added a wide knowledge and understanding of horticulture.

The castle of Sissinghurst was not a medieval castle. There was a late fifteenth-century house, part of which was incorporated in a large, grand Elizabethan house. Queen Elizabeth stayed three days there in 1573. The Baker family who built it lost their fortune in the Civil War, and it suffered

Sissinghurst Castle, Kent: the rose garden from the top of the tower.

Smallhythe Place, Kent.

progressively from neglect. From 1756 to 1763 it was used to house French prisoners, Edward Gibbon in his capacity of officer in the Hampshire militia being for a while in charge of their guards. The prisoners were overcrowded and badly treated, and damaged the interior. In 1800 much of the dilapidated house was pulled down and the material taken for use elsewhere. After acquiring the property in 1930 the Nicolsons saved much of what little remained and added the minimum of lighting and plumbing needed to make the buildings habitable by modern standards.

Sissinghurst was given to the Trust by the Treasury in 1966, having been accepted in payment of death duty after Lady Nicolson's death.

Smallhythe Place

KENT

two miles south of Tenterden

Smallhythe Place (page 71) was given to the Trust in 1939 as a memorial to Ellen Terry. The donor was her daughter, Miss Edith Craig, who was also responsible for collecting and arranging the exhibits now to be seen there. These include, in addition to memorials of her mother, many books, pictures and souvenirs of other famous actors and actresses.

Ellen Terry bought Smallhythe Place in 1899 when she was fifty-two, and it was her country home until she died there in 1928. Most of the rooms, including her dining-room, have now been given over to the display of the theatrical exhibits, but her bedroom has been kept as she had it. Many of the dresses she wore on the stage are preserved in the house, with her make-up basket, her books and many of her working scripts.

When making the collection of mementoes of other famous players, Miss Craig cast a wide net to draw in not only English actors from David Garrick to John Gielgud but Duse, Bernhardt and others from continental countries.

Smallhythe Place is a fifteenth-century timbered building with a red tile roof. It was originally connected with a shipyard, but after the sea receded became a farm. The building has been altered at different times but has not lost its original character.

Miss Craig converted the sixteenth-century barn into a theatre where she presented a number of plays and an annual star matinée. This is now used by the recently formed Ellen Terry Theatre Club, which presents plays there for its members.

Appendix

Properties not illustrated

Properties which are not illustrated and are not referred to in the notes that accompany the illustrations are noted below. In addition to the properties which it owns there, the Trust holds Restrictive Covenants over 9,987 acres and thirty-two buildings in these counties. (See note in Introduction.)

ESSEX

Danbury and Lingwood Commons, five miles east of Chelmsford, 300 feet above sea level. They cover about 200 acres.

Rayleigh Mount, six miles north-west of Southend. A castle mound of eleventh- and twelfth-century castles. Excavations carried out 1959–61.

Colchester. Bourne Mill, a mile south of the town. A fishing lodge of 1591, later converted to be a mill. Let.

Saffron Walden. The Sun Inn. Part fifteenth century. Headquarters of Cromwell and Fairfax in 1647. Now a shop and office.

Rainham Hall, south of the church. Built about 1729. Let.

Eastbury House, Barking, a quarter of a mile south of Upney station. Manor house of 1572. Let to Barking Corporation.

Also land at Blakes Wood, five miles east of Chelmsford, 80 acres mainly hornbeam and chestnut coppice; and at Dedham, Bridges Farm.

HERTFORDSHIRE

Barkway, four miles south of Royston, a small thatched house, probably 1687, called Berg Cottage. Not open. Also land at Hudnall Common (east of Little Gaddesden); Waterend Moor (east of Frithsden); and Little Heath (east of Berkhamsted).

BUCKINGHAMSHIRE

Ascott, two miles south-west of Leighton Buzzard. The house contains a fine collection of pictures including works by Rubens and other masters, collections of French and Chippendale furniture, and oriental porcelain. Given by Mr and Mrs Anthony de Rothschild.

On Coombe Hill, 1½ miles west of Wendover, a viewpoint (852 feet), the highest in the Chilterns.

Dorney Wood, south-west of Burnham Beeches. The house called Dorney Wood and 250 acres. Given to the Trust during the 1939–45 war on the condition that it is an official residence for a minister of the Crown.

Buckingham, Chantry Chapel, on Market Hill. Fine Norman doorway; rest rebuilt 1475. Was a school. Now used for meetings.

Long Crendon Courthouse, two miles north of Thame. Fourteenth-century part used as child welfare centre.

Boarstall Tower, between Bicester and Thame. Fourteenth-century gate-house altered sixteenth and seventeenth centuries, rest of house demolished.

Princes Risborough, manor-house, near the church. Seventeenth century.

Aylesbury. The Kings Head. Part fifteenth century. Let as an inn.

Ivinghoe. Pitstone windmill, half a mile south of Ivinghoe. Seventeenth century. Not open.

Stoke Poges, Gray's Monument, designed by James Wyatt in 1799. East of the churchyard.

Bradenham, four miles north-west of High Wycombe, a thousand-acre estate of farms, woodland and most of the village. The manor-house (not open) was for a time the home of Isaac Disraeli.

Also land at Whiteleaf Fields north-east of Princes Risborough; at Hogback Wood, west of Beaconsfield station; and at Medmenham, a farm north of the church.

BERKSHIRE

The Buscot estate between Lechlade and Faringdon, 3,800 acres of farm, woodlands and the village. Buscot Park houses the Faringdon collection of works of art.

Coleshill. South of Buscot, 3,600 acres embracing the village, farm and woodlands.

In the Manor of Cookham and Maidenhead, Maidenhead Thicket, North Town Moor and land at Cock Marsh and Winter Hill, Cookham Dean Common, Cookham Moor and Widbrook Common.

Falkland Memorial, south-west of Newbury on the Andover road, a nineteenth-century memorial to the Viscount Falkland who fell in the battle of Newbury. Given in 1897 by a local society.

Steventon, four miles south of Abingdon: Priory cottages, former monastic buildings converted into two houses.

Also land at Cothill, north-west of Abingdon, Ruskin Reserve, a small marshy woodland let to the Nature Conservancy; at Lardon Chase, north of Streatley, downs; in Windsor, The Goswells, three acres off Thames

Street, bought in 1910 to preserve the view of the castle; land on Ambarrow Hill, south of Crowthorne station; at Finchhampstead Ridges, west of Crowthorne station, 70 acres of woodland and heather with views; and at Pangbourne, meadowland on the south of the Thames.

MIDDLESEX

Morven Park. A Victorian house and 30 acres half a mile north of Potters Bar, now an old people's home. Gardens open.

LONDON

Blewcoat School, 23 Caxton Street, Westminster. An elegant school building of 1709. Now the office of the Trust's Membership Department.

40, 42 and 44 Queen Anne's Gate. Part of a street of Queen Anne houses. Now the Trust's headquarters offices.

The George Inn, Southwark, on the east side of Borough High Street. Built in 1677, the only remaining galleried inn in London. Still an inn. Occasional performances of Shakespeare's plays.

Sutton House, Hackney, 2 and 4 Homerton High Street. Early sixteenth century with later panelling. Let.

97–100 Cheyne Walk. Built 1674 and called Lindsey House. Now made into two. Fine seventeenth-century exterior. Not open.

33 Kensington Square. Built 1695. Not open.

Squire's Mount. A group of late eighteenth-century buildings on the south-west side of Hampstead Heath. Not open.

'Roman' Bath, 5 Strand Lane. Remains of a bath restored in the seventeenth century. Its claim to be of Roman origin now considered very dubious.

SURREY

Bookham. Two and a half miles west of Leatherhead, 450 acres of Bookham and Banks Commons. Woods and many birds.

Church Cobham. Cedar House, fifteenth century, altered later. Let.

On the south side of Esher, Claremont Woods, formerly part of the grounds of Claremont House (not N.T.). Managed by Esher U.D.C.

Frensham Common astride the Hindhead to Farnham Road (A 287). 660 acres of heathland including most of Frensham Great Pond.

North-west of Hindhead, Stony Jump, one of the Devil's Jumps.

Winkworth Arboretum. Three miles south-east of Godalming on the east side of B 2130. A hillside planted with rare trees and shrubs, a lake below. Ninety-five acres. Maintained by the Surrey, Hambledon and Godalming Councils.

Hydon's Ball and Hydon Heath. Three miles south of Godalming. One hundred and twenty-five acres of heath and woodland, most of it bought in 1915 as a memorial to Octavia Hill, one of the founders of the Trust.

In Godalming in Ockford Road, cottages given in 1925 to show how old cottages could be modernized. Not open.

Godalming Navigation. Opened 1760; now used by pleasure craft only. Given by the Commissioners of the Navigation.

Eashing Bridges. A bridge over the Wey 1½ miles west of Godalming, said to date from King John's reign. Witley and Milford Commons (370 acres) south of Milford between A 3 and A 286.

Shalford Mill, an eighteenth-century water-mill 1½ miles south-east of Guildford, given by Ferguson's Gang, anonymous benefactors who also gave property in the Isle of Wight and elsewhere.

Between Guildford and Dorking, Ranmore Common, also land at Abinger Roughs, at Blackheath, south of Chilworth station, at Hackhurst Down, north of Gomshall, and at Netley Park, east of Shere. The house at Netley Park (late eighteenth century) is let to the Holiday Fellowship.

Leith Hill. In the Leith Hill area, between A 25, A 24 and A 29, properties amounting to about 900 acres of heath and wood including the top of Leith Hill, the highest point in the south-east of England.

Holmwood Common, much of it wooded, a mile south of Dorking, given by Surrey County Council, Dorking Urban and Dorking and Horley Rural District Councils.

Between Reigate and Banstead Heath, 150 acres of open down copse and beechwood, mainly acquired with money raised locally.

At Gatton, north-east of Reigate, 200 acres of which half is woodland. Woodlands given in 1952 by Sir Jeremiah Colman.

Harewoods, a 2,000-acre agricultural estate including Outwood Common, at Outwood, three miles south-east of Redhill.

Selsdon Wood, 200 acres three miles south-east of Croydon.

Wandle Properties. Grouped under this heading are several properties on and near the River Wandle which provide valuable open space in a densely populated area. Among them are Watermeads and Morden Hall, which is let to the London Borough of Merton, on the east of Morden Road (A 24) and Mordenhall Road (A 297). Its park and gardens extend to 124 acres.

Sandhills, Bletchingley. Four hundred acres south of the village. Given by Lord and Lady Munster.

Also land at Sandhills Common, west of Witley station; at Thursley by the church, a memorial to the poet John Freeman; at Hambledon, land near the church, also Glebe House (not open); at Swan Barn Farm on the east of Haslemere; at Brockham east of Dorking (The Big Field); at Hatch Furlong, Ewell; at Chaldon, between Caterham and Merstham, Six Brothers Field, used as a sports ground; at South Hawke one and a half miles south of Woldingham and at Hanging Wood, Tandridge, both viewpoints; and at Park Downs, a mile south-east of Banstead an open space of 70 acres overlooking the Chipstead valley.

HAMPSHIRE

Mottisfont Abbey. Four and a half miles north-west of Romsey. The house was made from a twelfth-century priory after the dissolution of the monasteries. Major changes made in the eighteenth century included fine decoration of several of the rooms. More recently Rex Whistler added *trompe-l'œil* paintings in the drawing-room. Given by Mrs Gilbert Russell in 1957.

Sandham Memorial Chapel. Four miles south of Newbury just north of Highclere station. Built as a war memorial to a relation by Mr and Mrs J. L. Behrend in 1927. Inside the walls are covered by fresco paintings by Stanley Spencer.

Winchester City Mill, at the foot of High Street. Eighteenth century. Let to the Youth Hostels Association.

West Green House, a mile west of Hartley Wintney. Early eighteenth century. Given by Sir Victor Sassoon.

Hale Purlieu and Millersford Plantation, three miles north-east of Fordingbridge, 500 acres of heath and woodland.

Bramshaw Commons. Ten miles west of Southampton on the edge of the New Forest, south of A 36. A series of commons amounting to 930 acres.

Ludshott, to the south and west of Hindhead, property at Bramshott Chase, Ludshott Common, Waggoner's Wells and Passfield Common embracing about 900 acres.

At Curbridge, a mile below Botley, 70 acres of wood and farmland on the Hamble River.

Stockbridge, 200 acres to the east and south of the village given in 1946 with the lordship of the manor by the Misses Rosalind and Beatrice Hill.

At Sparsholt, three miles west of Winchester, two thatched cottages, not open.

Also land at Hightown Common, two miles east of Ringwood; at Woolton Hill, three miles south-west of Newbury, wood and farm land, a nature reserve; and at Newtown Common, three miles south of Newbury, a small plot of land off the Whitchurch Road.

At St Helen's, north-west of Bembridge. Land on St Helen's Common and St Helen's Duver.

At Ventnor. Land on Littleton Down and on St Boniface Down, above Ventnor, including the highest point on the island.

In West Wight. Land on Afton Down three miles south of Yarmouth; also on Brook Down, at Brook Chine, on Compton Down and Hanover Point, at Shippard's Chine, on Tennyson Down and Sudmoor Point. Fine views, and at Brook Chine and Shippard's Chine access to the sea.

Borthwood Copse, two miles west of Sandown, 50 acres of wood and field on Pheasants Hill. On the south coast, 170 acres on St Catherine's Point.

Twenty-four acres on St Catherine's Down. Views. Bought with Enterprise Neptune funds.

SUSSEX

Wakehurst Place. One and a half miles north-west of Ardingly. The garden of 120 acres and 400 acres of woodlands have been leased by the Trust to the Ministry of Agriculture and are being administered by the Director of Kew Gardens. The house, originally built in the late sixteenth century, has been very extensively altered. The property was bequeathed to the Trust by Sir Henry Price.

At Rye, Lamb House in West Street. A Georgian house which was the home of Henry James from 1898 to 1916. Given by his nephew's widow to be preserved 'as an enduring symbol of the ties that unite the British and American peoples'.

Black Down. One mile south-east of Haslemere and partly in Surrey. Six hundred acres of woods and down including the highest point in Sussex (918 feet).

Marley. About two miles south of Haslemere, land at Marley Common; also a viewpoint on Marley Heights to the south; and Shottermill Ponds, two hammer ponds.

Slindon Estate. Six miles north of Bognor Regis. A 3,500-acre agricultural estate stretching to the south downs. Access to the park and, by footpath, to other parts.

Drovers Estate. A 1,000-acre agricultural estate astride the Midhurst–Chichester road.

Chichester Harbour. Land at East Head, West Wittering, given by the West Sussex County Council.

Cissbury Ring, three miles north of Worthing. Views and the site of an Iron Age B hill fort.

Highdown Hill, three miles north-west of Worthing. Site of Bronze Age, Iron Age A1, Roman and Saxon occupation.

Warren Hill, eight miles north of Worthing, 250 acres of wood, farmland and Washington Common.

Bramber Castle, south-east of Steyning. Remains of Norman castle.

Shoreham Gap, 600 acres of down two miles north-east of Shoreham.

South of Frant, Nap Wood, a nature reserve let to the Sussex Naturalists' Trust.

Newtimber Hill, 240 acres of down and woodland five miles north-west of Brighton.

Crowlink, Michel Dene and Went Hill. Five miles west of Eastbourne, just south of Friston. Six hundred acres of cliff, down and farmland including part of the Seven Sisters. Also 58 acres to the east of Birling Gap forming the cliff approaches to Beachy Head.

Exceat Saltings, a small piece of land overlooking the Saltings south of Exceat Bridge, two miles east of Seaford.

Fairlight, 230 acres of cliff and farmland 4½ miles east of Hastings. Also land at Terwick, east of Rogate; at Sullington Warren, eight miles north of Worthing, a viewpoint; at Selsfield Common, four miles south-west of East Grinstead; on Lavington Common, west of Petworth; on Durford Heath, north-east of Petersfield; at Battle; at Ditchling Beacon, six miles north of Brighton, a viewpoint; at Wych Cross south of Forest Row.

KENT

At Appledore the Royal Military Canal, the 3½-mile stretch from Appledore to Warehorne.

At Petts Wood between Chislehurst and Orpington on the west of A 208. About 90 acres of wood and heath, the bulk of which was bought by public subscription in 1927 as a memorial to William Willett, founder of Summer Time. A further 230 acres of farm and woodland adjoining this property on the west, at Hawkwood, was given in 1957. In the 1930's two strips of land at Chislehurst were acquired as part of a scheme for preserving Chislehurst Common.

At Cobham, at the west end of the village, Owletts, a red brick house of Charles II's reign. Given in 1938 with cottages and orchards by Sir Herbert Baker.

Old Soar Manor. Two miles south of Borough Green. Solar block of a late thirteenth-century dwelling. Under guardianship of the Ministry of Works.

Otham. Three miles south-east of Maidstone. A late fifteenth-century yeoman's house called Stoneacre.

In the Westerham, Sevenoaks area, land with views on Ide Hill, Mariners Hill, One Tree Hill and Toys Hill.

Chiddingstone. In the village, four miles east of Edenbridge, a row of sixteenth- and seventeenth-century houses and the Castle Inn.

Coldrum Long Barrow between the Pilgrim's Way and the Folkestone Road, one mile east of Trottiscliffe, probably of Neolithic date.

Emmetts, two miles south of Brasted, 100 acres of farm and woodland including a 4-acre shrub garden.

A viewpoint on Gover Hill, three miles south-east of Ightham.

At Golden Hill, Harbledown, a small piece of land given as a playground for children.

At Loose, three miles south of Maidstone, Wool House, a fifteenth-century half-timbered house, not open.

On Oldbury Hill three miles south-west of Wrotham, 150 acres on which is an Iron Age hill fort refortified by the Belgae.

At Sole Street, a mile south-west of Cobham, Yeoman's House. Of timber construction. Not open.

The Leas, St Margaret's Bay. Ten acres of cliff, immediately in front of the Dover Patrol Memorial. Given by St Margaret's-at-Cliffe Parish Council.

Pegwell Bay, between Ramsgate and Sandwich. One hundred and fifty acres of saltings and mud flats bought from Enterprise Neptune funds. Part of a scheme for the protection of Pegwell Bay drawn up in consultation with the Kent Trust for Nature Preservation.

Also farmland at the foot of the downs at Wrotham Water one and a half miles east of Wrotham; woodland near Brasted at Scords Wood and Parsons Marsh about twelve miles to the south of the village; and Crockham Grange Farms, two miles south of Westerham, given to preserve the view from Mariners Hill.

Stourhead Park, Wiltshire: the Temple of Flora, and the lake in autumn.

2

ENGLAND
Western Counties

SOUTH WALES

Great Chalfield Manor, Wiltshire.

Great Chalfield Manor

WILTSHIRE

two and a half miles north-east of Bradford-on-Avon

Great Chalfield was built around 1480. It has never been altered or enlarged, most of the original building has survived and it provides a good impression of late Gothic domestic architecture. It was built by Thomas Tropnell, a local landowner who managed to improve his fortunes during the Wars of the Roses.

The property has changed hands by inheritance and purchase a number of times. Like other buildings of this style, it went completely out of fashion for a long period. But in 1840, before it had become too dilapidated, detailed plans for restoration were made for the then owner, who died before he could carry them out. But these plans, made by a pupil of Pugin, were used when restoration was carried out in 1910. The property was given to the Trust in 1943 by Major R. Fuller.

Avebury

WILTSHIRE

six miles west of Marlborough a mile north of A 4

Around 1800 B.C. Avebury (page 87) was a religious or ritual centre, visited by people from all over Britain and very probably from Europe. It is one of the most important Early Bronze Age monuments in Europe.

A ditch and outer bank enclosed an area five hundred yards in diameter. In this were erected over a hundred local stones to make an outer circle and two inner circles. From the south-east entrance to the circle an avenue of stones stretched for a mile and a half towards the south-east.

In the last three hundred-odd years excavations have been made. Finds from these excavations are in a museum near by. This and the circles are under the guardianship of the Ministry of Works.

Earlier generations have viewed the circles quite differently. Some stones were buried during the fourteenth century, apparently because the Church wished to put a stop to surviving heathen rituals there. The eighteenth century had a more utilitarian view and broke up some of the stones to build part of the village of Avebury.

The property was bought by the Trust in 1943 with the help of the Pilgrim Trust and Mr I. D. Margary. It includes, in addition to Avebury, Windmill Hill, a mile and a half to the north-west, where there are Early–Middle Bronze Age barrows.

The Trust also owns properties of archaeological interest in other parts of Wiltshire: Figsbury Ring, an Iron Age hill-fort four miles north-east of Salisbury, bought in 1930; Cley Hill, with an Iron Age hill-fort three miles west of Warminster, given by the Marquess of Bath in 1954; and White Barrow, a Neolithic earthen long barrow south of Tilshead (bought in 1909).

Opposite: Avebury, Wiltshire: part of the Great Stone Circle, looking south across the ditch to the outer bank.

Lacock Abbey, Wiltshire: the west front.

Lacock Abbey

WILTSHIRE

three miles south of Chippenham

Lacock Abbey presents four architectural styles. Parts of the thirteenth-century nunnery remain. These were preserved when other parts were converted to a Tudor dwelling-house in 1550. Alterations were made in 1754 in a Gothic style. Further changes were made in 1828. The different parts of the abbey—each of which is an interesting example of its own style and period—combine today to make the whole building one of romantic beauty.

The Tudor house was built by Sir William Sharington. He had travelled in Italy, and in his Lacock building introduced the new Italian architecture to England. For the eighteenth-century additions, Sanderson Miller was the architect.

Sir William Sharington died childless, and the abbey was inherited by his niece Mrs John Talbot. It remained in the possession of the Talbot family until it was given to the Trust, together with nearly the whole of Lacock village, by Miss Matilda Talbot in 1957. Fox Talbot, pioneer of photography, made his experiments at Lacock.

Key to Map

WESTERN COUNTIES & SOUTH WALES

1 Antony House
2 Arlington Court
Arlington Row: *see* Bibury
3 Ashleworth Tithe Barn
4 Avebury
5 Barrington Court
6 Bath
7 Berrington Hall
8 Betws Newydd
9 Bibury (Arlington Row)
10 Bigbury-on-Sea
11 Bishopston Valley
12 Blackdown Hills
13 Blaise Hamlet
Bodmin Moor: *see* Rough Tor
14 Bodrugans Leap
Bolt Head: *see* Salcombe
15 Boscastle Harbour
16 Bradley Manor
17 Bradnor Hill
18 Branscombe
19 Brean Down
20 Brecon Beacons
21 Breinton
22 Brilley
23 Bristol
24 Brockhampton
25 Brownsea Island
26 Bruton Dovecote
27 Buckland Abbey
28 Buzzards
29 Camel Estuary
30 Cerne Giant
31 Chapel Porth
32 Cheddar Cliffs
33 Chedworth Roman Villa
34 Chipping Campden Market Hall
35 Cilgerran Castle
36 Clevedon Court
37 Cleyhill
38 Clouds Hill
39 Clovelly
40 Coleridge Cottage
41 Combe Park
42 Combe Wood, Combe Raleigh
43 Compton Castle
44 Cornish engine (Rotative winding engine, Pool)
45 Cotehele House
46 Crackington Haven
47 Creech
48 Crickley Hill
49 Croft Castle
50 Crook Hill
51 Cubert
52 Dinton (Phillipps House)
53 The Dodman
54 Dolaucothi
Downhouse Farm: *see* Golden Cap Estate
55 Drakes Island
56 Dunkery Beacon (Selworthy)
57 Dyrham Park
58 East Titchberry Farm
59 Ebbor Gorge
60 Edens Hill
61 Erth Barton
62 Failand
63 Fal Estuary
64 Figsbury Ring
65 Flat Point
66 Fowey
67 Frocester Hill
68 The Gannel
69 Glastonbury Tor
70 Godrevy
71 Golden Cap Estate (Downhouse Farm)
72 Goodameavy
73 Great Chalfield Manor
74 Grey Wethers
75 Gunwalloe
76 Hardy Monument
77 Hardy's Cottage
78 Hailes Abbey
79 Heddon's Mouth (Trentishoe)
80 Helford River
81 Hembury
82 Hemmick Beach
Hen Tor: *see* Willings Walls Warrens
83 Henrhyd Falls
84 Hidcote Manor Garden
85 Holne Woods
86 Holnicote
87 Holt, The Courts
88 Hor Point
89 Horton Court
90 Kete
91 Killerton Garden
92 The Kymin
93 Lacock
94 Lamberts Castle Hill
95 Lamledra Farm
96 Lanhydrock House
Lantivet Bay: *see* Fowey, Polperro
97 Lanyon Quoit
98 Launceston
99 Lesceave Cliff
100 Lewesdon Hill
101 Little Haldon
102 Little Solsbury Hill
103 Llanborth Farm
104 Lochtyn
105 Lizard Downs
106 Lowland Point
107 Lydford Gorge
108 Lydstep Headland
109 Lympstone
110 Lynmouth
111 Lytes Cary
112 Manorbier
Marloes Beach: *see* St Bride's Bay
113 Marsland Mouth
114 May Hill
115 Mayon and Trevescan
116 Monks Steps
117 Montacute
118 Moretonhampstead Almshouses
119 Morte Point and Morte Bay
120 Morwenstow
121 Muchelney
122 Mullion
123 Mwnt
124 Nare Head
125 Newark Park
126 Notthill
127 Old Blundells School
128 Orcombe and Prattshayes
129 Painswick
130 Paviland Cliff
131 Paxtons Tower
132 Penard (Three Cliff Bay)
133 Penberth
134 Pencarrow
135 Pendarves Point
136 Pendower Beach
137 Pengethly Park
138 Pentire Head
139 Pepperbox Hill
Phillipps House: *see* Dinton
140 Pitton Cliff
141 Polperro
142 Ponterwyd
143 Poor's Acre
144 Port Gaverne
145 Porthminster
146 Portloe
147 The Quantocks
148 Rockbeare Hill
149 Rosemergy
Rotative winding engine, Pool: *see* Cornish engine
150 Rough Tor (Bodmin Moor)
151 St Agnes
152 St Anthony in Roseland
153 St Bride's Bay (Marloes Beach)
154 St David's Head
155 St Michael's Mount
156 Salcombe
157 Salisbury
158 Saltram
159 Sedgemoor
Selworthy: *see* Dunkery Beacon
160 Sharrow Point
161 Shute Barton
162 Sidmouth
163 Skenfrith Castle
164 Skirrid Fawr
165 Snowshill Manor
166 Southdown Farm
167 Stoke-sub-Hamdon Priory
168 Stonehenge Down
169 Stourhead
170 Stroud
171 Sugar Loaf, The
172 Tenby
Three Cliff Bay: *see* Penard
173 Thurba Head
174 Tintagel (Trebarwith Strand)
175 Tintinhull House

176 Tolpuddle
Trebarwith Strand: *see* Tintagel
177 Treen Cliff
178 Tregoning Hill
179 Trelis
180 Trenc
181 Treng
Trent
Hedd

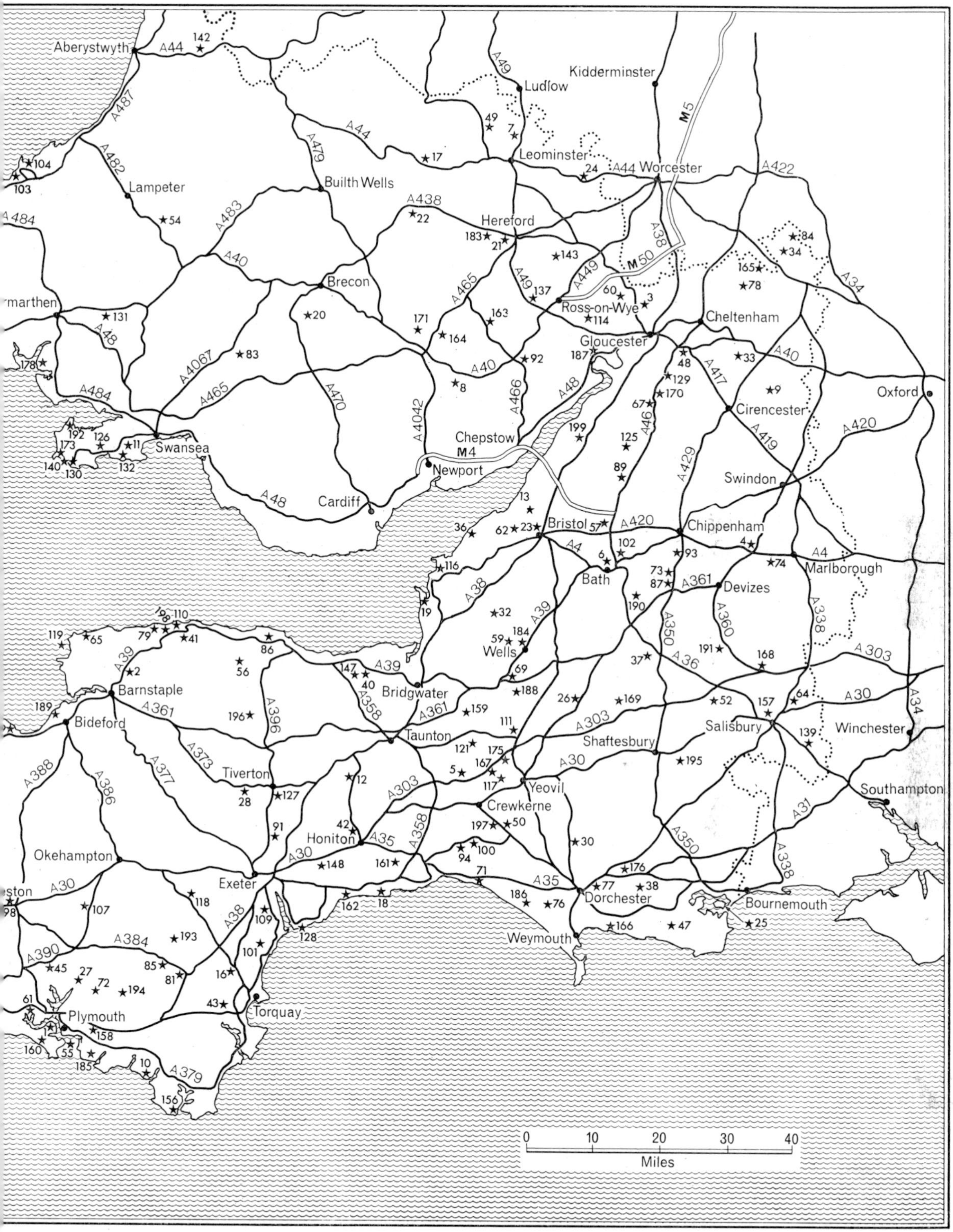

182 Trerice
183 The Weir, Swainshill
184 Wells
185 Wembury Bay
186 West Bexington
187 Westbury Court Garden
188 West Pennard Court Barn
189 Westward Ho!
190 Westwood Manor
191 White Barrow
192 Whiteford Burrows
193 Widdecombe-in-the-Moor Willings Walls Warrens (Hen Tor)
194 Win Green Hill
195 Winsford Hill
196 Winyard's Gap
197 Woody Bay
198 Wotton-under-Edge
199 Zennor

Lacock Village

WILTSHIRE

three miles south of Chippenham

When Miss Matilda Talbot gave *Lacock Abbey* to the Trust in 1944 she gave also the greater part of the village of Lacock. As landlord, the Trust is concerned to preserve the appearance of the village. But the buildings are let as private dwellings or as shops and the like, and are not open to visitors.

Every century from the thirteenth to the nineteenth has made contributions to the building of the village, each in its own characteristic architectural style. But there is here a neighbourliness about their contributions, and the sum of their efforts is a very beautiful village. As well as a diversity of architecture, there is a diversity of building materials to be seen. Some of the buildings are half-timbered with brick or other infilling, others are in the local Corsham stone, and some are brick built.

On the edge of the village is one of its finest buildings, a fourteenth-century tithe barn.

The village has not been dependent solely on agriculture. From the fourteenth century until the Industrial Revolution, while the west country wool trade flourished, Lacock and other villages had a prosperous cottage industry.

Phillipps House, Dinton

WILTSHIRE

nine miles west of Salisbury

The architect of Phillipps House (page 93) was James Wyattville, known as the architect who gave Windsor Castle its Gothic look. But at Dinton he was starting from scratch and designing a new house for a site which had been cleared of its earlier building. He produced a design in the neo-Grecian style, a two-storey building with a portico to set off its main frontage. The staircase-hall and some of the principal rooms are good examples of the style in which he built.

Lacock Village, Wiltshire.

The house was built between 1805 and 1815 for the Wyndham family, who owned the property from 1689 until 1916. It was given to the Trust with two hundred acres of parkland in 1943 by Mr Bertram Phillipps, who bought it in 1916. It is now let to the Y.W.C.A. as a holiday home.

In addition to Phillipps House the Trust owns Hyde's House, an early eighteenth-century house near the church in Dinton. It is not open. Also, a quarter of a mile east of the church, a stone Tudor house, and a seventeenth-century building called Lawes Cottage, once the home of the composer William Lawes.

Stourhead

WILTSHIRE

at Stourton, three miles north-west of Mere

Stourhead gardens have been called 'Henry Hoare's Paradise' after the Henry Hoare who created them, a grandson of the founder of Hoare's bank. For his *gardens* (page 95), one of the achievements of eighteenth-century garden design, he planted a valley with trees, dammed a stream to make lakes and built temples and a grotto. In the design for the garden he was trying to transfer into an actual garden landscape the picturesque scenery shown in paintings by French landscape painters. He was before his time in abandoning the formal style of layout, which was still popular, for the more naturalistic style which is today associated particularly with 'Capability' Brown. (Hoare made Stourhead gardens in 1740–50 and Brown did not set up as a consultant till 1749.) It is not known whether Hoare employed any architect or designer. According to his grandson, writing some years afterwards, he was his own designer. During the nineteenth century further plantings were made, and the gardens are now brilliant in spring with azaleas and rhododendrons.

Henry Hoare inherited Stourhead in 1725 from his father, another Henry. Both Henrys were most assiduous in their attention to the business of their bank, and the making of Stourhead, great though their interest and study in the arts, was a spare-time occupation.

Henry Hoare the first, like his son, had been an innovator. On buying the Stourhead estate, in 1714, he had built one of the first houses in the new Georgian style. He employed as architect Colen Campbell, who designed the Palladian building which is the central block of the present house. The

Westwood Manor,
Wiltshire.

Phillipps House, Dinton,
Wiltshire.

wings were added about 1800 by Richard Colt Hoare to house his collection of pictures, statuary and books. These wings were furnished in Regency style, and the furniture which the younger Thomas Chippendale made for them is still there.

The central block was gutted by fire in 1902, but the furniture was saved and put back after the interior had been restored in an exact copy of the original decoration. The statuary and pictures in the house—apart from the many family portraits, which are by painters of note—are mainly the collection made by Richard Colt Hoare and show the tastes of a wealthy, travelled connoisseur in the last part of the eighteenth century.

Stourhead was given to the Trust in 1947 by Sir Henry Hoare, the sixth baronet.

Westwood Manor

WILTSHIRE

one and a half miles south-west of Bradford-on-Avon

Westwood Manor (page 93) is a stone house in its own garden in the beautifully situated village of Westwood, which stands on high ground between two river valleys: those of the Avon and the Frome. It was built towards the end of the fifteenth century and retains some late Gothic windows. Alterations made in the sixteenth and seventeenth centuries included the embellishment of the interior with panelling and some fine Jacobean plasterwork.

In the Middle Ages Westwood belonged to the priory at Winchester, which leased it to tenants. At the dissolution of the monasteries it was used to endow the Dean and Chapter of Winchester, and continued to be leased to tenants until sold to a private owner by the Ecclesiastical Commissioners in 1861.

The house was altered and decorated by a succession of tenants. During the sixteenth century the property was rented by the Horton family, who were very prosperous clothiers. The property continued to be an agricultural holding. During the eighteenth and nineteenth centuries, when this style of building had little appeal for those wanting a country house, it seems to have served purely as a farm. By 1911 much of the panelling had been covered by wallpaper and the Great Parlour partitioned for use as an apple store. The late Mr E. G. Lister bought it and restored it with knowledge and discretion to its earlier state. On his death in 1956 he left the house with his collection of furniture to the Trust.

Stourhead, Wiltshire: a view in the gardens.

Brownsea Island, Dorset: a view of beach and woods taken from the castle landing-stage.

Brownsea Island

DORSET

in Poole Harbour about one and a half miles south-south-east of Poole

Brownsea Island and its woodlands make a fine contribution to the scenic attractions of Poole harbour, while visitors to the island are rewarded with magnificent views along the Dorset coast.

It extends to five hundred acres made up of *woodland*, sandy *beach*, heath, a marsh area and two lakes. There are several miles of woodland paths and glades, and a mile of bathing beach. Part of the island is managed as a nature reserve by the Dorset Naturalists' Trust, as there are rare wild flowers in the marsh, and the lakes are a sanctuary for wildfowl. This is open to guided parties at fixed times.

Lord Baden-Powell held the first Boy Scout camp here in 1907. Arrangements have been made with the Boy Scout and Girl Guide Associations for them to hold camps on the island, but there is no other camping. A

Clouds Hill, Dorset.

castle was built on the island in Henry VIII's time; but the present castle is a mainly Victorian mansion completed about 1900.

The Trust acquired the island in 1962 from the Treasury, who had accepted it in payment of death duty. A considerable endowment was needed, and this was raised by a public appeal, to which a number of charitable trusts contributed.

Clouds Hill

DORSET

nine miles east of Dorchester, one and a half miles east of Waddock crossroads

This is the cottage where T. E. Lawrence lived when he left the Royal Air Force in 1935. It was given to the Trust in 1937 by Mr A. W. Lawrence as a memorial to his brother, with some of the contents.

Downhouse Farm

DORSET

at Eype, about a mile south-west of Bridport

This 176-acre farm with thirty-five acres of grazing rights over Eype Down runs from the *undercliff* up to Thorncombe Beacon (508 feet). It was given in 1966 by R. C. Sherriff as his contribution to Enterprise Neptune, the Trust's appeal for coastal preservation. He had bought the farm a good many years earlier while in Hollywood and feeling homesick for England.

It forms part of the Trust's Golden Cap Estate, a twelve-hundred-acre property which extends for about five miles along the coast between Charmouth and Eypemouth. This Golden Cap property is made up of hill, cliff farmland, undercliff and beach and is served by fifteen miles of footpath, including a six-mile through route along the coast. There is also access by car to some of the viewpoints and to some of the beach. Part of the area is managed in consultation with the Dorset Naturalists' Trust, and visitors are particularly asked to remember that preservation of the wild life of animals and plants is of special importance here. The estate has been built up by gifts from a number of donors, most of them gifts to Enterprise Neptune.

Hardy's Cottage

DORSET

Higher Bockhampton, three miles north-east of Dorchester

This is the small thatched house where Thomas Hardy was born in 1840.

It was built by his grandfather and has been little changed externally. The walls were originally built in a composition of chalk, clay, straw and other materials which were much used in the south-west at that time. To give this weather protection they have been reinforced with brick facing or rendered cement.

Hardy grew up in the cottage, walking to school; first to the village school in Lower Bockhampton and then the three miles to Dorchester. He

Cliffs,
Downhouse
Farm,
near Bridport,
Dorset.

Hardy's Cottage,
Dorset.

Barrington Court, Somerset: the south front.

continued there while a pupil in the office of John Hicks, the Dorchester architect. He was twenty-two when he went to try his luck in London. He returned to the cottage five years later and again worked in Dorchester for a time before going to Yarmouth. He continued to visit the cottage both during and after his parents' lifetime, his last visit being in 1926.

The cottage was bought by the Trust in 1948 in accordance with Miss K. Hardy's will. A small collection of items of interest connected with Hardy was given to the Trust in 1965.

Barrington Court

SOMERSET

three miles north-east of Ilminster

Architectural historians point to Barrington as an exceptionally fine example of English domestic architecture of the sixteenth and seventeenth centuries, and since it was built so early in the period (in 1514–20) as probably a prototype. Its general plan, so far as domestic arrangements are concerned, follows that of the traditional medieval manor-house; but all the defensive features of a fortified manor-house were omitted. The experts see some French influence in the beautiful spiral chimneys and the sculptured finials which top the vertical lines of the building and provide decorative features of the exterior.

That there should be a trace of French influence about these details is not surprising. The man who had Barrington built, the second Lord Daubeney, had soldiered in France and had very likely been in Paris while his father was ambassador there. The house is made of the local golden stone from Ham Hill. Adjoining it is a brick stable block built in 1621.

Barrington has had its ups and downs in the hands of a number of different owners. During the nineteenth century it was a farmhouse and allowed to become dilapidated. It was bought for the Trust in 1907 and after the 1914–18 war the late Colonel A. A. Lyle, whose son now rents and maintains it, rehabilitated the house and installed oak panelling and other interior fittings which he had obtained from derelict houses.

Clevedon Court, Somerset.

Clevedon Court

SOMERSET

one and a half miles east of Clevedon on the Bristol road

Although alterations have been made at times, Clevedon Court (page 101) remains substantially a medieval manor-house. It was built about 1320, incorporating the tower of an earlier building. The plan of the building was in accordance with the fashion of the day, except that it included a chapel. It is on the first floor of the house and has a graceful south window. In Tudor times some comfort was added by providing the Great Hall with a fireplace and new windows. In the eighteenth century the Great Hall was given a new ceiling.

Clevedon was built by Sir John de Clevedon and has had several owners. It passed by marriage in Henry VI's reign to a Northamptonshire family called Wake. They sold it in 1630 to John Digby, first Earl of Bristol. After the death of the third and last earl it was bought in 1709 by Abraham Elton, Merchant Venturer, Mayor of Bristol, and M.P. for the city. It remained in the possession of the Elton family until 1961, when it was accepted by the Treasury in payment of death duty and transferred to the Trust.

The house contains a number of Elton family portraits and a collection of Elton ware. Sir Edmund Elton, who succeeded to the estate in 1884, established a pottery at Clevedon which enjoyed widespread popularity, urns, jars and vases receiving awards at exhibitions all over the world.

Lytes Cary

SOMERSET

two and a half miles south-east of Somerton

Lytes Cary is a stone-built manor-house with an added appeal to those interested in the history of gardening.

The house was not built all at one time but grew over quite a long period. The principal features are the fourteenth-century chapel adjoining the house, the Great Hall of about 1450, the Great Chamber of 1533 which has a fine

Lytes Cary, Somerset.

plasterwork ceiling, and the Great Parlour which has early seventeenth-century panelling.

The house was built by the Lyte family, who owned the property from the thirteenth century until the eighteenth.

Henry Lyte, who took over the house when his father retired to London in 1558, made a botanic garden here and in 1578 published his *Niewe Herball*, a translation from the Flemish which became a best-seller in the following thirty years. No trace of his botanic garden has survived, but during the last sixty years a beautiful garden in the Elizabethan style with lawns, clipped hedges and topiary has been established in its place. The Lytes sold the house about 1760, and during the nineteenth century it came to be neglected. But it was bought and restored in 1907 by Sir Walter Jenner (son of the Victorian physician), who laid out the present garden. He died in 1948 leaving the property to the Trust in his will.

Montacute, Somerset: the west front.

Tintinhull House, Somerset: the west front.

Montacute

SOMERSET

four miles west of Yeovil

Montacute is an outstandingly good example of an Elizabethan house, and the few changes made since it was built have not altered its character.

It is a tall, symmetrical house in Ham Hill stone with large windows, and makes a brave show—as it was intended to do. The interior is decorated with plaster friezes, heraldic glass and handsome chimney-pieces.

The architect has not been definitely identified, but a good deal of evidence points to William Arnold, a Somerset mason, who later designed Wadham College, Oxford, and had a hand in the building of several houses in the west country.

In 1590, when the house was built, the Montacute property belonged to Edward Phelips, a local man whose family had acquired it after the dissolution of the monasteries. He had the money and the ambition to build a fine house. He had already made money at the Bar, and went on to be Speaker of the House of Commons and Master of the Rolls.

Montacute remained in the possession of the Phelips family until 1931, when they sold it, and it was given to the Trust by Mr E. E. Cook through the Society for the Protection of Ancient Buildings.

In 1931 it was very sparsely furnished; but in recent years, with gifts and loans of paintings, tapestries and furniture, the Trust have been able to refurnish most of the rooms very handsomely.

Tintinhull House

SOMERSET

five miles north-west of Yeovil

Tintinhull House is a fine, small house in a beautiful garden. The layout of the latter was begun after 1900, and from 1933 onwards the late Captain F. E. Reiss and Mrs Reiss developed and improved it. It is a small garden where carefully placed trees and hedges provide a variety of delightful garden views. It contains a wide assortment of plants chosen and planted to ensure that every area is beautiful throughout the year.

The house is of dressed Ham Hill stone with a roof of local stone tiles. It was built about 1600 but around 1700 was given a new, more charming and elegant *west front.*

Mrs Reiss, who died in 1961, had given Tintinhull to the Trust in 1954.

Selworthy

SOMERSET

about two and a half miles west of Minehead and about half a mile north of A 39

Selworthy is one of several villages in the Trust's large Holnicote estate. This includes Dunkery Beacon, Selworthy Beacon, Bossington Hill, four miles of coast and, as well as Selworthy, most of Allerford, Bossington, Tivington and Luccombe villages, several hamlets and 6,700 acres of moorland, including 1,200 acres at Winsford Hill north of Dulverton.

Selworthy, Somerset, looking south towards Dunkery.

Arlington Court, Devon: the drawing-room.

Most of this twelve-thousand-acre estate was given to the Trust in 1944 by Sir Richard Acland, Bt.; but nearly two thousand acres, including Dunkery Beacon, had been given in the early 1930's by other donors.

Arlington Court

DEVON

seven miles north-east of Barnstaple

Arlington Court was built in 1822 for John Chichester to the design of Thomas Lee, a local architect who was later to design the Guildhall at Barnstaple. Outside it is a plain, rather severe building relieved by a semi-circular porch. Inside most of the rooms are as Lee left them; but in the 1860's the hall was enlarged by removing the rooms in the centre of the north side. At the same time the house was enlarged by the addition of a new wing, the attractive gardens were laid out, and a handsome stable block was built.

Bradley Manor, Devon: the east front.

The building contains furniture which was made for it by a Barnstaple cabinet-maker when the house was built, some family portraits, and a watercolour by William Blake signed and dated 1821. This is thought to have been brought to Arlington by John Chichester shortly after it was painted.

Miss Rosalie Chichester, who bequeathed the estate to the Trust, was born at Arlington in 1865 and lived there until her death in 1949.

It was her great-grandfather, Colonel John Chichester, who built the house. Before him the Chichester family had been in possession of the estate since 1384. It is not known when they first built a house there; but the foundations of what is probably a sixteenth-century building are visible in the park to the south of the present one.

Miss Chichester was an assiduous collector, with a special interest in ships and the sea, and accumulated during her long life collections of model ships, British and foreign shells, pewter, snuff-boxes and other objects. Her collections are on view in the house. She also made the large park an animal sanctuary.

The Trust has now established in the stables a small collection of carriages and horsedrawn vehicles, and hope to add shortly to Miss Chichester's collection a model of *Gipsy Moth IV*, in which her nephew, Sir Francis Chichester, sailed around the world.

Bradley Manor

DEVON

at the western edge of Newton Abbot

Bradley Manor is an interesting example of medieval domestic architecture. Most of the building dates from about 1420, when a thirteenth-century house was altered and enlarged. A chapel was included in these enlargements and this remains, together with the Solar, Great Hall and porch. The walls of the house are roughcast and the roof is slate. It is set in a valley of meadow and woodland.

The fifteenth-century building was the work of Richard Yarde, who inherited the earlier house from his grandmother. His descendants sold the property in 1750 and it changed hands again several times. Its style of architecture being out of fashion, the house was converted to be a farmhouse, with poultry kept in the chapel. In 1909 a descendant of the Yardes bought and restored it. In 1938 his daughter gave it to the Trust.

Buckland Abbey

DEVON

six miles south of Tavistock, and eleven miles north of Plymouth

Buckland Abbey (page 111) was founded in the thirteenth century as a Cistercian house. During the Middle Ages the monks had wide estates and built a large abbey church, presumably with cloisters, refectory and dormitories to scale. But it is not clear how these were laid out on the site. When the abbey was converted to be a secular dwelling-house after the dissolution of the monasteries, the abbey church became the hall of the new house, the monks' quarters were dismantled, and new kitchen and living quarters were built.

This conversion was carried out by Sir Richard Grenville of the *Revenge*, whose grandfather had bought the property in 1541. The date over the fireplace in the hall—1576—is taken as indicating that he completed the work in that year. But he did not stay at Buckland long. In 1580 he went to live at another of his family's properties. Shortly afterwards (1584) Buckland was bought by Sir Francis Drake. Drake was then rising forty, already famous and a comparatively wealthy man. He lived much at Buckland from then on, when not voyaging, but made no changes in the house. He took an active part in Plymouth affairs, being mayor in 1581 and later M.P. for the city.

Drake's brother inherited the property and it remained in his family's hands until 1946. They made some alterations to the interior during the eighteenth century and, it is thought, pulled down some part of the monastic buildings which had been left by Sir Richard Grenville.

The abbey was acquired and repaired by the Trust in 1948 with the help of private donors and the Pilgrim Trust. It has been leased to Plymouth Corporation and is maintained as a naval and Devon folk museum.

Opposite: Buckland Abbey, Devon.
Buzzards, Devon, in the valley of the Little Dart, near Tiverton.

Buzzards

DEVON

near Tiverton

A mile stretch of the Little Dart, covering about eighty acres of coppice and meadow, was given to the Trust in 1967. A secluded and undeveloped area, it has many wild flowers. Access is by footpath.

Compton Castle

DEVON

four miles west of Torquay

Compton Castle (page 112) was built as a fortified manor, intended to give protection to the food supplies and non-combatants of the neighbourhood, rather than to be a castle to withstand a full-blooded siege. But it had high walls and portcullises to protect the entrances. This was desirable when it

Compton Castle, Devon.

was first built, about 1320, as French raids on places so near to the coast—it is only a few miles inland from Tor Bay—were something to be taken into account. It was reconstructed and enlarged twice in the following two hundred years, but has remained a fortified dwelling-house.

In Queen Elizabeth I's reign the Gilberts, who had acquired the Compton estate by marriage early in the fourteenth century, were much involved both in the defence of the west country against the Spanish and in colonization of the New World. John Gilbert, Sheriff and Vice-Admiral of Devon, was knighted in 1571 and was engaged in organizing the defence of the county. His younger brother, Sir Humphrey Gilbert, was an enthusiastic supporter of the North West Passage idea, and in 1583 sailed as leader of the expedition which led to the colonization of Newfoundland.

Compton remained in the possession of the Gilbert family until 1800 but was in other hands during the nineteenth century. In 1930 it was bought back by Commander W. R. Gilbert, who gave it to the Trust in 1951.

Goodameavy

DEVON

six miles north-east of Plymouth and two miles south of Yelverton

This property on the south-eastern corner of Dartmoor covers nearly four hundred acres, including Dewerstone and Cadworthy woods, Dewerstone Rock and part of Wigford Down. Finds of archaeological interest have been made at the latter two places. It is fine walking country and there is free access by footpath to the Trust's moor and woods, though not to the farms.

The property was acquired in 1960, partly from the Treasury, which had accepted it in payment of death duty, and partly by purchase from two legacies.

Goodameavy, Devon, looking down the River Meavy.

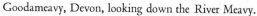

Killerton Garden

DEVON

on the Exeter – Taunton road (A 38), seven miles north-east of Exeter

Killerton Garden, which has been in the making and maturing for some 150 years, is a fifteen-acre hillside arboretum on the south slope of Killerton Clump. In addition to the spring and autumn glory of the trees and shrubs, it shows sheets of bulbs in spring, and the long herbaceous border is at its best in July and August.

It is part of the six-thousand-acre Killerton estate which was given to the Trust in 1942 by Sir Richard Acland, Bt.

The garden was laid out in its present form after the Napoleonic Wars by Sir Thomas Acland, tenth baronet. Succeeding generations of the Acland family have contributed to the plantings.

The climate is kind to shrubs and trees, of which there is a great variety. The higher slopes of the garden command fine views of the surrounding country.

Opposite: Killerton Garden, Devon.
Moretonhampstead, Devon: the almshouses.

Moretonhampstead Almshouses

DEVON

at the east edge of the town, on B 3212 by the churchyard

These almshouses are built of granite over an open colonnade and have a thatched roof. They were built in 1637 and given to the Trust by the Moretonhampstead Almshouse Charity in 1952. They have been let, and are not open.

Another charming arcaded granite building in this style—Church House, Widdecombe-in-the-Moor—also belongs to the Trust. It is a fifteenth-century building, given in 1933 by local subscription. Part of it is now used as a cottage, and part as the village hall.

Saltram, Devon: the west front,

Saltram

DEVON

three and a half miles east of Plymouth

Saltram, which also presents many other delights, has two particular distinctions; the Saloon and *dining-room* are Robert Adam at his best, and the pictures in the house include a splendid collection of Reynolds portraits.

The house was built in the middle of the eighteenth century, altering and incorporating parts of a Tudor house which preceded it on the site. It was given a plain exterior but a very decorative interior. The first part of this building was carried out between 1743 and 1750 by John and Lady Catherine Parker. It is not known whom they employed as architect. But the quality of the decoration of the rooms for which they were responsible shows that they employed craftsmen of the highest skill. In 1768 their son John (later Baron Boringdon) engaged Robert Adam to make extensive alterations to the east wing. Some further work was carried out in 1818, when the porch was added. There have been no material changes since then.

Saltram, Devon: the Adam dining-room.

The various collections in the house—furniture, pictures, pottery and porcelain—are immensely interesting. The John Parker who employed Robert Adam as his architect was responsible for a great part of them. He was probably advised on his choice of pictures by Sir Joshua Reynolds, who was his friend and a frequent visitor to Saltram House. Reynolds's portrait of Parker's two children is still in the position their father chose for it, over the chimney-piece in the morning-room. John Parker kept accounts, though not, unfortunately, in great detail. But they do record purchases from Chippendale and Wedgwood of furniture and vases now in the house.

The house stands in a beautifully landscaped park through which, unfortunately, a new motor road is now to be built. The Trust appealed against the proposal; but a Joint Select Committee of both Houses of Parliament decided in favour of the Ministry. Park, house and principal contents were accepted by the Treasury in payment of death duty in 1957 and given to the Trust.

Trentishoe

DEVON

on the coast about seven miles east of Ilfracombe, five miles west of Lynton

The Trust owns about two miles of the coastline between Ilfracombe and Lynton. Trust properties there cover a thousand acres of woodland, moorland and cliff at Woody Bay and leading down from *Trentishoe Common* to the sea at Heddon's Mouth, and between Lynton and Heddon's Mouth. Most of this has been acquired in recent years with the help of the Exmoor Society and the Devon County Council.

Antony House

CORNWALL

five miles west of Plymouth

Antony (page 120) was built between 1711 and 1721, the centre block in stone and the two wings, joined to it by colonnades, in brick. Except for the addition of a nineteenth-century porch it has not been altered since. It has not been established who was the architect, but it is agreed that he achieved a most successful design.

The rooms are panelled, and some of them contain furniture which is contemporary with the house and has always been there. They also contain some fine china and an unusually interesting collection of family portraits.

The Carew family came to Antony in 1492, and in the present house are portraits and treasures both of generations who lived at Antony before this

Trentishoe, Devon: a view from Trentishoe Common.

house was built and of those who have lived there since. In the *entrance hall* is a portrait of Richard Carew, the Elizabethan author of the *Survey of Cornwall*, with a chest and other furniture which probably came from the house of his time. His book gives a vivid picture of Cornwall at the period of the Armada.

In the garden, where there is a fine maidenhair tree, are a collection of stone carvings from the North West Frontier of India and a temple bell from Burma. These were brought to Antony by General Sir Reginald Pole-Carew, who campaigned in India and Burma.

Antony was given to the Trust in 1961 by Sir John Carew Pole.

Antony House, Cornwall: the east front, and *below*, the entrance hall.

Bodmin Moor, Cornwall. Rough Tor: the view to the south-west.

Rough Tor

CORNWALL

three miles south-east of Camelford

As a memorial to men of the 43rd (Wessex) Division who fell in the 1939–1945 war, a stretch of Bodmin Moor was given to the Trust in 1957. Rough Tor (1,312 feet) is the second highest point in Cornwall. On its westerly slopes there are remnants of human settlements which are thought to be of an Early–Middle Bronze Age date.

Access to Rough Tor is by vehicle to the edge of the Moor (from Camelford by the Jubilee Drive) and thence on foot.

Crackington Haven

CORNWALL

half way between Boscastle and Bude

Here the Trust owns a three-mile stretch of the wild and unspoiled part of the north coast of Cornwall. This covers Crackington Haven, Cambeak, High Cliff—the highest in Cornwall (731 feet)—and Pencannow or Pentenna Point (400 feet). High Cliff was the setting for episodes in Hardy's novel *A Pair of Blue Eyes.*

The property is made up of farmland, cliff and foreshore, and access is by footpath only. The high points command superb views along the coast.

The major part of the property was given, in 1959, in memory of Flight-Lieutenant A. G. Parnall and air crews who gave their lives in the Battle of Britain, by Flight-Lieutenant Parnall's brother. Additional land was nobght in 1959.

Opposite: Crackington Haven, Cornwall, looking from Pencannow Point towards Cambeak.
Boscastle Harbour, Cornwall.

Boscastle Harbour

CORNWALL

three and a half miles north-east of Tintagel on the Bude road (B 3263)

There are fine views from the surroundings of Boscastle Harbour, and many cliff flowers. Part of the harbour works were built by Sir Richard Grenville in 1584. Other parts had to be rebuilt in 1962 by the Trust. These had been originally made about 1820 but were blown up in 1941 by a drifting mine. The harbour belongs to the Trust, as do about 270 acres of adjoining cliffs including the 317-foot Willapark Headland. The harbour was given to the Trust in 1955 by Mr T. P. Pulford, and the following year additional land was given by another donor. The Palace Stables at the head of the harbour have been let to the Youth Hostels Association.

There are two other Trust properties close to Boscastle Harbour. At Forrabury Common (adjoining it) sixty-seven acres were bought in 1955–7

with monies given for purchases in the west of England. Here there persists a survival of Celtic agricultural planning—a 'Stitchmeal' system of land holding. The Trust own thirty-four of the forty-two 'stitches' into which the area is divided.

In the Valency Valley (two miles north-west) a hundred acres were given in 1958 by the Treasury, who had accepted them in payment of death duty.

Helford River

CORNWALL

between Falmouth and the Lizard

The Trust owns forty-three acres of farmland and wooded cliffs near Mawnan church on the north side of the mouth of the Helford, fifty acres of Rosemullion Head north of the river mouth and several other properties in this very beautiful estuary. These properties were given between 1939 and 1963 by various donors. Among them is the garden at Glendurgan four miles south-west of Falmouth, a gift of members of the Fox family, where there are tender shrubs, a walled garden and a water garden.

Helford River, Cornwall, near Mawnan on the north side of the river mouth.

Cotehele House, Cornwall: the courtyard.

Cotehele House

CORNWALL

eight miles south-west of Tavistock on the west bank of the Tamar

When Sir Richard Edgecumbe and his son, who succeeded him, rebuilt their home between 1490 and 1520 they continued the plan of the medieval manor that they were improving and enlarging. Alterations and additions made since then have not touched their principal work, so Cotehele provides basically a most authentic example of a medieval house. The interior is embellished by the tapestries, needlework, furniture, pewter and brass collected during the seventeenth century. The tapestries which decorate the walls include Brussels and Flemish work as well as products of Soho and Mortlake. The furniture includes some unusually interesting English pieces.

Lanhydrock House, Cornwall: the gatehouse and house seen from the park and, *below*, the great gallery.

There is also a collection of arms and armour in the hall. The chapel clock is a great rarity. It was installed in about 1489 when the chapel was completed. It is a pre-pendulum clock, powered by two ninety-pound weights, which has never been converted to pendulum working.

The gardens are on many different levels as they descend to the valley below the house. There are ponds and rills, old yew hedges, terraced flower borders, a tulip tree, golden ash and other fine trees, a medieval dovecote, and shrubs which provide colour through the season.

Cotehele continued in possession of the Edgecumbe family until 1947, when it was offered to the Treasury in payment of death duty, accepted and given to the Trust—the first property to be acquired by the Trust in this way. The contents of the house are on loan from Lord Mount Edgecumbe's trustees.

Lanhydrock House

CORNWALL

two and a half miles south of Bodmin

Lanhydrock House overlooks the beautiful valley of the River Fowey. It stands in a park of about 250 acres, largely wooded. The park trees were planted during the eighteenth and nineteenth centuries. The delightful gardens, near the house, were given their present layout in 1857.

The house itself was built between 1630 and 1651. The north wing and the *gatehouse* remain from this original building, but the rest, which had been altered in 1780, was badly damaged by fire in 1881. It was rebuilt, not as a new building, but as a replica of what had been burned.

The *great gallery*, in the north wing, retains its charming plasterwork. On the ceiling and over the two fireplaces the plasterers illustrated many of the well-known Old Testament stories, and did so most vividly. The craftsmen have not been identified, but it is believed that they did other work in the neighbourhood.

The contents of the house include Mortlake and Brussels tapestries, and a number of portraits, some of them by Kneller and Romney.

In the garden are some bronze garden urns by Louis XIV's goldsmith Louis Ballin. These were brought to this country from the Château de Bagatelle in Paris during the last century, and to Lanhydrock when the gardens were laid out in 1857. The general plan of this nineteenth-century garden has been retained, but it has been largely replanted and now contains many very fine magnolias, azaleas, camellias, hydrangeas and other trees and shrubs. Mr Gladstone and Lord Rosebery each planted a copper beech by the tennis courts.

In the Middle Ages Lanhydrock had belonged to the priory at Bodmin. The tithe barn, in the garden, remains as evidence of this ownership. It changed hands several times after the dissolution of the monasteries. It was bought in 1620 by Sir Richard Robartes, who came of a family which had prospered as merchants and bankers connected particularly with the Cornish tin trade. He began the seventeenth-century house. This was completed by his son, who had a long and active public life, attaining high rank in the Parliamentary forces during the Civil War and holding a number of important offices after the Restoration, including that of Lord President of the Council. The house and park remained in the ownership of the family until given to the Trust in 1953 by the seventh Viscount Clifden.

Lantivet Bay

CORNWALL

east of Fowey between Polruan and Polperro

Trust properties in this Pencarrow Head, Lantic Bay and Lantivet Bay area cover nearly a thousand acres of cliff, farmland and beach. They include Pencarrow Head, from which there are wide ranging views, the coves of Lantivet Bay and the farmland surrounding Lansallos church. There is access by footpaths. These properties were acquired between 1936 and 1965 by gift and public subscription, including the purchase of land at Lansallos Barton Farm in 1956 from funds subscribed to Enterprise Neptune, the Trust's appeal for preservation of the coast.

Trelissick

CORNWALL

four miles south of Truro astride B 3289

This 370 acres of *park*, farm and woodland includes woods on the west bank of the Fal above and below King Harry Passage, and Round Wood on the east bank. The park, from which there are beautiful views of the estuary, is open to visitors at advertised times. Trelissick House is not open.

Given to the Trust in 1955.

Lantivet Bay, Cornwall, looking eastwards across the bay with Lansallos church in background.

Trelissick, Cornwall, looking from the park to the estuary of the River Fal.

St Michael's Mount

CORNWALL

half a mile south of Marazion

When Sir John St Aubyn bought St Michael's Mount in 1660 he came into possession of a group of buildings standing in an enclosure against the central pinnacle of the rock. Some were monastic, some secular, the Mount having been in the previous 500 years both monastery and fortress or at times a combination of the two.

Edward the Confessor founded a chapel here in 1044 in a grant to the Benedictine Abbey of Mont Saint Michel in Brittany. In 1154 there was a church and quarters for 13 brothers.

Later in the century, while Richard I was on Crusade, some of John's partisans seized the Mount to hold as a fortress. It reverted to monastic use but was again treated as a stronghold during the Wars of the Roses, during the Cornish rebellion against Edward VI and during the Civil War.

Since Sir John's purchase in 1660 it has led a peaceful existence.

The monastic church is of the late fifteenth century but probably incorporates masonry of a much earlier church. The other buildings have been remodelled and added to at different times since 1660, most recently in 1878.

The Mount, which is an island at high tide, is itself a romantic sight and from its terraces affords splendid views towards Land's End and the Lizard.

The Mount continued in the ownership of the St Aubyn family until 1964 when the third Lord St Levan gave it to the Trust.

Trebarwith Strand

CORNWALL

one and a half miles south of Tintagel

In addition to land on the cliffs overlooking Trebarwith Strand, the Trust have several other properties near Tintagel—a viewpoint on Barras Nose to the north of King Arthur's Castle; land between Tintagel church and the sea, from which there are fine views; a viewpoint on Penhallick Point given

St Michael's Mount, Cornwall.

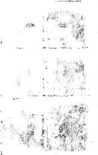

Trebarwith Strand, near Tintagel, Cornwall.

Trerice, Cornwall: the hall.

to mark the Coronation in 1953; and in Tintagel the small fourteenth-century house known as the Post Office. It was used from 1844 to 1892 as the G.P.O.'s letter-receiving office for the district. The building is now open to the public.

These properties were acquired between 1897 and 1962 by public subscriptions and the gifts of a number of donors.

Trerice

CORNWALL

three miles south-east of Newquay

Trerice is an Elizabethan stone manor-house, built about 1570 on the site of an earlier house, and has been very little altered. The *hall* and solar (now the drawing-room) have fine ceilings and fireplaces. There is no record of who executed the excellent plasterwork in these rooms, but it is thought, from the evidence of similar work done at that time in other houses in Cornwall and parts of Devon, that it was a local craftsman.

The builder of the house, Sir John Arundell, had inherited Trerice from his father and with it the means to rebuild. His father, another Sir John, had a remarkable career in the service of the Crown and profited by it. He was knighted at the battle of the Spurs, was Esquire of the Body to Henry VIII, and also served both Edward VI and Mary. The Arundells supported the Crown during the Civil War with much gallantry and loss, but recovered something of their position after the Restoration. Trerice passed during the eighteenth century to a nephew of the fourth Lord Arundell, and from him to the Acland family of Killerton in Devon. The property was sold in 1915 and the house changed hands several times. The Trust bought it in 1953 with money bequeathed by Mrs Annie Woodward, and restored it with the help of Mr J. F. Elton and a grant from the Historic Buildings Council.

Rotative Winding Engine, East Pool and Agar Mine, Pool

CORNWALL

on south side of Camborne–Redruth road, A 30

Engines of this kind (page 134) were among the first applications of steam power to industry. The Trust acquired five nineteenth-century examples in 1967 with the help of the Cornish Engines Preservation Society, which has been looking after them for some time, and with further help from the local and county councils and the Ministry of Works.

East Pool and Agar mine, Cornwall:
rotative winding engine.

They are the most recent additions to the list of Industrial Monuments preserved by the Trust. Other properties in this category are the *Stratford-upon-Avon Canal*, the eighteenth-century limekilns at *Beadnell*, near Seahouses in Northumberland, and the eighteenth-century cotton-mill and cottages at *Styal*, south of Manchester.

The engine illustrated is the type of winding engine in general use in Cornish mines during the last century. There is free parking space adjoining the engine.

It was built in 1887 by Holman Bros to the design of F. W. Michell and used for hoisting men and ores.

It is a double-acting rotative engine of thirty inches cylinder bore by nine feet stroke, designed to work at from twenty-seven to thirty revolutions per minute and at a rope speed of a thousand feet per minute.

Ashleworth Tithe Barn

GLOUCESTERSHIRE

about six miles north of Gloucester, one and a half miles east of Hartpury

A stone-roofed fifteenth-century tithe barn with two projecting porch bays. It is 120 feet long. Given to the Trust in 1956.

The Trust owns seven other tithe barns distributed over Berkshire, Cornwall, Devon, Somerset, Wiltshire, Worcestershire and Yorkshire.

Ashleworth Tithe Barn, Gloucestershire.

Arlington Row, Bibury

GLOUCESTERSHIRE

on the south side of A 433

This row of seventeenth-century stone cottages was acquired in 1949 with the help of the Bristol and Gloucestershire Archaeological Society. Rack Isle, a four-acre field opposite to them, was given to the Trust in the same year. It was used as a drying ground when wool was a cottage industry here.

Blaise Hamlet

GLOUCESTERSHIRE

four miles north of central Bristol, just north of B 4057

These cottages (page 139), grouped round a green, were built in 1809 by John Harford, to house pensioners of the Blaise estate.

They are picturesque, all different, and designed by John Nash. Given to the Trust in 1943.

Chipping Campden Market Hall

GLOUCESTERSHIRE

in Chipping Campden on B 4081 opposite the police station

The Trust had this charming Jacobean open arcade re-roofed in the early 1950's. It was bought in 1944 with the help of the Midland Counties Trust Fund, Campden Trust and others.

The Trust also owns thirteen acres of meadow in Chipping Campden between the churchyard and the station; and at Dover's Hill, on the right of the Weston-sub-Edge road (B 4035), 180 acres of a natural amphitheatre where Dover's Games were held from 1612 to 1852.

Arlington Row, Bibury, Gloucestershire.

Chipping Campden, Gloucestershire: the market hall.

Dyrham Park, Gloucestershire: the east front.

Dyrham Park

GLOUCESTERSHIRE

seven miles north of Bath and twelve miles east of Bristol

Dyrham was built at the end of the seventeenth century, part of it being designed by a well-known architect, William Talman, and part by an otherwise unknown French architect called S. Huduroy. It is a fine building and has been described as looking, for all its parkland setting, as though it might be a town house. Inside the house the rooms are panelled, and there are tapestries and leather wall-hangings. The contents include Delftware tulip holders, Dutch paintings and Dutch furniture contemporary with the house.

Blaise Hamlet, Gloucestershire.

Sir William Blathwayt, who built the house, knew Holland well. He made a very highly successful career as a civil servant and spent much time in Holland, being as a young man a secretary at the embassy at The Hague and later, while Secretary at War, accompanying King William to Flanders on a number of campaigns. He came to Dyrham when he married Mary Wynter, whose family had owned the estate since Tudor times.

The house that he had built has been very little altered. The formal gardens that he had made were transformed into parkland late in the eighteenth century and some fine trees have survived.

Blathwayts remained in possession of Dyrham until 1956, when house and contents were sold to the Ministry of Works, who transferred them to the Trust in 1961.

In 1967, with the co-operation of the university and education authorities in Bristol, the Trust held at Dyrham a study course for teachers on the history and furnishing of the house, and following this a study room was established there for teachers and their pupils.

The ruins of Hailes Abbey, Gloucestershire.

Hailes Abbey

GLOUCESTERSHIRE

two miles north-east of Winchcombe, a mile east of the Broadway road (A 46)

The abbey is in ruins but enough remains standing, as the photograph on this page indicates, for the visitor to reconstruct in the mind's eye some idea of the beautiful medieval building.

The abbey was founded in 1246 by King John's second son, Richard

Earl of Cornwall, in fulfilment of a vow made when he escaped shipwreck on the Scillies. He endowed the abbey liberally.

The ruins were given to the Trust in 1937 with neighbouring meadowland. It is under the guardianship of the Ministry of Works. There is a museum containing tiles, bosses found in the ruins, maps, plans and other objects connected with the abbey.

Hidcote Manor Garden

GLOUCESTERSHIRE

at Hidcote Bartrim four miles north-east of Chipping Campden

'By that time I had become so wildly intoxicated by the spilling abundance of Hidcote that I was no longer in any mood to worry about exact naming, but only in the mood to enjoy the next pleasure to be encountered'—thus

Hidcote Manor Garden, Gloucestershire.

the late Lady Nicolson (Vita Sackville West) in the Trust's guide-book. Many a less learned gardener has had the same feeling on a visit to Hidcote.

It is a modern garden, planned and planted—apart from a cedar tree and some beeches—since 1905. That was the year in which the late Major Lawrence Johnston acquired the manor-house and the surrounding fields. The garden he made is formed of a series of small gardens divided by hedges of different species. These contain a variety of trees, plants and shrubs, including many rarities, their arrangement being as Lady Nicolson described it.

The garden was given by Major Johnston to the Trust in 1948. It is preserved under a joint arrangement between the Trust and the Royal Horticultural Society. This arrangement was applied first to Hidcote and later to *Nymans* and a number of other gardens belonging to the Trust.

Snowshill Manor

GLOUCESTERSHIRE

three miles south of the west end of Broadway

Snowshill is a stone-built sixteenth-century Cotswold manor-house to which alterations and additions were made in the early parts of the seventeenth and eighteenth centuries. By 1919 it had been in use as a farmhouse for 140 years, and was in need of much repair. The late Mr Charles P. Wade bought it, carried out the necessary repairs, made the present very agreeable garden and amassed the immensely varied collections which are to be seen in the house today. Mr Wade gave house, garden and contents to the Trust in 1951. He was an architect and artist-craftsman with a special curiosity concerning craft tools and the products which earlier generations made with them. He tried his own hand at using period tools. He lived in Snowshill without electric light and slept there in a Tudor bed.

His intense interest in collecting did not lead him to seek works of art, but bygones of almost every description from this and other countries. In the Music Room, which he panelled himself, he put coaching horns, eighteenth-century hurdy-gurdies, guitars, cellos, bassoons, drums, hautboys, barrel organs, harps and lyres. In other rooms the exhibits include ship models, lacquer cabinets, clocks, navigational instruments, lacemakers' lamps, spinning-wheels, hand-shuttles, bicycles and children's toys.

Snowshill Manor, Gloucestershire.

Berrington Hall, Herefordshire, from the north-west.

Berrington Hall

HEREFORDSHIRE

three miles north of Leominster

Berrington Hall is a late eighteenth-century house (about 1780) designed by one of the leading architects of that time, Henry Holland Jnr. It stands in a park laid out by 'Capability' Brown. There have been no significant alterations to the exterior of the house, and practically none at all inside.

It consists in a rectangular main block, rather austere, with a large portico; and three pavilions to house the laundry and other domestic offices. A square water-tower was built at the back of the house during the nineteenth century, and the quadrants joining the pavilions to the main block were altered.

The tone of austerity is not continued inside the house. Here Holland gave the principal rooms splendid fireplaces, beautifully decorated ceilings and fine doors and doorcases.

The site chosen for the house looks down on its own park and beyond that

Berrington Hall, Herefordshire: the drawing-room.

to extensive views of the Welsh hills, many miles away in Brecon and Radnor.

Practically nothing is known of the history of Berrington before Thomas Harley bought the estate about 1775, but there are traces of a medieval house about half a mile from the present one. Thomas Harley was a banker and government contractor. He was Lord Mayor of London during the Wilkite riots. He spared no expense in the building of Berrington, as the surviving accounts show. Holland's estimate for construction was £14,500, a large one for that time. Brown was paid £1,600. Harley's daughter, who inherited the estate from her father, married the second Lord Rodney, son of Admiral Rodney.

In the dining-room are contemporary battle pictures of Admiral Rodney's engagements. The Rodneys continued at Berrington until they sold it in 1900 to Mr Frederick Cawley (later Lord Cawley). In 1957 it was accepted by the Treasury in payment of death duty and transferred to the Trust with some of the contents.

Croft Castle

HEREFORDSHIRE

five miles north-west of Leominster

Croft affords a variety of interest and beauty—the castle itself and the little church close by, the avenue of Spanish chestnuts, the trees and waters of the Fish Pool Valley and the Iron Age hill fort on the ridge to the north of the castle.

The castle as seen today consists of the walls and towers of the fourteenth–fifteenth-century castle and an eighteenth-century central structure. It looks very much a castle from the outside. Inside, the hall and gallery were made in the eighteenth century on what had been an open courtyard. The walls of the eighteenth-century 'Gothic' staircase and the ceilings of some of the other rooms have delightful plasterwork. Some of the rooms are lined with panelling brought from other houses. There is an interesting collection of family portraits and Croft family heirlooms, the property of Lord Croft.

The small stone church beside the castle has a bell turret and cupola of the late seventeenth–early eighteenth century. But the church itself is much older: how much older is not known, but it was certainly altered in 1515 or, as the contemporary report says, was 'enlarged or more beautifully made'.

The Spanish Chestnut Avenue, a single row, about half a mile long, of 350-year-old trees, is a unique feature of the grounds—indeed there is nothing like it in the British Isles. There are many other fine trees, including Indian cedar, California redwood and immense oaks. The Fish Pool Valley is an excellent example of the late eighteenth-century school of landscaping,

Croft Castle, Herefordshire.

which insisted on 'nature's negligent disguise'. It was planted with mixed deciduous trees.

Croft Ambrey, the Iron Age hill fort, commands a view of fourteen counties. Recent excavations have established that it was occupied from the fourth century B.C. until the Roman Conquest.

There was a Croft at Croft at the time of Domesday and the family continued there until 1750. A gap followed until they bought it back in 1923. The Trust, aided by a grant from the Ministry of Works, bought it in 1957, Lord Croft and other members of the family providing an endowment for maintenance.

The Sugar Loaf

MONMOUTHSHIRE

north-west of Abergavenny

The Sugar Loaf rises to 1,950 feet and there is a track to the summit. About two thousand acres of the hill, which commands views of the Usk valley, were given to the Trust in 1936 by the first and second Viscountesses Rhondda as a memorial to the first viscount.

The Sugar Loaf, Monmouthshire: seen from Hatteral Hill on the Black Mountains.

Brecon Beacons, Breconshire, from the mountain road across Mynydd Illtyd on the north-west.

Brecon Beacons

BRECONSHIRE

About eight thousand acres, being the main part of this mountain massif in South Wales, were given to the Trust in 1956 by the chairman of the Eagle Star Insurance Company.

Two sandstone peaks face north and slope southwards. The highest point is Pen-y-fan (2,907 feet).

There are widespread views, extending south to the Bristol Channel, northwards (reputedly) as far as Cader Idris sixty miles away, and eastwards to another Trust property, *The Sugar Loaf* near Abergavenny in Monmouthshire. There is access to the whole area.

Marloes Beach

PEMBROKESHIRE

in St Bride's Bay between St David's Head and Milford Haven, on the southern arm of the bay near the island of Skomer

In addition to 520 acres at Marloes, the Trust has several other properties on the Pembrokeshire coast at St David's Head, in Whitesands Bay, at Solva and on Lydstep Headland between Tenby and Manorbier.

Some of this land was acquired after a public appeal, helped by the Pilgrim Trust, in 1939; the rest has been given by various donors.

Opposite: Whiteford Burrows, Glamorganshire.
Marloes Beach, Pembrokeshire, looking from east to west.

Three Cliff Bay

GLAMORGANSHIRE

seven miles south-west of Swansea on the east side of Pwlldu Head

The Trust has property here (page 152) and at other places on the unspoiled coasts of the Gower Peninsula. See note on *Whiteford Burrows.*

Whiteford Burrows

GLAMORGANSHIRE

in the north-east part of the Gower Peninsula

Whiteford Burrows, the little peninsula which juts out northwards at the eastern end of the Gower Peninsula, is made up of sand burrows and salt marsh. Its plant and bird life is of great interest. Six hundred and seventy acres here were bought in 1966 with money subscribed to Enterprise Neptune, the Trust's appeal for coastal preservation.

Three Cliff Bay, Penard, Glamorganshire.

The Trust's first acquisition in the Gower Peninsula was made in 1933. There have been further gifts by various donors at intervals since then, and purchases from Enterprise Neptune funds. The largest of these was the acquisition, in 1967, of seventeen miles at the western extremity, protecting Rhossili Down and Beach, Worm's Head, Llanshydian Marsh and foreshore between Thurba and Oxwich. In earlier years gifts were made of viewpoints in the south of the Peninsula at Notthill, Paviland Cliff, Pitton Cliff, Port Eynon Point and Thurba Head; of 150 acres in the Bishopston Valley six miles south-west of Swansea; and of land at Penard a little farther west adjoining Pwlldu Head.

Appendix

Properties not illustrated

Properties which are not illustrated and are not referred to in the notes that accompany the illustrations are noted below. In addition to the properties which it owns there, the Trust holds Restrictive Covenants over 9,710 acres and thirteen buildings in these counties. (See note in Introduction.)

WILTSHIRE

Holt, three miles east of Bradford-on-Avon, The Courts. Richly decorated façade of about 1700. Gardens open; not house.

Salisbury, Mompesson House. Built 1701 and has its original panelling and plasterwork. Also Joiners Hall, which retains a sixteenth-century timbered façade. Not open.

Stonehenge Down. Stonehenge belongs to the Ministry of Works, but 1,400 acres of the surrounding farmland belong to the Trust.

Viewpoints at Pepperbox Hill, five miles south-east of Salisbury, and Win Green Hill, five miles south-east of Shaftesbury.

Grey Wethers, three miles west of Marlborough, at Piggle Dene on the north side of the Bath road and at Lockeridge Dene a mile to the south of it, small pieces of land on which are sarsen stones known locally as Grey Wethers.

Warminster, Boreham Field, six acres on the south of the Warminster–Salisbury road. Given by Major E. P. Yeates.

DORSET

The Cerne Giant, the 180-foot-high figure cut in the chalk on Giant Hill near Cerne Abbas.

Tolpuddle, seven miles north-east of Dorchester. The Tolpuddle Martyrs Tree was given to the Trust in 1934.

Viewpoints at Crook Hill, Beaminster; at Lewesdon Hill three miles west of Beaminster; and at West Bexington, Lime Kiln Hill.

Hardy Monument, on the Martinstown–Portisham road six miles south-west of Dorchester, an 1846 memorial to Admiral Hardy, flag captain of *Victory*.

Southdown Farm, Ringstead Bay, seven miles south-east of Dorchester. At Creech, an eighteenth-century folly, three miles west of Corfe Castle.

Winyards Gap, four miles south-east of Crewkerne, woodland given as a 1939–45 war memorial.

Golden Cap estate, eight acres called The Saddle, a col between Golden Cap and Langdon Hill. Bought with funds given to Enterprise Neptune by an anonymous donor.

Black Ven Cliff, Charmouth, fifteen acres of cliff-land adjoining existing property. Bought from Enterprise Neptune funds.

SOMERSET

At Bath, the eighteenth-century Assembly Rooms, gutted by fire in 1942 but now restored; Rainbow Wood Farm, a mile south-east of the town and farmlands a half-mile north of the farm; on Little Solsbury Hill 2½ miles north-east of the town, a flat hill top with an Iron Age hill fort.

On Blackdown Hills, two miles south of Wellington and half a mile east of the Wellington–Hemyock road, a viewpoint which commands in clear weather views of the Welsh hills; and half a mile west of this the Wellington Monument, an obelisk of 1817 commemorating the duke's exploits.

Viewpoints at Monks Steps, Kewstoke on the north edge of Weston-super-Mare; and on Tor Hill just east of the city of Wells.

Land on Brean Down two miles south-west of Weston-super-Mare.

Woodspring Priory, near Weston-super-Mare. A coastal farm on which stands a group of fifteenth-century Augustinian priory buildings. Bought after public appeal for funds.

Half a mile south of Bruton, Bruton Dovecote, a sixteenth-century dovecote.

At Cheddar Cliffs, a hundred acres on the north side of the gorge.

Coleridge Cottage, in Nether Stowey, where Coleridge wrote *The Ancient Mariner*.

At Bristol, 360 acres at Failand four miles west of the town centre.

At Glastonbury, the summit of Glastonbury Tor, and three miles east, the fifteenth-century West Pennard Court Barn.

At Muchelney, 1½ miles south of Langport, Priests' House, late medieval.

The Quantocks. A fine viewpoint on Longstone Hill, west of Holford, and land at Holford Fields, three miles west of Nether Stowey, at Shervage Wood two miles west of Nether Stowey, and at Willoughby Cleeve half a mile west of Holford.

Sedgemoor, on Turn Hill four miles north of Langport, a viewpoint across the battlefield; also land at Burrow Mumps, north-east of Athelney station; on Cock Hill between Glastonbury and Bridgewater; on Ivythorn Hill, south of Street; and on Red Hill, three miles west of Langport.

Stoke-sub-Hamdon Priory, between Yeovil and Ilminster north of A 3088, a fifteenth-century building formerly a chantry house.

Ebbor Gorge, a hundred acres of wooded limestone gorge three miles north-west of Wells given by Mrs G. W. Hodgkinson in memory of Sir Winston Churchill. Mostly leased to the Nature Conservancy.

King John's Hunting Lodge, Axminster. A merchant's house of about 1500 which will be used as a local museum. Given by the Treasury.

DEVON

Branscombe, half way between Sidmouth and Seaton, farm, woodland and a mile of foreshore. Also twenty-three acres on Weston Cliff, bought from Enterprise Neptune funds; at Dunscombe, between Sidmouth and Branscombe, 240 acres of farmland, bought from Enterprise Neptune funds; and Higher Dunscombe Cliff, between Sidmouth and Branscombe, ninety acres, bought from Enterprise Neptune funds.

Drake's Island, in Plymouth Sound opposite the Hoe, leased from the Crown Estate Commissioners and being developed as an Adventure Training Centre.

At Hembury and at Holne Woods, ten miles west of Newton Abbot, woodlands on the west side of the River Dart.

Hen Tor and Willings Walls Warrens, 2,800 acres of open moorland on the south-west flank of Dartmoor overlooking the headwaters of the River Plym. Plym Bridge Woods, 120 acres of wooded valley of the Plym, bought in 1968.

Lydford Gorge, half way between Okehampton and Tavistock, 90 acres of the valley of the Lyd.

Lynmouth, Watersmeet, about half a mile east of Lynmouth, land on both sides of the East Lyn valley and astride the Hoar Oak Water.

Old Blundell's School, Tiverton. The seventeenth-century grammar school buildings now converted into dwelling-houses.

Salcombe. Properties around Salcombe harbour, from Bolt Tail and Bolt Head to the west to Prawle Point to the east, cover more than eleven miles of coast-line. Acquired bit by bit since 1929 by public subscription and from individual donors. One and a half miles south-west of Salcombe is Sharpitor, a modern house in which a museum of local interest has been established.

Gammon Head, north-west of Prawle Point, fifty-three acres of a rocky promontory, given by Lt-Col. E. A. Rose and his family in memory of George, Joanna and James Oakes.

Shute Barton, three miles south-west of Axminster. A medieval manor-house with late Gothic windows. Part was demolished in the eighteenth century. Open by appointment only.

Westward Ho! Kipling Tors. Eighteen acres of the gorse-covered hill of *Stalky and Co.*

Also, at Bigbury-on-Sea, a viewpoint on Clematon Hill; at Clovelly a viewpoint on Mount Pleasant, given as a 1914–18 memorial; land at Combe Park near Lynton and at Combe Wood, Combe Raleigh, near Honiton; East Titchberry Farm, east of Hartland Point, with a mile of cliff; at Flat Point west of Ilfracombe, near the village of Lee, coast and cliff-land; at Golden Cove, Berrynarbor, about 2½ miles east of Ilfracombe, wooded cliff-land; Damage Cliffs, three miles west of Ilfracombe, a hundred acres of hillocky cliff, bought from Enterprise Neptune funds with the help of Devon County Council and the Northcott Devon Foundation; on Lambert's Castle Hill 4½ miles east of Axminster the 842-foot hill top and surrounding land; at Little Haldon, three miles north-west of Teignmouth, heathland with views of Dartmoor; at Lympstone seven miles south-east of Exeter, land overlooking the estuary of the Exe; land at Marsland Mouth near Welcombe Mouth; on Morte Point and around Morte Bay, north-west of Barnstaple, nine properties amounting in all to about twelve hundred acres of headland, farmland and sand dunes, several of them gifts of the late Miss Rosalie Chichester of Arlington Court; at Orcombe and Prattshayes 2½ miles east-south-east of Exmouth, cliff-land and foreshore; on Rockbeare Hill three miles west of Ottery St Mary; in Sidmouth, part of The Byes, a public walk by the river, and Peak Hill Field; land and foreshore at Wembury Bay, five to six miles south-east of Plymouth; Holdstone Down, halfway between Coombe Martin Bay and Heddons Mouth, five acres of moorland and cliff bought from the Holberton Fund; Bridford Wood, north-east of Moretonhampstead, eighty acres of oak-covered hillside, bought with a legacy from Miss Gwendolen Pelly and a donation from the Devon County Council.

CORNWALL

The Trust owns twelve thousand acres in Cornwall, most of this land being coastal. Acquisitions have been made recently through Enterprise Neptune, the Trust's appeal for the preservation of the coast; but before the national appeal was launched Trust supporters in Cornwall had already established a Cornwall coast fund. Several beautiful parts of both north and south coasts are shown on pages 119, 123, 129, 131. Among other parts where the Trust has property are: Penberth Cove and Treen Cliff near Land's End, with the famous Logan Rock; north-west of Wadebridge, at Pentire Head and Portquin Bay, five hundred acres of cliff and farm land including Pentire Point and the Rumps; on the south coast, Mullion Cove and the site on the cliff a mile to the west of the village where Marconi set up the wireless transmitter which sent out the first transatlantic wireless signal; at St Anthony-in-Roseland, south-east of St Mawes coastal farmland, the thirty-five acres on St Anthony Head, from which the Trust has removed the very unsightly buildings put there for anti-aircraft defence during the 1939–45 war; St Mawes estuary, Tregassick Farm, a 140-acre farm, bought from the Muller and Ronald Baker funds; Trengwainton, two miles west of Penzance, a garden with a magnificent collection of shrubs and tender plants; an eighty-acre property on the Lizard Downs, including the east side of Kynance Cove; at Beagles Point, on the Lizard Peninsula, Treleaver Farm of 110 acres, bought from the Jolly Fund; Predannock, 640 acres of cliff and farm land on the west side of the Lizard peninsula, bought with Enterprise Neptune funds and a local appeal.

There is also National Trust land at Chapel Porth, 1½ miles south-west of St Agnes; at Cubert, four miles west of Newquay; at the Dodman, four miles south of Mevagissey; at Erth Barton, four miles west of Saltash; at Lanteglos near Fowey; at The Gannel near Newquay; between Godrevy and Portreath cliff and farmland extending for over six miles; at Gunwalloe Towans, a mile north-west of Mullion village; Lamledra Farm, west of Gorran Haven, two miles south of Mevagissey; at Morwenstow, six miles north of Bude; at Pendower Beach, Nare Head south-west of Tregony; at Pendarves Point, six miles south-west of Padstow, cliff-land including Park Head; St Eval, the headland which dominates this part of the Cornish coast at Pendower Beach, a mile south of Veryan; at Polperro; at Rosemergy and Trevean Cliffs on the north side of the Land's End–St Ives road (B 3306); at St Agnes, three stone cottages (not open) and heathland which commands fine coastal and inland views; at Sharrow Point, five miles west of Tor point; on Trencrom Hill, 4½ miles north of Penzance, where there is a well-preserved Iron Age B hill fort; and smaller parcels of land at Bodrugan's Leap, 1½ miles south of Mevagissey; in the Camel Estuary; in the Fal Estuary; on St Catherine's and St Saviour's Points near Fowey; also farmland on the east side of Polridmouth Cove and fifty-seven acres on Gribbin Head; at Hemmick Beach, four miles south of Mevagissey; at Hor Point and Hellesveor Cliff, 1½ miles west of St Ives; at Lesceave Cliff, five miles west of Helston; Zennor Head, north-west of St Ives, 4½ acres traversed by the coastal footpath, bought from the Cornwall Coast Fund; Rinsey Cliff, near Helston, thirty-five acres of cliff-land embracing two small coves, a gift to Enterprise Neptune by Mr H. K. Wigzell; at Lowland Point, on the east side of the Lizard peninsula; at Mayon and Trevescan Cliffs between Sennen Cove and Land's End; at Port Gaverne, seven miles north of Wadebridge; at Porthminster Point, on the south edge of St Ives; at Portloe on the south-west arm of Veryan Bay; at Zennor, five miles north-west of St Ives; at Lanyon Quoit, four miles north-west of Penzance, a huge granite capstone, remains of a long barrow; Bodigga Cliff, east of Looe, forty acres of cliff-land and foreshore, given by Metropolitan Railway Country Estates Ltd; Rinsey Cliff, Crackington, sixty acres of rough grazing and cliff-land on the Cornish Coast Path, bought from Enterprise Neptune funds; The Dizzard, sixty acres of cliff-land north-east of Crackington Haven, given by the Duchy of Cornwall; Tregardock, south of Tintagel, sixty acres of cliff-land, access on foot only, given by the Four Winds Trust; Frenchman's Creek, Helford River, a mile-long strip on the eastern bank of the Frenchman's Creek of Daphne du Maurier's novel, bought after public appeal for funds.

In Launceston, a Georgian house in Castle Street, to be a town museum.

GLOUCESTERSHIRE

Chedworth Roman villa, three miles north-west of Fossebridge. Mosaic pavements and a site museum. The villa was rediscovered in 1864.

Horton Court, three miles north-east of Chipping Sodbury. A Cotswold manor-house, altered in the last century, retaining its twelfth-century hall.

Viewpoints at Crickley Hill, the Scrubbs, six miles east of Gloucester; at Frocester Hill near Nympsfield between Stroud and Dursley; at May Hill, nine miles west of Gloucester; and at Haresfield Beacon, about three miles north-west of Stroud.

In addition to the cottages at Blaise Hamlet north of Bristol (photograph on page 138), Westbury College, in Westbury, three miles north of the centre of the city, the fifteenth-century gatehouse of the college of priests of which John Wyclif was a prebend. Also King George's Field, a mile south-east of Avonmouth, used as a recreation ground; land at Frenchay Moor, five miles north-east of the city; at Shirehampton Park, four miles north-west of the city, part used as a golf-course; and at Leigh Woods on the left bank of the Avon, by Clifton Suspension Bridge, 160 acres including the Iron Age promontory fort of Stokeleigh.

At Upleadon, 2½ miles east of Newent, a piece of land on Edens Hill.

Newark Park, 640 acres of wood and farmland 1½ miles east of Wotton-under-Edge on a spur of the Cotswolds.

In Painswick, a small Cotswold town house now a bookshop.

Near Stroud, in addition to the property at Haresfield Beacon noted above, land at Besbury Common, half a mile north of Minchinhampton; at Hyde Commons, three miles south-east of Stroud; 580 acres of Minchinhampton Commons, north of Nailsworth, with earthworks thought to be first century A.D.; land on Littleworth Common, adjoining Minchinhampton

Commons; 240 acres of Rodborough Common, a mile south of Stroud; land at Stockend Wood on Scottsquar Hill, two miles south of Painswick; and at Watledge Hill between Nailsworth and Pinfarthing.

At Wotton-under-Edge, some steeply sloping pasture land on the northern outskirts.

Westbury Court Gardens, nine miles south-west of Gloucester. A late seventeenth-century Dutch water garden. Given to the Trust in 1967 by Gloucestershire County Council. Not open until restoration work is completed.

HEREFORDSHIRE

Brockhampton, about two miles east of Bromyard, a two-thousand-acre agricultural estate. Lower Brockhampton (house) is a late fourteenth-century moated manor-house. Hall open.

The Weir, Swainshill, five miles west of Hereford. Garden and views.

Bradnor Hill, 1½ miles north-west of Kington, 340 acres of common land partly used as a golf-course.

Brilley, on the Herefordshire-Radnorshire border between Hay-on-Wye and Kington, 350 acres of farm and woodland, wide views.

Pengethly Park, a farm and woodland four miles west of Ross.

Poor's Acre, land in Haugh Wood, six miles south-east of Hereford.

Breinton Springs, three miles west of Hereford, fourteen acres of wood and farmland north of the River Wye.

MONMOUTHSHIRE

Skenfrith Castle, six miles north-west of Monmouth. Norman ruins.

Viewpoints at Betws Newydd, four miles north of Usk; Coed-y-Bwynydd, on the Kymin, a mile east of Monmouth; and on the summit of Skirrid Fawr, three miles north-east of Abergavenny.

BRECONSHIRE

Henrhyd Falls, eleven miles north of Neath, just north of Coelbren Junction. Waterfall and wooded ravine.

CARDIGANSHIRE

Lochtyn, about twelve miles north-east of Cardigan, immediately north-east of the village of Llangranog. A two-hundred-acre farm with 1½ miles of beautiful cliffs.

Mwnt, four miles north of Cardigan, about twenty acres of coastland.

Ponterwyd, twelve miles east of Aberystwyth, a 230-acre sheep farm above the Rheidol gorge.

Llanborth Farm, ninety acres with half a mile of cliff and access to Penbryn beach, about ten miles north-east of Cardigan. Bought in 1966 from Enterprise Neptune funds with the help of the Goldsmiths' Company.

Cwmtydi, Caerllan Farm of seventy acres, with a half-mile of coastline on the east side of Cwmtydi inlet. Access to cliffs. Bought from Enterprise Neptune funds.

CARMARTHENSHIRE

Dolaucothi, at Pumpsaint, between Llanwrda and Lampeter, a 2,400-acre agricultural estate. Given in 1941 by Mr H. T. C. Lloyd-Johnes as a memorial to the Johnes family, owners since the time of Henry VII, and particularly to Lieutenant-General Sir James Hill-Johnes, V.C. The gold-mine at Dolaucothi has been worked intermittently since Roman times.

Tregoning Hill, a viewpoint on the east headland of the Towy estuary, a mile south of Ferryside.

Paxton's Tower. A folly, seven miles east of Carmarthen, built 1811 as a memorial to Nelson. Fine views. An acre adjoining Paxton's Tower given as a car park by the Landmark Trust.

PEMBROKESHIRE

Cilgerran Castle, three miles south of Cardigan on the Teifi. A thirteenth-century ruin under the guardianship of the Ministry of Works.

Tenby. Tudor merchant's house, late fifteenth–nearly sixteenth century, now used as a National Trust Information Centre.

A hundred and sixty acres at Kete, a mile of coast west of Dale with views of Skomer and Skokholm islands.

Manorbier Cliff, forty-eight acres of cliff, with views, bought in 1967 with Enterprise Neptune funds.

Solva, to the east of Solva harbour 270 acres covering a mile and a half of coast. Bought with Enterprise Neptune funds.

Oxburgh Hall, Norfolk.

3

ENGLAND
Midland Counties and East Anglia

Blickling Hall, Norfolk: the south front.

Blickling Hall, Norfolk: the library in the Long Gallery.

Blickling Hall

NORFOLK

one mile north-west of Aylsham

Blickling stands in a lovely setting of lawns and formal garden. It is a fine symmetrical building of mellowed rose red brick with many gables, chimneys and pinnacles. It was built about 1620, on the site of an earlier house, for Sir Robert Hobart, the Lord Chief Justice. Although the architect has not been finally identified, there is good evidence to suggest that it was Robert Lyminge, who had designed another very famous and not dissimilar Jacobean house, Hatfield House, some few years before. During the later part of the eighteenth century alterations were made to the north and west fronts, and some changes were made in the interior. As a result the State Bedroom and the Peter the Great Room are now good examples of the style of elegance of the 1780's; but the *Long Gallery* (page 163) retains its elaborate Jacobean plasterwork ceiling.

Of special interest among the furnishings of the house is the tapestry which gives the Peter the Great Room its name. This was woven in St Petersburg in 1764 and represents Peter the Great at the battle of Poltawa. It was given by the Empress Catherine to John Hobart, second Earl of Buckinghamshire, who was ambassador to Russia from 1762 to 1765.

Beyond the formal gardens there is a landscaped park with a mile-long lake fringed by magnificent trees.

Blickling passed by marriage last century to the eighth Marquess of Lothian. When the eleventh Marquess, Philip Kerr, died in 1940 while serving as ambassador in Washington he left the property to the Trust.

Blakeney Point and Scolt Head

NORFOLK

respectively eight miles east of Wells and three miles north of Burnham Market

The north coast of Norfolk between Hunstanton and Weybourne is completely unspoiled and of the greatest interest to scientists. Before the Fishmongers' Company and anonymous donors gave the Trust its thousand-acre Blakeney Point property in 1912, Dr Oliver and others from University College, London, had already done valuable scientific work there over many years. Under the Trust's ownership it became the first nature reserve in Norfolk. It is administered by the Trust.

Scolt Head Island (1,600 acres) was bought for the Trust in 1923 with funds raised by the Norfolk Naturalists' Society. In 1953 it was leased to the Nature Conservancy.

The area is one of shingle ridges, sand dunes and salt marsh and is subject to rapid physical change. Consequent variations in its plant life and the distribution of animal and insect populations provide unusual scope for ecological studies. Its bird population, in addition to winter and summer migrants, includes nesting colonies of tern, oyster-catcher and ringed plover.

These properties are maintained as Nature Reserves and students are

Blakeney Point, Norfolk: the ternery.

welcome—about a hundred organized school and college parties visit each year—provided they keep strictly to the rules. The importance of this proviso is highlighted by a note in the Trust's 1967 *News Letter*: 'This is the first time for some years that Sandwich tern have stayed through the season on the Point in any numbers, and the Warden is to be congratulated on achieving this by diligently keeping visitors from disturbing the nests.'

The Trust has published a detailed guide to these properties, compiled by experts in the different subjects which can be studied there.

In 1967 the Trust bought, with Enterprise Neptune funds, the manor of Brancaster from the Brancaster Memorial Trust. This covers over two thousand acres of tidal foreshore, marsh, dunes and saltings to the west of Scolt Head Island.

Oxburgh Hall

NORFOLK

seven miles south-west of Swaffham at Oxborough

The house (page 171) was built in 1482, at a time of transition from the fortified manor-house or castle to the later unfortified country house. It still retains the general outline of the original building, although from time to time parts of the house have been damaged and restored or altered, and additions have been made.

The Great Tower, which remains completely unchanged, is a truly impressive sight, rising eighty feet straight from the edge of the moat. The detail of the brickwork is as impressive as the proportions of the tower, and the layman has no difficulty in accepting Pugin's dictum that it is 'one of the noblest specimens of the domestic architecture of the fifteenth century'.

Inside the tower on the first floor is the King's Chamber, so called because Henry VII lodged there when he visited Oxburgh in 1497. Displayed in this room are some panels of needlework embroidered and signed by Mary Queen of Scots. These are among the very few known examples of her work. They were brought to Oxburgh in 1793 by a daughter of Viscount Montague of Cowdray, who married a Bedingfeld. Oxburgh, which was built by the Bedingfeld family and has been their home for more than 480 years, was given to the Trust by the Dowager Lady Bedingfeld in 1952.

4 South Quay, Great Yarmouth

NORFOLK

For about 350 years 4 South Quay had a succession of owners, including mayors and prominent merchants of Yarmouth. It was built in 1590 on the site of an earlier building. Its seventeenth-century owners gave the rooms oak panelling and fine chimney-pieces. The present outside appearance of the house dates from about 1810. The front was at that time in need of repair, and the owner encased it in white brick and enlarged the windows.

4 South Quay, Great Yarmouth, Norfolk.

It was given to the Trust in 1943 and has been leased to Yarmouth Corporation as a museum. Recently some seventeenth-century glass panels of ships and fishing scenes have been incorporated in windows overlooking the courtyard.

Key

MIDLAND COUNTIES AND EAST ANGLIA

1 Abbey Gatehouse, Ramsey
2 Alport Height
3 Angel Corner
4 Anglesey Abbey
5 Aston Wood
6 Attingham Park
7 Bale Oaks
8 Benthall Hall
9 Blakeney Point
10 Blickling Hall
11 Brackley Park
12 Bredon Tithe Barn
13 Bullfer Grove
14 Burnham Overy Mill
15 Cawston Duelling Stone
16 Chadwich
17 Charlecote Park
18 Charnwood Forest
19 Children's Field, Knowle
20 Clent Hill
21 Clumber Park
22 Clump Farm
23 Cofton Hackett
24 Coombe End Farm
25 Coughton Court
26 Curbar Gap
27 Derwent Estate
28 Dovedale
29 Downs Banks
30 Duffield Castle
31 Dunstable Downs
32 Earlswood Moat House
33 Eccles Pike
34 Edale (Mam Tor)
35 Farnborough Hall
36 Flatford Mill
37 Frankley Beeches
38 Grantham House
Great Yarmouth: *see* 4 South Quay
39 Greyfriars
40 Groveley Dingle
41 Guildhall, Lavenham
42 Gunby Hall
43 Hanbury Hall
44 Hardwick Hall
45 Harvington Hall
46 Hawksmoor
47 Hopesay Hill
48 Horsey Windmill
49 Houghton Mill
50 Ickworth
51 Kencot Manor Farm
52 Kinver Edge
53 Kinwarton Dovecote
54 Knowles Mill
55 Kyson Hill
56 Lantern Pike
Lavenham: *see* Guildhall, Lavenham
57 Letocetum
58 Long Mynd, The
59 Longshaw
60 Lyveden New Build
Malvern Hills: *see* Midsummer Hill, Malvern Hills
Mam Tor: *see* Edale
61 Manifold and Hamps Valleys
62 Market Cross, Colston Bassett
63 Market House, Winster
64 Melford Hall
65 Midsummer Hill, Malvern Hills
66 Miller's Dale
67 Morville Hall
68 Moseley Old Hall
69 Outney Common
70 Oxburgh Hall
71 Packwood House
72 Peckover House
73 Priest's House
Ramsey Abbey Gatehouse: *see* Abbey Gatehouse, Ramsey
74 Riley Graves
75 St George's Guildhall
76 Scolt Head
77 Sharpenhoe
78 Shining Cliff Wood
79 Shugborough
80 Sling Pool
81 South Leigh
82 4 South Quay, Great Yarmouth
83 South Ridge Farm
84 Stanton Moor Edge
85 Staunton Harold Church
86 Stratford-upon-Avon Canal (Southern Section)
87 Sudbury Hall
88 Taddington Wood
89 Tattershall Castle
90 Thorington Hall
91 Town Walls Tower, Shrewsbury
92 Upton House
93 Watlington Hill
94 West Runton
95 Wichenford Dovecote
96 Wicken Fen
97 Wightwick Manor
98 Wilderhope Manor
99 Willington Dovecote
Winster Market House: *see* Market House, Winster
100 Woolsthorpe Manor

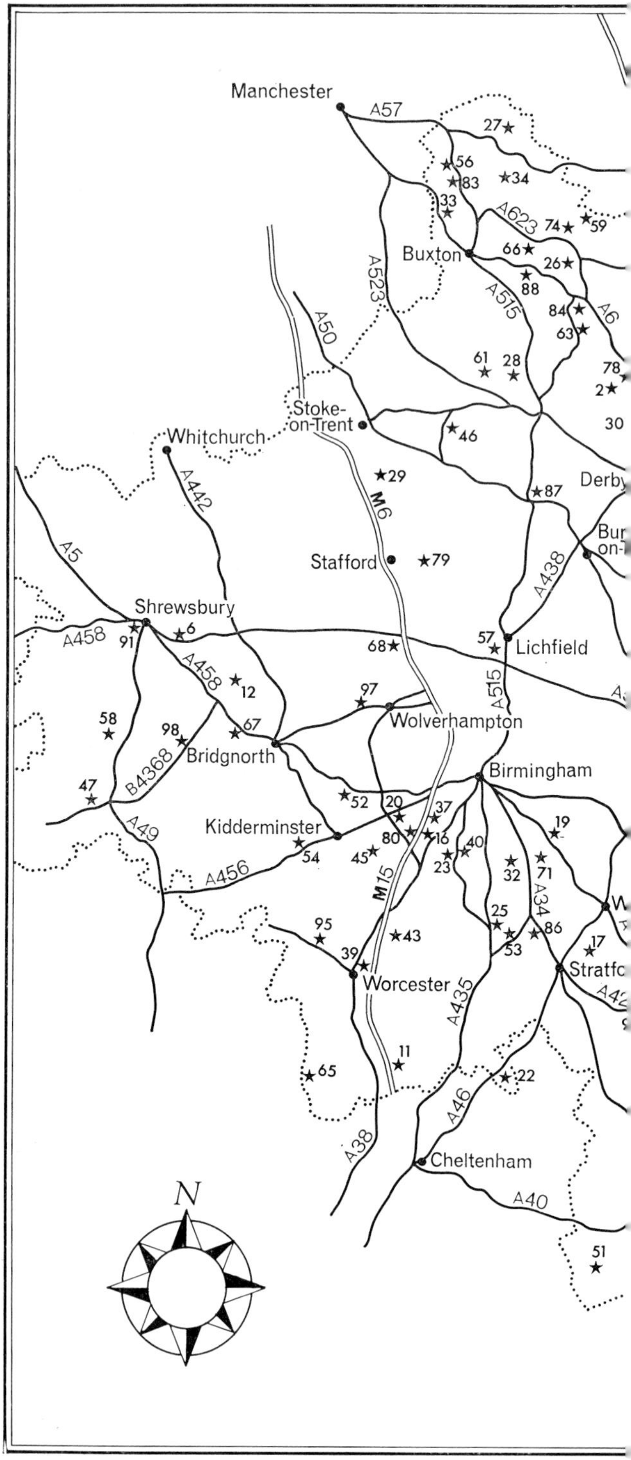

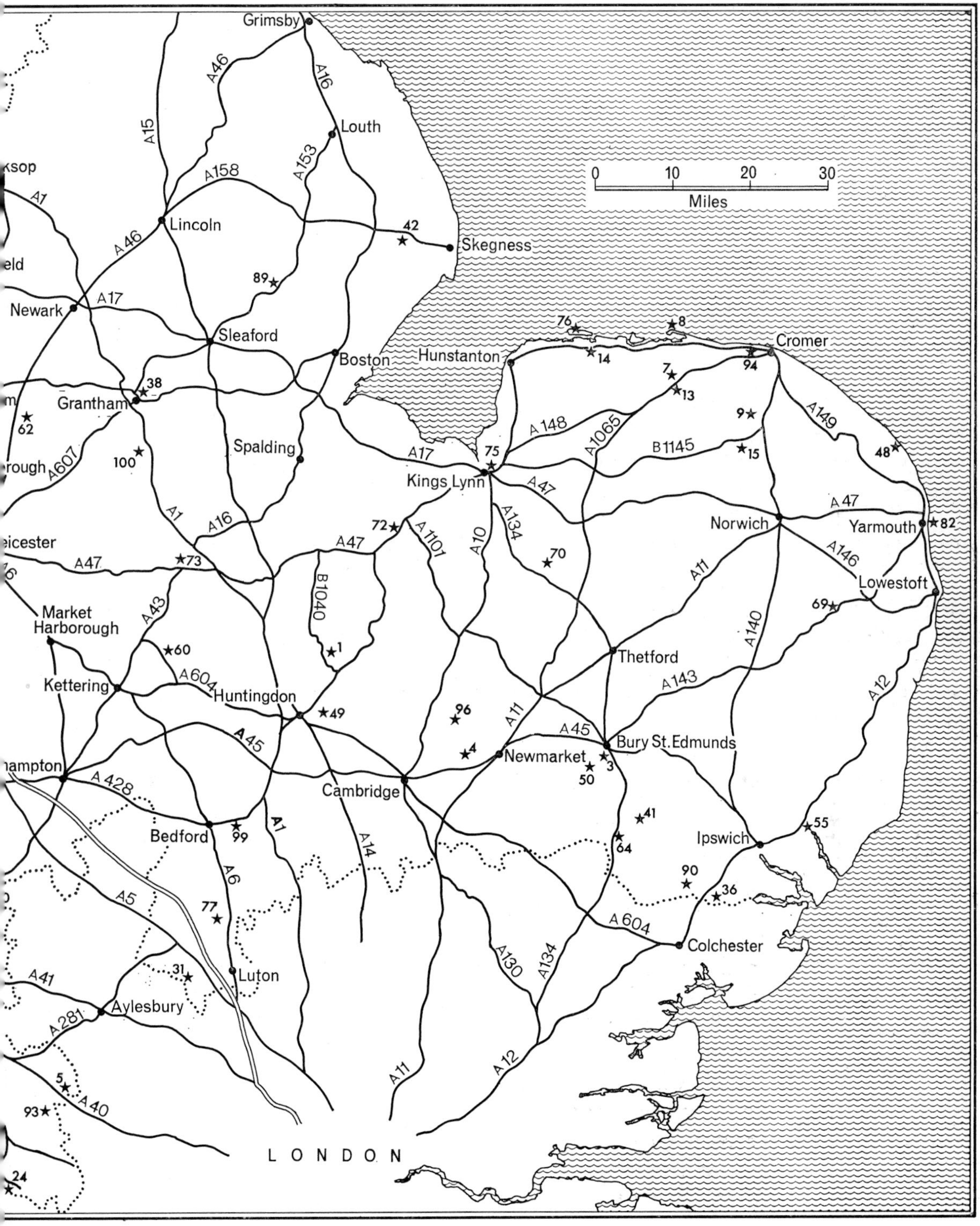
Grimsby
Louth
Skegness
Lincoln
Newark
Sleaford
Boston
Grantham
Spalding
Hunstanton
Cromer
Kings Lynn
Norwich
Yarmouth
Lowestoft
Thetford
Bury St. Edmunds
Newmarket
Cambridge
Huntingdon
Market Harborough
Kettering
Bedford
Luton
Aylesbury
Ipswich
Colchester
LONDON
0
10
20
30
Miles
A46
A16
A15
A153
A158
A7
A17
A607
A1
A47
A43
A604
A45
A428
A5
A6
A41
A281
A40
A14
A11
A10
A1101
B1040
A134
A148
A1065
B1145
A149
A146
A140
A143
A12
A130

Horsey Windmill, Norfolk.

Horsey Windmill

NORFOLK

about eleven miles north of Yarmouth

Horsey mill is a fine landmark and vantage point for those who go up it to admire the views to Horsey Mere and out to sea. It was built in 1912 as a drainage mill on the site of an earlier mill. It was struck by lightning in 1943, and although it has been restored it is no longer used for drainage purposes.

The Trust's whole Horsey property extends to seventeen hundred acres and includes farmlands as well as Horsey Mere, marshes and marrams. The mere is accessible by boat, but as it is a breeding ground for marsh birds access is not unrestricted.

The Trust bought the property in 1948 with the help of a public subscription and a grant from the Pilgrim Trust.

Oxburgh Hall, Norfolk.

Flatford Mill, Suffolk.

Flatford Mill

SUFFOLK

ten miles south-west of Ipswich, a mile south of East Bergholt

Flatford (page 171) is the mill of Constable's 'Hay Wain' and of other of his pictures. The mill and millhouse were built in the eighteenth century and belonged to his father. Constable himself worked in the mill for about a year.

The Trust bought the mill in 1943 but were reimbursed some years later by a benefactor.

The mill and a nearby half-timbered building of the fifteenth century are let to the Field Studies Council and used by them as a Field Study Centre.

Melford Hall

SUFFOLK

three miles north of Sudbury in Long Melford

In the Middle Ages Melford belonged to the abbots of Bury St Edmunds. After the dissolution of the monasteries it was granted to William Cordell, a local man who became Speaker of the House of Commons and later Master of the Rolls. He built virtually a new house, though incorporating in it some parts of the old one. When exactly it was built and who was employed on the work is not known. But presumably it was finished by 1578 because in that year Cordell entertained Queen Elizabeth at Melford and did so, according to contemporary accounts, most sumptuously. Although the inside has been much altered since her visit, the outside must have appeared to Elizabeth as very much the attractive brick manor-house one sees today.

The internal changes and additions were made at two different periods. In the 1730's and 40's the Elizabethan screens in the hall were replaced by Doric columns, a large staircase was introduced and the hall redecorated. At this period the Blue Drawing Room was given a carved wood chimney-piece and an ornamented ceiling of mid-Georgian style. Then in 1813 a

Melford Hall, Suffolk.

library was added, fitted with Regency bookcases and furnished with chairs and tables designed for the room.

The contents of the house, which are varied and interesting, reflect something of its history and that of the families who have been its owners. The andirons in the Hall probably belonged to the earlier monastic house, perhaps to the twelfth-century abbot. William Cordell had them remounted and added his crest. Beside them are two Nonsuch chests, so called because of the illustrations of Nonsuch Palace which decorate them; reputedly a gift to her host from the visiting Queen Elizabeth. Other rooms contain fine furniture and family portraits of the Parker family. The house was bought by Sir Harry Parker in 1786 and remained in the ownership of the family until 1960, when it was accepted by the Treasury in part payment of death duties and given to the Trust. Sir Harry devoted himself to the administration of the estate. His father, brother and nephew, all named Hyde Parker, were all admirals of gallantry and distinction. In the Library are paintings of their actions, executed by Dominique Serves, marine painter to George III, and charts used by them in engagements in which they took part. The second Admiral Hyde Parker was knighted for forcing the boom in the attack on New York in 1776. Later he was in command at the battle of Copenhagen, and it was to a signal from him that Nelson turned a blind eye.

Ickworth

SUFFOLK

three miles south-west of Bury St Edmunds

Ickworth (pages 176–77) was built most unusual in plan and generous in size. The central portion is a lofty rotunda, and curved corridors lead from this to the two wings. The height of the rotunda is a hundred feet and the length of the whole building two hundred yards.

This plan was devised by a remarkable man, Frederick Augustus Hervey, Bishop of Derry, who became Earl of Bristol in succession to his brother in 1779. He was an enthusiastic traveller and collector of works of art—such a well-known traveller that many of the Hotels Bristol in continental countries are named after him. It was his intention that one wing should contain pictures, the other sculpture, and that the rotunda be used as living quarters. But he did not live to finish the house (he began it in 1794 and died in Italy in 1803) and his son, who finished the building, changed the internal arrangement. He made the East Wing his residence and furnished the rooms in the rotunda as entertaining rooms.

Although the marble group which the earl bishop commissioned from Talman stands in the entrance hall, his art collection did not all find its way to Ickworth. He had assembled much of it in Rome, and this was confiscated after 1798 when the French invaded Italy. But other members of the Hervey family, both before and since his time, accumulated furniture, porcelain and, notably, silver of the highest quality; so Ickworth, as he intended, houses magnificent collections. The paintings include a Velasquez portrait of a son of Philip IV of Spain and family portraits by Reynolds, Gainsborough, Angelica Kauffmann and other famous artists. Among the subjects of these portraits are the famous beauty and wit Molly Leppell, who was the bishop's mother, and Lady Elizabeth Foster, later Duchess of Devonshire, who was his daughter.

The Guildhall, Lavenham, Suffolk.

The house stands in a setting of magnificent beeches, cypresses and cedars. It was acquired by the Trust in 1956, having been accepted by the Treasury in part payment of death duties.

The Guildhall, Lavenham

SUFFOLK

Lavenham Guildhall was built in the 1520's by the Guild of Corpus Christi. This was a trade guild, concerned with the wool trade which had flourished in Suffolk for two centuries, but also concerned to celebrate the

Ickworth, Suffolk: the dining-room.

Opposite: Ickworth, Suffolk; the north portico.

Anglesey Abbey, Cambridgeshire: the north front.

festivals of the Church. On feast days they processed from their fine half-timbered hall to church or—as, for example, at Corpus Christi—held their celebration in the hall.

But the guild did not long survive the suppression of the religious houses, and before the end of the century their Guildhall had become parish property.

Through most of the seventeenth century it was used as the town hall. Thereafter it became at different times a prison, a workhouse and a wool store.

Although the inside suffered from these vicissitudes and not much of the original panelling and carving has survived, the outside remains a good example of the rather ornate style of half-timbered building in fashion under Henry VIII.

It was rescued in 1887 by Sir Cuthbert Quilter, who undertook the repair of the building, and in 1951 his son, with the aid of the Lavenham Preservation Society, gave it to the Trust.

Funds for upkeep were raised by a local appeal supported by the Pilgrim Trust, and it is now used by Lavenham for public meetings and other social activities.

A view in the gardens of Anglesey Abbey.

Anglesey Abbey

CAMBRIDGESHIRE

six miles north-east of Cambridge

There have been three phases in the long life of Anglesey Abbey. First, it was a foundation of the Augustinian Order; the Canons' Parlour, built in 1236, remains the dining-room of the house of today. Secondly, after the dissolution of the monasteries, when part of the building was pulled down, it was rebuilt as an Elizabethan manor-house; substantially the house which is there today. Thirdly, in 1926 the late Lord Fairhaven and his brother bought it, made some alterations to the interior, and during the following forty years transformed the grounds and created there a *garden* of outstanding interest. Earlier owners had planted trees, including cedars, which are now

Wicken Fen, Cambridgeshire: evening light.

mature. Lord Fairhaven extended these plantings and established a rose garden, flowering trees and herbaceous plants. To mark the eight hundredth anniversary of the founding of the abbey he erected a commemoration urn. Sections of the gardens are laid out in formal style with statuary, grass and trees.

Lord Fairhaven was also a collector of pictures. When he died in 1966 he left the abbey and gardens to the Trust, together with the exceptionally fine paintings (including works by Claude, Cuyp, William Etty and Constable) which hang there.

Wicken Fen

CAMBRIDGESHIRE

ten miles north-east of Cambridge

Wicken Fen is a famous nature reserve where for many years naturalists have studied the plants, insects and birds of the fenlands. It has been described as 'an open-air laboratory for biological study in its widest sense'. It is much visited not only by specialists but also by school parties and by the general public. There is a resident warden and visitors are required to keep strictly to the rules for access to different areas.

In 1967 the committee which administers the fen for the Trust launched an appeal for funds to improve facilities for study, and to create a new marshland reserve. This reserve, to quote the committee, 'will produce a new range of aquatic and marsh communities, providing a valuable breeding habitat and migration refuge for many species of birds'.

The first gift to the Trust of a part of the fen was made in 1899 and further gifts have been made since. The property now extends to about seven hundred acres.

Peckover House, Wisbech

CAMBRIDGESHIRE

Peckover House (page 183) is one of the Georgian houses in Wisbech overlooking the River Nene. The stables are to the side, and there is a garden at the back. The house was built in 1722 in brick for a local family called Southwell. The exterior, except for some detail of the garden front which may have been added later in the century, remains unaltered. Inside the house a great deal of remarkably fine decoration was added to the rooms between 1730 and 1750. All the rooms are panelled; the fireplaces have carved overmantels. There is a good Georgian staircase. In the pale blue, grey and white drawing-room the overmantel is described in the Trust's guide-book as 'a *tour de force* of applied carving, outstanding in its elegance and grace'.

Towards the end of the eighteenth century the house was bought by Jonathan Peckover, founder of the local bank, which was merged with Barclays in 1896. During the nineteenth century the Peckovers added the two low wings on either side of the house. They also laid out the garden and planted some rare trees, including a maidenhair tree which has flourished. In the glasshouse orange trees bear good fruit. The house and garden were given to the Trust in 1943 by the Hon. Alexandrina Peckover.

The Trust also owns the much plainer early eighteenth-century houses on either side of Peckover House, Nos. 14 and 19 North Brink. These were accepted by the Treasury in payment of death duties and transferred to the Trust in 1949.

Houghton Mill

HUNTINGDONSHIRE

midway between Huntingdon and St Ives

Houghton Mill (page 184) is a timber water-mill on the River Ouse given to the Trust by the River Ouse Catchment Board and the borough councils of Huntingdon and Godmanchester in 1939. An external fire escape has been added to the building, which is one of those which the Trust has let to the Youth Hostels Association (others are Wilderhope in Shropshire, Winchester City Mill and the Palace Stables at the head of Boscastle Harbour in Cornwall).

Ramsey Abbey Gatehouse

HUNTINGDONSHIRE

at the south-east edge of Ramsey

The remains of the fifteenth-century gatehouse of the Benedictine abbey (page 185) were given to the Trust in 1952.

Peckover House, Wisbech, Cambridgeshire: the chimney-piece in the drawing-room.

Houghton Mill, Huntingdonshire.

Ramsey Abbey Gatehouse, Huntingdonshire.

Gunby Hall

LINCOLNSHIRE

seven miles west of Skegness

Gunby Hall was built for Sir William Massingberd in 1700 in brick of a beautiful deep plum colour. A north wing was added in 1873 to allow of improved internal arrangements, and this includes a drawing-room which follows successfully the style of the earlier rooms.

Failing any evidence other than the design of the house itself, it is supposed that the architect was a mason or builder who had studied the work of Sir Christopher Wren's school.

Whoever may have designed the house, Tennyson has supplied its apt description in the verse which ends with the line 'A haunt of ancient peace'. Indeed he may well have had Gunby particularly in mind, since there is preserved at the house a copy of the verse written in his own hand, signed and dated 1849.

Among the contents of the house are two portraits by Reynolds and a book of special interest. This is one of the few surviving autographed copies of Boswell's *Life of Johnson.* It was given to Bennet Langton, whose son married the Gunby heiress in 1784.

Gunby was given to the Trust by the Massingberd family in 1944.

Grantham House, Grantham

LINCOLNSHIRE

Grantham House stands in the centre of the town, across the road from Grantham church. Its twenty-five acres of garden and grounds lead down to the river and across it to meadows through which there is a public right of way. From this there are views of the beautiful church.

The house and its outbuildings are stone with tiled roofs. It has been altered a number of times and its architectural features date from several different periods. The central hall survives from the original building of about 1380; sixteenth-century windows face the church; the garden front was made over about 1734.

Gunby Hall, Lincolnshire.

Grantham House, Grantham, Lincolnshire.

Woolsthorpe Manor, Lincolnshire.

It was built by a family of wool merchants called Hall and was known as Hall Place. It has changed hands several times, the eighteenth-century alterations being made by Anne, Lady Cust, whose son, Sir John Cust, was Speaker of the House of Commons. The house and grounds were given to the Trust in 1944 by the late Misses Winifred and Marion Sedgewick. Not open to the public at the time of writing.

Woolsthorpe Manor

LINCOLNSHIRE

seven miles south of Grantham

Woolsthorpe Manor, which was given to the Trust in 1943 through the Royal Society and the Pilgrim Trust, who provided funds for its repair, is preserved as a place of historic interest. Isaac Newton was born in this small early seventeenth-century house in 1642. He returned here from Cambridge during the plague years 1665–6 at a time when, in his own words, he was 'in the prime of my age for invention'. He conceived his idea of universal gravitation at this time, and traditionally it was in the garden of Woolsthorpe that he was prompted to it by seeing the fall of an apple from a tree.

Tattershall Castle

LINCOLNSHIRE

three and a half miles south-east of Woodhall Spa

Tattershall (page 190) is a fortified manor-house built about 1440 by Ralph Cromwell, who had become Treasurer of England some years before. It is fully entitled to the name 'castle' not only because it was built on the site of a medieval castle, but also because the defensive features of a castle were included in its design. The introduction of gunpowder had made such castles vulnerable, but Cromwell may have thought it sensible for an unpopular minister in an unsettled time to defend himself at least against less sophisticated attack. The great hundred-foot brick tower of his stronghold still stands.

At the same time he was mindful both of comfort and of the display he thought proper for a great officer of state. The rooms in the four stages of the tower have good windows and fine fireplaces; and from examination of the site and contemporary building accounts it is clear that the castle had spacious, well equipped kitchens.

Tattershall, like *Bodiam Castle* in Sussex, was saved from ruin by Lord Curzon. When it came up for sale in 1910 it had been uninhabited for two

Tattershall Castle, Lincolnshire.

hundred years and was decaying. American speculators bought it and sold the fireplaces, which it was proposed to send to America. At that point Lord Curzon stepped in, and saving both castle and fireplaces employed Mr William Weir to restore the castle as far as possible to its original state. In his will Lord Curzon left Tattershall (and Bodiam) to the Trust.

Clumber Park, Nottinghamshire: the lime tree avenue.

Clumber Park

NOTTINGHAMSHIRE

two and a half miles south-east of Worksop

Clumber Park, a fine and extensive piece of late eighteenth-century landscaping, was made from a part of the old forest of Sherwood and some adjoining heathland. It covers 3,800 acres, of which about 2,000 are woodland and contains Hardwick village and farm, an eighty-acre lake and a three-mile-long *lime avenue.* Before the park was laid out the land was described as 'a black heath, full of rabbits, having a narrow riving running through it with a small boggy close or two'. When the Dukes of Newcastle had the park made they also had built a mansion, with terraces and fountains to grace it, by the lake. This has been demolished, except for one small portion now used as a restaurant, and the chapel and the stables. Clumber was acquired by the Trust in 1946 through public appeal and the sale of timber, and with the help of eight local authorities.

Clumber Chapel was designed by one of the architects of the Gothic revival, G. F. Bodley, and has been described as Bodley's 'cathedral in miniature'. It was built by the seventh Duke of Newcastle (between 1886 and 1889) as his private chapel and for the use of the people of Clumber Park. It is in the Decorated style of the fourteenth century. Its tower and spire rise to 180 feet. It contains some beautifully carved limewood statues of the evangelists, saints and archangels; stained-glass windows by C. E. Kempe; and some fine quality metalwork, much of which was wrought by blacksmiths on the estate. Services are held in the chapel on Sundays in the summer.

Dovedale

DERBYSHIRE

four to seven miles north-west of Ashbourne

On the Derbyshire-Staffordshire border, in the Dove, Manifold and Hamps valleys and the hills which divide them, Trust properties embrace a variety of areas of unspoiled country (pages 193–94). Altogether two thousand acres there belong to the Trust, and over a further three thousand acres protective covenants have been granted. In addition to the three places illustrated, the Trust has property in Dovedale which includes the remarkable rock formations known as Jacob's Ladder and the Twelve Apostles. At Ilam, in Staffordshire, the park and woodland on both sides of the Manifold and the home farm are Trust property. The nineteenth-century Ilam Hall is let to the Youth Hostels Association.

A little farther north on the east bank of the Dove (at High Wheeldon about five miles south-east of Buxton), some thirty acres on the hills bounding the upper reaches of the river were given in 1947 as a memorial to men of Derbyshire and Staffordshire who fell in the 1939–45 war.

In the Manifold valley the Grindon and Swainsley estates cover nearly nine hundred acres of farmland to the west of Alstonfield, reaching up to Grindon Moor and Welton Hill. On the right bank of the Hamps between

Hall Dale, Derbyshire: the entrance, just above Dovedale, on the Staffordshire side of the River Dove.

Bunster Hill, Derbyshire: a view taken from the Ilam–Blore road showing Bunster Hill, which stands between Dovedale and Ilam.

Mill Dale, Derbyshire: Viator's Bridge at the top end of Dovedale.

Sparrowlee and Beeston Tor, the Throwley Estate includes Oldpark Hill and parts of Beeston Tor.

These Derbyshire and Staffordshire properties were acquired by the Trust during the 1930's and since the last war by the generosity of many donors, notable among them being the late Sir Robert McDougall.

Hardwick Hall

DERBYSHIRE

six and a half miles north-west of Mansfield

Hardwick Hall (page 196) is much praised by critics as a masterpiece of Renaissance building, its interior embellished by a wealth of magnificent plasterwork, and it has a unique collection of tapestries and needlework. In a brief account of the house Sacheverell Sitwell wrote of the Great High Chamber that in his opinion it is 'the most beautiful room not in England alone, but in the whole of Europe'.

To less learned visitors, too, Hardwick is immensely satisfying; a grand, impressive building, richly decorated, splendidly furnished and with fine gardens laid out in a series of walled courtyards. It had suffered very little change for three hundred years and more. Some of the contents listed in the present day guide-books are also to be found in the inventory that 'Bess of Hardwick' had made when she moved into her new house in 1601. Her descendants, who became Earls and then Dukes of Devonshire, added to her furniture and tapestries during the seventeenth century. But since then little has been changed, because Chatsworth became their preferred family home. So Hardwick remains outside as Bess built it, and inside substantially as it looked in 1688.

It is not known who was the architect, but it is likely that Bess herself (who, when she came to this task, was an experienced and indeed compulsive builder) worked with Robert Smythson. He had been working at Wollaton Hall not far away, and among his papers are plans which look like Hardwick. It took from 1591 to 1597 to build and decorate. But Bess (born Elizabeth Hardwick and married four times, lastly to the Earl of Shrewsbury; hence the initials ES on the towers) was a lady of prodigious determination. Also, in her fourth widowhood she controlled the considerable wealth which her four husbands had bequeathed to her. Further, she seems to have done some advance planning. Thus the Brussels tapestries, in the High Great Chamber,

Hardwick Hall, Derbyshire: the west front.

she had bought a few years before the building was begun, and the detail of the room was evidently planned to display them.

There is a wealth of interesting portraits in the house. They include three of Bess herself, two of Mary Queen of Scots and others of Queen Elizabeth, Lord Burghley, James I and Thomas Hobbes the philosopher, who was tutor to the Earl of Devonshire and died at Hardwick in 1679.

Hardwick was accepted by the Treasury in part payment of death duties on the death of the tenth Duke of Devonshire and transferred to the Trust in 1959.

Winster Market House

DERBYSHIRE

four miles west of Matlock

The market house at Winster, a town noted for its mumming dance, was built just before or just after 1700.

It was repaired and given to the Trust in 1906 after a local appeal.

Winster Market House, Derbyshire.

Mam Tor

DERBYSHIRE

one mile west of Castleton

Mam Tor commands wide-ranging views of the Peak District. Below it on its west side is the village of Castleton at the head of the Hope Valley; to the east is Edale; while to the north it looks up from its 1,700-foot summit to the 2,000-foot flat top of Kinder Scout. In the Edale area the Trust owns more than 1,100 acres, including several hill farms, 470 acres of Mam Tor and the nearby Winnats Pass, the limestone gorge which leads down to Castleton.

At the top of Mam Tor there is a hill fort. Excavations were started recently and preliminary results suggest a date early in the Iron Age.

In Edale an Information Centre has been set up jointly by the Trust and the Peak District National Park.

The Trust bought the Mam Tor property in 1944, using a legacy from Miss Ethell Marples supplemented by gifts from her relations, who wished the property to be a memorial to her. The Winnats property was bought in the same year with funds raised by the Sheffield and Peak District branch of the Council for the Preservation of Rural England.

Moseley Old Hall

STAFFORDSHIRE

four miles north of Wolverhampton

Moseley Old Hall (page 200) is one of the houses in which Charles II hid while he was a fugitive after the battle of Worcester. It stands on the edge of Cannock Chase and was then very isolated. The King arrived from Boscobel early on 8th September 1651 and stayed till the evening of the 9th. He was received by Lord Wilmot, who was in hiding, Thomas Whitgreave, to whose family the hall belonged, and John Huddlestone, a priest who was living there in the guise of tutor to Whitgreave's nephews. There are three accounts of his visit, one given by the King himself to Pepys and the others

Mam Tor, Derbyshire.

written by Whitgreave and Huddlestone. Whitgreave's loyalty was rewarded in 1666 by the grant of an annuity.

The hall was built in 1600, a black-and-white building of oak beams and plaster. In 1870, when the timber was in need of extensive repair, it was encased in brick. Inside there is oak panelling, and in the King's Bedroom the four-poster bed in which Charles slept. By the fireplace in this room is the secret hiding-place in which, at a pinch, two people can crouch.

The Whitgreaves let the hall as a farm during the nineteenth century, and it continued as one till 1940. In that year Mr Wiggin bought it and began much-needed renovation. He died before he could complete the task, but his holding operation made preservation possible. His widow gave the hall to the Trust in 1962. The Wolverhampton National Trust Centre and Staffordshire County Council have provided funds for maintenance by appeal and grant. The King's Bed, which had remained in the hall until 1935, was bought by the late Sir Geoffrey Mander and returned to the hall when the renovations had been finished. More recently the garden has been remade to a seventeenth-century pattern and stocked with plants in cultivation in that century.

Moseley Old Hall, Staffordshire.

Wightwick Manor, Staffordshire: the hall.

Wightwick Manor

STAFFORDSHIRE

three miles west of Wolverhampton

As an inscription over the front door records, the house was begun in the year of Queen Victoria's jubilee. Mr Theodore Mander, a Wolverhampton industrialist and mayor of the city, employed as his architect Edward Ould, to build a half-timber house with elaborately carved gables and timbers on a base of red sandstone. They used William Morris wallpapers and materials for the interior decoration. Mr Mander's son, the late Sir Geoffrey Mander, who gave the house and its contents to the Trust in 1937, added nineteenth-century pictures, furniture, books and manuscripts to his father's collection.

Fine craftsmanship went into the making of the house, and its decoration exemplifies the tastes of the period. In addition to the Morris tapestry and wallpapers, there is much stained glass by C. E. Kempe and tiles by William de Morgan. The very interesting collection of pictures in the Great Parlour and other rooms includes drawings and paintings by Burne-Jones, Holman Hunt, Madox Brown, Millais and Rossetti. There are some Chinese vases and books from Rossetti's house in Cheyne Walk and a decorated cupboard and a bed from No. 2 the Pines at Putney, the home of Theodore Watts-Dunton and Swinburne.

Shugborough

STAFFORDSHIRE

five and a half miles south-east of Stafford

Shugborough (page 203) grew to its present size and was given its splendidly decorated principal rooms in three stages. First, William Anson built a square three-storey block in the 1690's; this forms the centre of the building. Then in the eighteenth century two immensely knowledgeable patrons, employing distinguished architects, made extensive additions and alterations. First, in the middle of the century Thomas Anson added to the house and employed James Stuart to erect the remarkable buildings in the park. In the

1790's Thomas William Anson (later created Viscount Anson) employed Samuel Wyatt to make further alterations and additions.

The principal rooms contain a variety of interesting French and English furniture, china, busts, tapestry and paintings.

The Thomas Anson who made the mid-eighteenth-century additions at Shugborough was the elder brother of the famous Admiral Lord Anson. The admiral was a wealthy man and probably helped to finance his brother's projects. Dying childless, he left his brother his heir. So it is fitting that one of the garden monuments can be taken as commemorating the admiral. It is a Chinese pavilion built from sketches brought back by one of the officers who accompanied him on his eventful four-year voyage round the world.

The house, park and contents were accepted by the Treasury in part payment of death duties on the death of the fourth Earl of Lichfield, and in 1966 were transferred to the Trust. They have been leased to the Staffordshire County Council, who have now established a county museum in the stable block.

Attingham Park

SHROPSHIRE

four miles south-east of Shrewsbury

At Attingham (pages 204–5) the house and park result from two exercises in late Georgian elegance. First, the building of the house by the first Lord Berwick and the architect George Steuart; second, the planning of the park and additions to the house by Nash and Humphrey Repton for the second Lord Berwick. George Steuart was commissioned to design a house that would, among other things, look impressive when seen from the road beyond the park. So Attingham, which was built with exceptional speed between 1783 and 1785, has giant columns to the portico of the main block, and extends for nearly four hundred feet between the pavilions at either end. Nash's contribution to the house was to fill in part of the courtyard to make the *picture gallery*. In doing this he made use of a building technique which in 1807 was a novelty—the glazed roof of the gallery has a frame of cast iron.

The internal decoration of the house is most impressive, with its elegant chimney-pieces, pier-glasses, scagliola columns in the hall and expert plasterwork in the ceilings of the principal rooms. These rooms also contain pictures and furniture of interest.

Shugborough,
Staffordshire.

Shugborough,
Staffordshire:
the dining-room.

Attingham Park, Shropshire: the picture gallery.

Attingham was left to the Trust in his will by the eighth Lord Berwick, who died in 1947. Most of the house has been leased to the Shropshire County Council as a College of Adult Education.

Benthall Hall

SHROPSHIRE

four miles north-east of Much Wenlock

From the outside, Benthall is a good example of sixteenth-century domestic architecture. It is built largely of brick faced with ashlar stone, and with its gables and moulded brick chimney-stacks makes a pleasing appearance. Records of its building have been lost, but it was probably first built in about 1538 and then altered later in the century. These alterations may have been prompted by a desire to provide hiding-places for priests, of which the house contains several. There is no history of these having been used, but the Benthall family were Roman Catholics.

Attingham Park, Shropshire.

Improvements were made inside the house in the seventeenth century, the dining-room being panelled and a fine *staircase* (page 206) installed, its large newel posts carrying carvings of grotesque heads.

Benthall stands high above the River Severn within a mile of the Severn Gorge. During the Civil War it was first held for two years for the King by Lawrence Benthall, then surprised and taken by Parliamentary forces, who used it as a base from which to prevent supplies being carried by river to the

Benthall Hall, Shropshire: the early seventeenth-century staircase.

Royalists in Worcester and Bridgnorth. The house does not seem to have suffered during these military operations, but outbuildings were destroyed.

In 1844 the house was sold to a neighbouring estate and occupied till 1934 by various tenants. One of them, the botanist George Maw, author of *The Genus Crocus*, planted many rare plants in the garden, and some of his uncommon crocus plants naturalized and still flower there. In 1934 a descendant of the builders bought back the house, and in 1958 she gave it to the Trust, other members of the Benthall family providing endowment.

Wilderhope Manor, Shropshire.

Bredon Tithe Barn, Worcestershire.

The Long Mynd, Shropshire, above Carding Mill valley looking north-east.

The Long Mynd

SHROPSHIRE

fifteen miles south of Shrewsbury

The modern wayfarer on these magnificent moorlands is a very long way from being the first to tread them. The Portway, the track which runs the length of the crest of the Long Mynd, is believed to be older even than the barrows which stand beside it. But like those before him, the walker can enjoy superb views to the Black Mountains in Breconshire, or across Shropshire or the Cheshire plain.

The Trust's 4,500-acre property here was bought by public subscription in 1965. A further 650 acres to the south of it, Minton Hill, was added shortly afterwards.

Wilderhope Manor

SHROPSHIRE

eight miles south-west of Much Wenlock

Wilderhope (page 207) is a limestone building of about 1585 with seventeenth-century plaster ceilings, standing on the southern slope of Wenlock Edge in remote, wooded country. It was built by a local family called Stillman who occupied it until 1742. It later changed hands a number of times but was not enlarged or altered to any extent. At the time that it was given to the Trust (1936) by the W. A. Cadbury Trust, extensive repairs were carried out. It has been leased to the Youth Hostels Association.

Bredon Tithe Barn

WORCESTERSHIRE

three miles north-east of Tewkesbury, north of B 4080

This (page 207) is a fifteenth-century stone barn. It is 132 feet long and has five porches, one with unusual stone cowling. Given to the Trust in 1951.

The Trust owns nine other tithe barns distributed over Berkshire, Cornwall, Devon, Gloucestershire, Somerset, Wiltshire, Worcester and Yorkshire.

Clent Hill

WORCESTERSHIRE

three miles south of Stourbridge

Clent Hill (page 211) is not far from Birmingham, Stourbridge and Kidderminster, and is much visited by townspeople in search of a walk and a good view. It provides wide views of both the Wrekin and the Malvern Hills. The

Trust property covers 355 acres of Clent Hill and Walton Hill Commons, including some woodland and enclosed land let for grazing. There are many bridle and foot paths. The property was given to the Trust in 1959, part by the Worcestershire County Council, part by Bromsgrove Rural District Council and part by the Feeney Trustees. No less than twenty-four local authorities contribute to its upkeep.

Midsummer Hill, Malvern Hills

WORCESTERSHIRE

Part of Midsummer Hill, where there is an Iron Age hill fort, was given to the Trust in 1923 in memory of a son killed in the 1914–18 war.

The Trust also owns small pieces of land on Broad Down, 1½ miles to the north of Midsummer Hill; on Castlemorron Common on the eastern slope of the Malvern Hills; and at Tack Coppice on the bridle road from Hollybush to Chase End Hill.

Hanbury Hall

WORCESTERSHIRE

two and a half miles east of Droitwich

Hanbury Hall (page 212) is a fine English country house of the 1690's and has a painted staircase by James Thornhill, who later painted the cupola in St Paul's Cathedral.

It was built for Thomas Vernon by William Rudhall. Thomas Vernon was a very eminent lawyer and for some years M.P. for the city of Worcester. He made a considerable fortune which he used to increase his family's property and to build Hanbury. His architect, William Rudhall, is not known for any other building. It has been suggested that he may have worked in some capacity for William Talman, the architect of *Dyrham*,

Clent Hill, Worcestershire.

Midsummer Hill, Malvern Hills, Worcestershire.

Hanbury Hall, Worcestershire.

Uppark and other houses of the period, since much of Hanbury is very suggestive of Talman's work.

The building of the house was finished in 1701 and the Thornhill paintings must have been executed a little later. The evidence for this is that he included in his composition political allusion to the trial of Dr Sacheverell, which took place in 1710.

The author of the Trust's guide to Hanbury refers to a painted staircase as having been 'a status symbol for a rich man' of the time. In the one which Thornhill executed for Thomas Vernon, and in addition to the portrait of Dr Sacheverell, the ceiling shows an assembly of classical deities, and the walls the story of Achilles. Thornhill also painted the ceiling of one of the principal rooms in the house.

The eighteenth-century garden has not survived; but on the west side of the house the orangery still stands. It is contemporary with the house.

Hanbury Hall remained in the hands of Thomas Vernon's family until it was acquired by the Trust in 1953 under the will of Sir George Vernon, the second and last baronet.

Charlecote Park, Warwickshire: the house with the gatehouse in the foreground.

Charlecote Park

WARWICKSHIRE

four miles east of Stratford-upon-Avon

Charlecote Park is the place where Shakespeare reputedly poached deer. His subsequent appearance before the magistrate, the story continues, gave him the model for Mr Justice Shallow in *King Henry IV* and *The Merry Wives of Windsor*. The Sir Thomas Lucy to whom this tradition applies built Charlecote in 1558 and entertained Queen Elizabeth to breakfast there in 1576 on her way to Kenilworth. Falstaff's comment to Shallow—''Fore God you have a goodly dwelling and a rich'—applies very well to the house Sir Thomas built.

Since his time it has been enlarged and a good deal altered both inside and out; but the general outline of the Elizabethan building remains. The *gatehouse* (page 213), which guards the approach to the front, was built a little earlier than the house itself and has remained unaltered. The plum-red brick in which it was made has mellowed beautifully.

The park, which still harbours the descendants of Sir Thomas's deer and with them Spanish sheep imported in the eighteenth century, was laid out in its present form by 'Capability' Brown.

There are a number of interesting family and other portraits in the house, including a contemporary picture of Queen Elizabeth I.

The late Sir Montgomerie Fairfax-Lucy gave Charlecote to the Trust in 1946.

Coughton Court

WARWICKSHIRE

two miles north of Alcester

The principal architectural feature of Coughton is the gatehouse, a formidable and solidly proportioned stone building of 1509. We do not see it today exactly as it was first built because the stone wings adjoining the central portion were added in a 1780 version of Gothic, probably in place of some earlier work, but they contribute satisfactorily to the impressiveness of the whole frontage.

The other parts of the house are in contrast, consisting of Elizabethan half-timbered upper storeys on ground storeys of brick. Two wings of this construction are set at right angles to the gatehouse and form a court behind it. Originally they were joined by a third wing and the court was entirely enclosed.

Inside the house, the dining-room has exceptionally fine panelling of different periods and an elaborate chimney-piece in marble and timber.

The contents of the rooms belong to Sir Robert Throckmorton, a descendant of the Sir George Throckmorton who built the gatehouse in 1509. They include porcelain, some notable furniture, portraits and an interesting exhibition of Throckmorton family muniments. Among the family portraits is a picture of Sir Nicholas Throckmorton, father of Bessie Throckmorton, who was a lady in waiting to Queen Elizabeth and married Sir Walter Raleigh. On the first floor of the gatehouse, in what is now the Drawing Room, the arms of Catesby and others concerned in the Gunpowder

Coughton Court, Warwickshire.

Plot are displayed in heraldic glass. The Throckmortons were not directly implicated in the plot, but according to tradition the wives of some of the plotters assembled in this room to await the outcome of the affair.

During the Civil War Coughton was seized by Parliamentary forces, who were in turn bombarded by Royalist forces. How much damage this caused is not known because when the damage was repaired after the Restoration, alterations were made in the interior of the house. In 1688 it was in trouble again. The Throckmortons have always been Roman Catholics, and when King James II fled the country a Protestant mob from Alcester destroyed the entire east wing. This was not restored; but towards the end of the eighteenth century the site was cleared and the moat, which till that time had surrounded the house, was filled in.

In 1946 Coughton was given to the Trust by Sir Robert Throckmorton and leased back to him.

Farnborough Hall

WARWICKSHIRE

six miles north of Banbury

Farnborough is a trim, classical mid-eighteenth-century stone-built house which incorporates some part of the late seventeenth-century house which stood on the site. Inside, the *hall* and dining room have fine stone and marble fireplaces and rococo ceiling and wall decoration; the staircase is lit by an oval dome in which the lights are decorated by a bold wreath of fruit and foliage. In the grounds, which look up to Edge Hill three miles away, there are two charming eighteenth-century garden temples and an obelisk.

Ambrose Holbech bought Farnborough in 1683 and it was probably his grandson, William Holbeach, who carried out the remaking of the house between 1745 and 1755. There are no records of the work; but the names of a stonemason and of a plasterer employed by him are known, and it looks as though he acted as his own architect.

The house and grounds were acquired by the Trust in 1960, having been accepted by the Treasury in part payment of death duties.

Packwood House

WARWICKSHIRE

one mile east of Hockley Heath

The main part of the house (page 219) was built about 1560 by a yeoman who seems to have called it his 'Great Manciant House'. He built a typical mid-sixteenth-century black-and-white house which has since been rendered over. About 1670 his lawyer grandson made the excellent brick-built additions to provide stables and outbuildings. In between those dates, during the Commonwealth, this same lawyer planned and established the extraordinary topiary work in the garden, representing the Sermon on the Mount: clipped yews stand for the multitude and larger yews for the Twelve Apostles.

The house contains a great deal of interesting tapestry and furniture. This was collected for preservation at Packwood by Mr G. Baron Ash, who gave house and collections to the Trust in 1941.

Farnborough Hall, Warwickshire.

Below: the entrance hall.

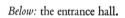

Stratford-upon-Avon Canal, Warwickshire: volunteers on maintenance work at Lock 22.

Stratford-upon-Avon Canal (Southern Section)

WARWICKSHIRE

The Southern Section of the Stratford Canal runs from Stratford, where it is connected by a lock to the River Avon, thirteen miles north-west to Lapworth, where it links up with the other section of the Stratford Canal. This in turn is linked to the Grand Union. The Trust owns the freehold of the whole of this thirteen-mile Stratford to Lapworth Section and its towpath.

Packwood House, Warwickshire.

It is open to boats, and as it passes through the Warwickshire countryside presents both those in boats and walkers on the towpath with many pleasing views.

It is also of interest to students of industrial archaeology and to those concerned with the restoration and maintenance of inland waterways. The canal, with its thirty-six locks, twenty cast-iron split bridges and two large cast-iron aqueducts was a very considerable engineering feat for the period in which it was built: 1793–1815. It was bought by railway interests in the nineteenth century and its traffic dwindled. By 1930 it was derelict and in 1958 proposals were made for it to be dismantled. The Stratford-upon-Avon Canal Society and the Inland Waterways Association opposed this plan and in 1961 the Trust leased the canal from the British Waterways Board. There followed three years of rehabilitation. This formidable task

Upton House, Warwickshire.

was carried out by a handful of full-time staff aided by a great many volunteers working at week-ends or during their holidays, by R.E. and R.A.F. units and by men from H.M. prisons. The money needed to finance the work was £61,000. Towards this the Ministry of Transport made a grant of £20,000, and £33,000 was raised by public appeal.

The canal was formally reopened to traffic in the summer of 1964 by H.M. Queen Elizabeth the Queen Mother, President of the National Trust. Volunteers, including young people, continue to give help in maintenance and improvement tasks, as the picture on page 218 shows.

Upton House

WARWICKSHIRE

seven miles north-west of Banbury

Upton House was built in 1695 of the orange-gold local stone, and in spite of some alterations retains outwardly the appearance of a house of the period. The interior has been completely remodelled to display exceptionally fine collections of pictures and porcelain. It is this collection which provides the principal interest of Upton House.

These collections were made by the second Lord Bearsted, who gave them to the Trust with the house and its terraced gardens in 1948. The pictures,

Staunton Harold Church, Leicestershire.

of which there are nearly two hundred, range over a wide variety of schools, British, Dutch, Flemish, French, German, Italian and Spanish, and include works by Pieter Brueghel, El Greco and many other masters. In the porcelain collection there are many very fine English porcelain figures and a number of good Sèvres pieces.

For Warwickshire, *see also* Kinwarton Dovecote, page 227.

Staunton Harold Church

LEICESTERSHIRE

five miles north-east of Ashby-de-la-Zouch

Staunton Harold is one of the very few churches built during the Commonwealth. Its general appearance outside is that of a Gothic building; but inside the panelling, painted ceiling, pulpit, lectern and pews are of the seventeenth century. It has been very little altered, the pulpit even retaining its original cushions and hangings.

There is an inscription over the door reading: 'In the year 1653 when all things Sacred were throughout ye nation Either demolisht or profaned Sir Robert Shirley, Barronet, Founded this church; whose singular praise it is, to have done the best things in ye worst times, and hoped them in the most callamitous. The righteous shall be had in everlasting remembrance.'

This Sir Robert, whose family had been at Staunton Harold for two hundred years, had succeeded to the baronetcy in 1646. He had been several times imprisoned for complicity in Royalist plots. After the building of the church the authorities ordered him to find the money to raise a regiment. This, they argued, he must be well able to do if he could afford to build a splendid church. He refused and was sent to the Tower, where he died in 1656, leaving money for distressed Royalists. The chapel was given to the Trust in 1954 by his descendant the twelfth Earl Ferrers.

The beautiful silver-gilt communion plate, bearing the date mark 1654, made by a goldsmith at Gloucester, is at the Victoria and Albert Museum.

Lyveden New Build

NORTHAMPTONSHIRE

four miles south-west of Oundle

Lyveden New Build (or Bield) was, for all its eccentric plan and decoration, evidently intended to be, among other things, a comfortable family house. It was never finished and has had virtually to fend for itself since building stopped in 1605. The fact that the shell has deteriorated so little is a great tribute to the masons who built it.

Lyveden New Build, Northamptonshire.

As a house to be lived in, it would have had kitchen, buttery and servants' quarters in the basement, Great Hall and a parlour on the floor above and Great Chamber and bedrooms on the floor above that. The only odd thing about the domestic layout was the entrances. The front door is six feet above ground and was to be approached by a flight of steps; the back door, opening into the basement, was approached by an underground passage.

But the achievement of domestic comfort was not Sir Thomas Tresham's main purpose. This was that Lyveden New Build should be symbolical of the Passion. It is in the shape of a cross of equal arms, a bay window at the end of each arm. Running round the outside are two friezes. On one of these were depicted, among other things, Judas' money-bag surrounded by the thirty pieces of silver, the crown of thorns, the sponge, the spear and the seamless garment between three dice. On the other were cut sentences from the Vulgate and other references to the Passion. Sir Thomas also incorporated mathematical arrangements in his plan. The arms of the cross are equal squares which enclose another of the same size, making five equal squares;

Kinwarton Dovecote, Warwickshire.

the bay windows start five feet from the corner of the building and have five faces each five feet in length. The letters of the wording on the frieze are spaced one to a foot, and the length of lettering to each arm is eighty-one feet, or nine times nine.

So far as is known Sir Thomas kept to himself the ideas which prompted him to such eccentricity in his building. Lyveden was not his only essay in this field. He also had built a triangular lodge at Rushton to set forth the doctrine of the Trinity. What is known of him is that he came of a family which had been long established in Northamptonshire, and that he himself spent a good deal of time in prison. He was brought up a Protestant, but

Willington Dovecote, Bedfordshire.

became a Roman Catholic in 1580 and fell foul of the religious laws. During his imprisonments he developed his fancies and his mystic ideas, and when at liberty applied them to his buildings. Just after his death his son was involved in the Gunpowder Plot and imprisoned, and later the estate passed into other hands. The building was left untouched except for the removal of the floor timbers, which were taken away to another house during the Commonwealth.

Lyveden New Build was bought by the Trust by means of a public subscription in 1922. It has not been restored, but has been given weather protection.

Watlington Hill, Oxfordshire.

Watlington Hill

OXFORDSHIRE

one mile south-east of Watlington

Watlington Hill, in the Chilterns, part open down and part coppice, commands fine views of Oxfordshire. The Trust was given over a hundred acres of the hill in 1941 and 1957 by the fourth Lord Esher and his father and mother, who also gave the beech woods surrounding Watlington Park, a mile to the south.

Dovecotes

Kinwarton — *Willington*

WARWICKSHIRE — BEDFORDSHIRE

respectively one and a half miles north of Alcester and four miles east of Bedford

The birds that lived in dovecotes were actually pigeons, and were not fed but foraged abroad for their own food. This foraging naturally led them to any cultivated fields there might be in the neighbourhood: so the keeping of pigeons in the Middle Ages was not a free-for-all, but a privilege reserved to the lord of the manor, in some cases a layman, in others a churchman. Of the two dovecotes illustrated here, that at Kinwarton (page 224) probably belonged to the Abbey of Evesham, which had property where the dovecote stands, near Alcester. That at Willington (page 225) was built by Sir John Gostwick, Cardinal Wolsey's Master of the Horse.

It has been established, from the evidence of the architectural detail of the arch over the doorway, that the Kinwarton dovecote was built about the middle of the fourteenth century. These circular dovehouses were furnished inside with an ingenious contrivance called a *potence* (French for gallows). To a vertical beam in the centre of the building several horizontal beams are attached at different heights, and at the extremity of each, close to the wall, is a length of ladder. The vertical beam pivots so that the horizontal beams with their ladders can be moved round the wall, giving access in turn to all the nesting boxes—in this case five hundred of them. Kinwarton is unusual in that this useful piece of equipment has survived. Kinwarton was given to the Trust in 1958.

Sir John Gostwick's Willington dovecote is a much bigger building and has fifteen hundred nesting boxes. Close by it are stables and a barn, also Trust property, built at the same time as the dovehouse. The dovehouse and the other buildings were given to the Trust, by different donors, in 1914 and 1947 respectively.

The Trust preserves also another fifteenth-century dovecote, at Bruton in Somerset.

Appendix

Properties not illustrated

Properties which are not illustrated and are not referred to in the notes that accompany the illustrations are noted below. In addition to the properties which it owns there, the Trust holds Restrictive Covenants over 9,448 acres and twenty buildings in these counties. (See note in Introduction.)

NORFOLK

Burnham Overy, a mile north of Burnham Market. Burnham Overy Water Mill (eighteenth century) and the Tower Windmill (1816). Not open.

King's Lynn. St George's Guildhall. An early fifteenth-century building and the largest surviving medieval guildhall in England. Was long put to theatrical use and following recent repairs is being so used again.

At West Runton between Sheringham and Cromer, seventy acres including the highest point in Norfolk. This is in what has long been known locally as the Roman Camp. Excavations have revealed nothing Roman.

Additional land given by Mrs S. R. Warren in memory of her husband.

Cawston Duelling Stone, close to the old Woodrow Inn on the Norwich–Holt road near Cawston. It is inscribed H.H. and was set up near where Sir Henry Hobart of Bickling Hall was fatally wounded in a duel in 1698.

At Bale Oaks, five miles south of Blakeney, a group of ilexes near to the church and at Bullfer Grove, 4½ miles south-west of Holt, eight acres of woodland. Both given in 1919 by Sir Lawrence Jones.

SUFFOLK

Bury St Edmunds. Angel Corner, an eighteenth-century house let to the corporation. Gershom-Parkington collection of clocks kept here.

Thorington Hall, two miles south-east of Stoke-by-Nayland, an oak framed plastered house of about 1600. Converted into studios. Not open.

Kyson Hill, three-quarters of a mile south of Woodbridge, four acres of parkland overlooking the Deben.

Outney Common, Bungay. Six acres of common by the Waveney.

Dunwich Heath, south of Dunwich, 200 acres of cliff and heath with a mile of beach. Bought with money given to Enterprise Neptune by the H. J. Heinz company.

BEDFORDSHIRE

Dunstable Downs, 285 acres on the Chilterns two miles south of Dunstable, including the Tree Cathedral close to Whipsnade village green. Also twenty acres known as Dell Fields, acquired with contributions from members of the Camping Club of Great Britain, local Girl Guides and Bedfordshire County Council.

Sharpenhoe, The Clappers, 136 acres and a viewpoint 1½ miles south-west of Barton in the Clay.

NOTTINGHAMSHIRE

Colston Bassett, five miles south of Bingham. Market Cross. Eighteenth century on a medieval base. Given by the Society for the Protection of Ancient Buildings.

DERBYSHIRE

Sudbury Hall, six miles east of Uttoxeter on A50. A seventeenth-century brick-built house with fine interior decoration including an overmantel by Grinling Gibbons and ceiling paintings by Laguerre. Formerly the property of the Lords Vernon. Accepted by the Treasury in part payment of estate duty and transferred to the Trust in 1967. Lord Vernon has given an endowment, and both the Historic Buildings Council and the Derbyshire County Council have offered grants towards maintenance. Not open.

Hope Woodlands between Glossop and Sheffield, about six miles east of Glossop, the sixteen-hundred-acre Hope Woodlands Estate given to the Trust with Hardwick Hall. Weathering has recently exposed here a section of Roman road, just off A 57 near Doctors Gate Culvert.

Derwent Estate. Thirteen miles west and north-west of Sheffield, six thousand moorland acres, partly in Yorkshire.

At Eyam (five miles east of Tideswell) on a hillside half a mile east of the village, the Riley Graves where seven members of one family were buried in 1665 when the village, stricken by the plague, heroically isolated itself.

Hathersage, Longshaw: about a mile south-east of Hathersage on the south side of A 625, a thousand acres of moor and woodland extending from the Fox House Inn to Surprise View. Acquired mainly in 1931–6 by subscription. Froggatt Wood: seventy-six acres of wood and pasture on the west of B 6054 given in the 1930's by the Sheffield and Peak District Branch of the Council for the Preservation of Rural England.

Miller's Dale, two miles south of Tideswell, sixty-four acres astride the River Wye.

Alderwasley, Shining Cliff Wood, two hundred acres of woodland on the west bank of the Derwent, four miles north of Belper.

Taddington, fifty acres of wooded slope on the south side of the Buxton–Bakewell road 1½ miles east of Taddington.

Duffield Castle, 2½ miles south of Belper. Foundations of a Norman keep razed in 1266.

Viewpoints at Alport Height, two miles south-east of Wirksworth; Curbar Gap, two miles north of Baslow; Eccles Pike, 1½ miles west of Chapel-en-le-Frith; Hayfield at South Ridge Farm, a quarter of a mile south of Hayfield; Lantern Pike, 1½ miles north-west of Hayfield, thirty-two acres given as a memorial to Edwin Royce, a Past President of the Manchester Ramblers' Federation; Stanton Moor Edge, four miles south-east of Bakewell, a twenty-seven acre, three-quarter-mile-strip with views over the Derwent valley; and Wolfscote Hill, 1½ miles south of Hartington.

Alsop Moor Plantation, sixteen acres on the Ashbourne–Buxton road eight miles north of Ashbourne. Also land in Biggin Dale and in Wolfscote Dale.

STAFFORDSHIRE

Downs Bank, 1½ miles north of Stone, 166 acres of moorland given as a war memorial in 1946 after local appeal.

Hawksmoor, 1½ miles north-east of Cheadle, 250 acres of woodlands and open space.

Kinver Edge, four miles west of Stourbridge, two hundred acres of heath and woodland given as a family memorial in 1917. Site of an Iron Age promontory fort. Also cave dwellings, one of them a pre-Reformation hermitage, which were inhabited till 1900.

Letocetum, at Wall on the A 5 two miles south-west of Lichfield: here was a Roman posting station on Watling Street near the intersection with Ryknild Street. The bath house now belongs to the Trust. It has been excavated and a site museum houses the finds. Under guardianship of the Ministry of Works.

SHROPSHIRE

In Shrewsbury, Town Walls Tower. Fourteenth century. Last remaining watch tower. Not open.

Hopesay Hill, three miles west of Craven Arms, 130 acres let as a sheepwalk.

Morville Hall, 3¼ miles west of Bridgnorth. Elizabethan with eighteenth-century additions. Open by written appointment.

WORCESTERSHIRE

Properties near Birmingham. Chadwick Manor Estate, four miles north of Bromsgrove on the edge of Birmingham, stands astride the Worcester road: four hundred acres of farm and woodland, given to the Trust in 1927 by two members of the Cadbury family. It was the first gift to the Trust of a large open space to be preserved as an agricultural estate. There are public footpaths and at Highfield (870 feet) there are views to the Malvern Hills.

Nearby there is another commanding height, Frankley Beeches, an eight-hundred-foot hill top crowned with beech trees. This was given to the Trust by the Cadbury firm. Due south of Birmingham at Groveley Dingle are 170 acres of wood and farmland with some footpaths for the walker and views of the Lickey Hills. Given to the Trust in the 1930's. Forty acres of farmland at Cofton Hackett, a mile south-west of Groveley. At Sling Pool, five miles north of Bromsgrove in a valley running down from the Clent Hills, a pool with tree-covered banks. For Clent Hill see photograph on page 211.

Clump Farm, half a mile south-east of Broadway. Seventy-nine acres of farmland. Public footpath with views over the Vale of Evesham.

At Harvington, four miles south-east of Kidderminster, an acre and covenants over other land. This was given to protect Harvington Hall, a sixteenth-century house belonging to the Roman Catholic diocese of Birmingham.

A mile and a half north-west of Bewdley, Knowles Mill and four acres of orchard.

Worcester. Grey Friars, fifteenth-century timber-framed house with later additions. Given by Mr and Miss F. E. Matley Moore, who also gave three fifteenth–sixteenth-century houses on Friary Street, now let as shops. Five and a half miles north-west of the town, Wichenford Dovecote, seventeenth century, half-timbered.

WARWICKSHIRE

Knowle. Children's Field. A three-acre field for games nine miles south-east of Birmingham near Knowle church. Given in 1910 by the Rev. T. Downing.

Earlswood Moat House, on the south edge of Birmingham a mile east of Earlswood Lakes station. Small fifteenth-century house with sixty-five acres of pasture and woodland. Not open.

LEICESTERSHIRE

Ulverscroft, six miles south-west of Loughborough: an eighty-acre nature reserve.

NORTHAMPTONSHIRE

Priest's House, Easton-on-the-Hill, about two miles south-west of Stamford off A 43. A pre-Reformation priest's lodge.

At Brackley, a three-acre open space on the east side of the High Street. Managed by the corporation.

OXFORDSHIRE

Aston Wood, $1\frac{1}{2}$ miles north-west of Stokenchurch, a hundred acres of beech wood astride the Oxford road. Mainly the gift of Sir Edward Cadogan.

Greys Court, three miles west of Henley. A sixteenth-century manor house with a medieval tower in the grounds and gardens of unusual interest. Given with an endowment by Sir Felix and Lady Brunner.

Also Coombe End Farm, 2½ miles north of Pangbourne; two seventeenth-century cottages at South Leigh, 2½ miles east of Witney, not open; and Kencot Manor Farm, five miles south of Burford, a small seventeenth-century house with two acres, not open.

The Lake District: Little Langdale Tarn, from the east, with Blake Rigg in the background on the left.

4

ENGLAND
Northern Counties

NORTH WALES

NORTHERN IRELAND
Isle of Man (Appendix)

Lindisfarne Castle, Northumberland.

Lindisfarne Castle

NORTHUMBERLAND

The castle stands on Holy Island, just off the Northumbrian coast between Berwick and Bamburgh. Holy Island came into history in the seventh century when it was the seat of a bishopric. In the twelfth century there was a Benedictine monastery here.

The castle came afterwards. It was built in Edward VI's reign as a defence against the Scots. With the accession of James I its point was lost, and after a successful siege by Parliamentary forces during the Civil War it was neglected until 1900. In that year it was taken in hand by Sir Edwin Lutyens, commissioned by Mr Edward Hudson. Lutyens converted the Tudor castle into a dwelling house.

Lindisfarne was given to the Trust in 1944 by Sir Edward de Stein and his sister.

The Farne Islands

NORTHUMBERLAND

The Farne Islands are about ten miles south of Berwick-upon-Tweed, a mile and a half to five miles off the coast. According to the state of the tide there are fifteen to twenty-eight or more of them. The largest (the Inner Farne) is sixteen acres in extent at low tide, much of it bare rock rising to seventy or eighty feet. Its cliffs are similar to those in the photograph on page 240, which is of Staple Island.

They are a breeding-place for seals and for a host of sea birds—eider-duck, guillemot, puffin, fulmar, petrel and another fifteen or more species. Access is allowed, except that landing on some of the islands is forbidden during the breeding season. Visitors are required to keep strictly to the rules which have been made to preserve the islands as a bird sanctuary.

The known history of the islands begins in the seventh century when St Aidan was a visitor, and later St Cuthbert established his hermit cell on the

Beadnell Bay, Northumberland.

Inner Farne. On this island are remains of a thirteenth-century monastery. There have been lighthouses since Charles II's time, and the Longstone Lighthouse, built in 1826, was the home of Grace Darling.

Acquired after a public appeal in 1925.

Beadnell Bay

NORTHUMBERLAND

about seven miles north-north-east of Alnwick

Fifty-five acres of the sand dunes and rough grazing in Beadnell Bay south of the Long Nanny were bought in 1966 from Enterprise Neptune funds.

Wallington, Northumberland.

Wallington

NORTHUMBERLAND

twelve miles west of Morpeth

Wallington is built on a site where previous owners had erected a medieval castle and then, in extension of it, a Tudor house. Both of these were pulled down to make way for another house in 1688. They provided some of the stone from which it was built and its cellars are the foundations of the medieval building. The builder was Sir William Blackett of County Durham, who had inherited and made a lot of money from mines and shipping and bought the Wallington estate to provide himself with a place in the country. He already had a large town house in Newcastle. He built the present square house at Wallington—120 feet square—but left it fairly

The Farne Islands, Northumberland: guillemots on Staple Island.

spartan inside. His son put in the staircase and brought in Italian craftsmen to do the fine plasterwork in the principal rooms. He also built the stables and clock tower. It seems that he first intended the clock tower to be a chapel, for thus it appears on the plans.

Then in the eighteenth century the Trevelyans came to Wallington from Cornwall on the marriage of a Trevelyan to a Blackett heiress. At that time the centre of the square of which the house consists was still a courtyard. But in the following century, when Pauline, Lady Trevelyan, made Wallington a salon which attracted such writers and artists as Swinburne, Ruskin and Millais, Ruskin suggested that the courtyard be roofed. This was done and the former courtyard became a picture gallery.

In 1942 Sir Charles Trevelyan, who had been President of the Board of Education in the first Labour Government, gave the house and its contents to the Trust.

The Roman Wall, Northumberland, seen from Cuddy's Crag near Housesteads.

The Roman Wall

NORTHUMBERLAND

The Trust preserves Housesteads, one of the seventeen forts that were spaced along Hadrian's Wall: and about three and a half miles of the wall.

Housesteads (that is its modern name: it was Borcovicum in fifteenth-century lists) was built at the same time as the wall, A.D. 122–30. It housed an infantry unit a thousand strong and had temples, shrines, a bath-house and quarters for women and children. In the museum, which contains antiquities found near by, there are models of what it was like in full occupation. Today's visitor can admire the wonderful views from the site or, if imaginatively inclined, gaze at them through the eyes of a Roman sentry.

The property was given to the Trust in 1930 and the fort and museum are under the guardianship of the Ministry of Works.

Penshaw Monument

COUNTY DURHAM

half way between Sunderland and Chester-le-Street east of A 183

This Doric temple was erected in 1844 as a memorial to John George Lambton, first Earl of Durham, Governor General of the British provinces in North America in 1838 and author of the Durham Report.

Given to the Trust in 1939 by the third Earl.

Washington Old Hall

COUNTY DURHAM

Washington Old Hall is a small manor-house of the early seventeenth century in which were embodded parts of an earlier house which had stood on the site. The original house was built in the twelfth century and from 1183 until 1613 was the home of George Washington's ancestors.

Washington is an old village in the northern industrial and mining area of County Durham, the surrounding country now very built up. In its centre is a village green and just off the square, below the church, which is on a little hill, stands Washington Old Hall.

It was rescued in 1936, when it had become dilapidated, by a committee formed for the purpose. With help from both sides of the Atlantic it was restored and furnished, and in 1956 transferred to the Trust. It has been let to the Washington Urban District Council and is used by the people of Washington as a community centre.

Washington Old Hall,
County Durham.

Penshaw Monument,
County Durham.

Buttermere Valley

CUMBERLAND

roughly half way between Whitehaven and Keswick

In this part of the Lake District the Trust owns three lakes (*Buttermere*, *Crummock Water* and Loweswater), several areas of woodland and the waterfall at Scale Force about three-quarters of a mile up Scale Beck south-west from Crummock Water. Much of this property was bought by public subscription in the 1930's, some since the last war, and some was given by Dr G. M. Trevelyan and other donors.

Fishing and boats are to let on all three lakes.

Derwentwater and Borrowdale

CUMBERLAND

south of Keswick

Two of the Trust properties in this part of the Lake District are illustrated. At *Watendlath* (photograph on page 247), a mile and a half north-east of Rosthwaite on the flank of Borrowdale, the hamlet with the land surrounding and common rights over two thousand acres to the south was bought in 1960–2. The purchase was made from funds bequeathed by several donors. The *Castlerigg Stone Circle* (photograph on page 247), two miles east of Keswick just south of the old Penrith road, is under the guardianship of the Ministry of Works. It is a free-standing megalithic circle of unhewn local boulders; thirty-eight stones, five of which are fallen. It is about a hundred feet in diameter. Only eight of the stones are more than five feet high. There is an interior rectangular setting of smaller stones. A stone axe was found here in the 1870's. Some excavation carried out in the 1880's found only charcoal. The circle was given to the Trust in 1913 by Canon Rawnsley and others.

In this Derwentwater and Borrowdale area Trust properties amount to more than five thousand acres of the woodland, farmland and hillsides. At Brandelhow, on the west side of the lake, is the Trust's first acquisition in the

Buttermere Valley,
Cumberland.
Dry stone walling.

Buttermere Valley,
Cumberland.
Buttermere and
Crummock Water
from Green Crag.

Great Gable and the Innominate Tarn, Cumberland.

Opposite: Castlerigg Stone Circle, Cumberland.
Watendlath Village, Cumberland, before the larch wood was felled.

Lake District—some wood and parkland with adjacent foreshore bought by public subscription in 1902. There are two landing stages here at which motor launches call. At Castle Crag (900 feet) between Rosthwaite and Grange is one of several famous viewpoints. The summit of Castle Crag was given by Sir William Hamer as a memorial to his son, who was killed in the First World War. On the east side of the lake, Calf Close Bay and Friars Crag were bought by public subscription in 1922 as a memorial to Canon Rawnsley, one of the founders of the Trust. Seatoller Farm, its land and woods surrounding the hamlet of Seatoller, has fell land reaching to the top of Honister Pass.

These various properties have been acquired at intervals since 1902 from public subscriptions, from a variety of donors, including the Rev. H. H. Symonds, and in one instance from the Treasury, which had accepted Seatoller Farm in payment of death duty.

Scafell Pike, Cumberland: Glaramara and Scafell Pike viewed from Castle Crag.

Scafell Group

CUMBERLAND

between Borrowdale, Eskdale and Wastwater, Cumberland

The photograph of *Scafell Pike* above was taken from another Trust property, Castle Crag between Rosthwaite and Grange. Of this Scafell Group the Trust holds altogether about 2,500 acres. Forty acres on Scafell Pike itself (3,210 feet and the highest summit in England) were given in 1920 as a war memorial for the Lake District. In 1923 the Fell and Rock Climbing Club gave about twelve hundred acres above the fifteen-hundred-foot mark near Styhead Pass as a war memorial to club members. Other land has been given by private donors. *Great Gable* (photograph on page 246) is part of the group.

Langdales, Westmorland: Langdale Pikes, from Elterwater.

Langdales

WESTMORLAND

west-north-west of Ambleside

The section in the Trust's list of properties which is headed 'Langdales' notes the property belonging to the Trust at the head of Great Langdale, which consists of several farms and the Dungeon Ghyll Hotel; and other property, some adjoining the shore of *Elterwater*, some in Little Langdale, some at the head of Great Langdale. Four of the Great Langdale farms were given by Dr G. M. Trevelyan. Side House Farm, at the head of Great Langdale, was bought in 1963 with the help of Mrs Moorman and Trinity College, Cambridge as a memorial to him. Two of the farms in Little Langdale were bequeathed to the Trust by Mrs W. Heelis (Beatrix Potter).

The 'Langdales' section also refers the reader to another entry headed 'Lord Lonsdale's Commons'. *Langdale Pikes* (photograph on page 249) are included in Lord Lonsdale's Commons, which comprise the high land from the slopes of Helvellyn to the head of Great Langdale, and at the lower level White Moss and Elterwater Commons with parts of Grasmere Lake and Rydal Water, in all nearly seventeen thousand acres. These the seventh Earl of Lonsdale leased to the Trust in 1961 for a peppercorn rent for thirty-five years or his lifetime, whichever is the longer.

Dora's Field

WESTMORLAND

a mile and a half north-west of Ambleside on the north side of A 591

Dora's Field, which was formerly known as the Rash Field, lies opposite Rydal Water and extends to about an acre and a half. It belonged for a time to Wordsworth, who bought it in 1826 and planted daffodils there for his daughter. It was given to the Trust by his grandson in 1935.

The house where Wordsworth was born—in Cockermouth and now known as Wordsworth House—also is Trust property. It is a mid-eighteenth-century building and its original staircase, fireplaces and panelling remain. Wordsworth in *The Prelude* referred to the garden, which leads from the back of the house to the Derwent. The property was acquired by the Trust after a public appeal in 1938.

Sizergh Castle

WESTMORLAND

three miles south of Kendal

The name Sizergh, like other names in Cumberland and Westmorland, has its origin in the Scandinavian occupation of northern England in the ninth and tenth centuries. The first part, now reduced to Siz, had a variety of

Sizergh Castle, Westmorland: the pele tower.

Dora's Field by Rydal Water, Westmorland.

spellings such as Sirith in its easy days, and was a personal name. The second part, erg, meant a summer pasture. The core of Sizergh Castle is the fourteenth-century *pele tower*. A pele was a tower within a stockade. Before the Union of 1603 those who lived near the Scottish border thought it sensible to take their own security measures, and many of these pele towers, as well as castles, were built. The tower at Sizergh has nine-foot-thick walls which still rise sixty feet to the battlements. Its fourteenth-century fireplaces and windows have remained unaltered during all the additions and changes which have been made through the centuries to render the castle a more convenient and handsome dwelling house. There is a variety of interest in the other parts of the building and their contents. The Great Hall, built in 1450, was altered and decorated between 1558 and 1575, and has a large Tudor fireplace. During this same period the wings, with their fine panelling and interior decoration, were added to the castle. Some further changes were made late in the eighteenth century. The castle contains English and French furniture of different periods, silver and china and, in addition to family portraits, a collection of Stuart portraits and Stuart and Jacobite relics. The Strickland family acquired Sizergh by marriage in 1239 and it has continued to be their main residence ever since. Sir Thomas Strickland who had been Keeper of the Privy Purse to the Queen in Charles II's reign, and his second wife who was a member of the household of James II's queen, went into exile with James II and his family in 1688. Lady Strickland acted as governess to the young prince and the Stuart portraits in the Dining Room were given to her by the Queen. Sir Thomas's son was allowed to return to England and Sizergh in 1700.

In 1950 Mr H. Hornyold-Strickland and his wife and son gave the castle and contents to the Trust.

Ullswater

CUMBERLAND AND WESTMORLAND

The Trust owns some very beautiful property around Ullswater, including parts of the lake shore, and was most actively engaged at all levels in the battles of the early 1960's that preserved the lake from being converted into a reservoir.

The photograph on page 253 is from Glencoyne Park, a Trust property to the west of the lake running up to Stybarrow Dodd (2,760 feet) and Raise (2,885 feet). On the same side of the lake, Gowbarrow Park ($2\frac{1}{2}$ miles north of Glenridding, between the Penrith and Dockray roads) includes the

Ullswater, Westmorland.

sixty-five-foot-high waterfall of Aira Force and a mile of the lake shore. South of Patterdale at the bottom end of the lake the Trust has farmlands in the valley including Hartshop Hall farm and open spaces on the fells above which run up to the Kirkstone Pass. This property, which includes the whole of Brotherswater, was given by the Treasury in 1947 having first been accepted in payment of death duty—the first property acquired by the Trust in this way. On the east shore of Ullswater, Side Farm runs for a mile northwards from Goldrill Beck at the south-east corner.

Beningbrough Hall, Yorkshire: the garden front.

Beningbrough Hall

YORKSHIRE

eight miles north-west of York

Viewed from the outside Beningbrough has the taciturnity that is popularly supposed to be characteristic of Yorkshire people. Also, a Yorkshireman might add, it is solid, dignified and spiced with a touch of unconventionality. It is a compact building made of small bricks ($9'' \times 2\frac{1}{8}''$). There are two storeys and an attic floor with eleven windows at each level. Steps lead up to the doors on both the main entrance and the *garden front.* The porches above these doors carry stonework beautifully executed.

The house was built about 1716. There is no solid evidence of who may have been the architect; but some unusual detail in the design is to be found elsewhere in buildings designed by Thomas Archer, so it has been suggested that he made rough plans and a local builder worked from them. Certainly there were at that time some excellent builders and wood-carvers in York and some very fine work was put into Beningbrough—notably the staircase.

East Riddlesden Hall, Yorkshire: the Great Barn.

The wide treads of this are parqueted and the balustrade, with its slim uprights, looks as though it has been wrought in iron. In the Drawing Room, Saloon and State Bedroom is a wealth of delightful and most expertly executed wood-carvers' decoration.

When the Trust acquired the property in 1958 (from the Treasury which had accepted it in payment of death duties) it was empty of furniture. But gradually this state of affairs is being remedied.

East Riddlesden Hall

YORKSHIRE

one mile from the centre of Keighley on the west side of the Bradford road

East Riddlesden Hall (page 255) is a late seventeenth-century manor which, apart from having been blackened by industrial grime, looks much as it did when it was completed in 1692. It has some contemporary panelling and plasterwork and now houses a collection of seventeenth-century furniture, portraits and domestic bygones.

The Great Barn—illustrated on page 255—is much older than the present hall and is one of the finest medieval barns in the north of England. It is 120 feet by 40 feet in area, its oak pillars being on stone bases.

Nostell Priory

YORKSHIRE

six miles south-east of Wakefield

One of the many remarkable things about Nostell is that one of its two architects, James Paine, was only nineteen when he began the work. He went on to be one of the foremost of mid-eighteenth-century architects, but to give him this commission seems an act of great perception as well as boldness on the part of Sir Rowland Winn. Paine and Sir Rowland, who was himself a man of architectural knowledge and taste, spent eight years building and decorating the central block and other parts of a larger plan for a Palladian house. But they did not finish; when Sir Rowland died in 1765 his son (also Sir Rowland) had new ideas and employed Robert Adam to add a north wing, planned to harmonize with the central block. Adam also designed the stable block. Since then the exterior of the house has been little changed.

The interior of the house was also a form of combined operation. The proportion and layout of the rooms come from Paine's design and he was responsible for the decoration of some of them. Adam contributed the larger part of the decoration of the rooms and put into them some of his best work.

Nostell Priory, Yorkshire.

In the library and other rooms where he needed painted murals or ceilings or stucco he engaged Antonio Zucchi, Angelica Kaufmann and Joseph Rose.

The two graceful staircases, by Paine, have elaborately moulded walls and ceilings and are carried to the top of the house. For the Library Adam designed very elegant bookcases and there are mural paintings of mythological subjects. For the Tapestry Room and for the *Saloon* he designed beautiful pier-glasses. The Dining Room and the State Bedroom were joint operations. In the Dining Room Paine provided the white marble Palladian chimney-piece and the door cases; Adam added wall panels and a plaster frieze of satyrs' masks and vines. In the State Bedroom the rococo ceiling is by Paine and Adam introduced the Chinese wallpaper.

The furniture is as remarkable as the interior decoration. Much of it is by Thomas Chippendale, some of the pieces being to designs by Adam and intended for the places they still occupy. Thus the Chippendale side tables in the Saloon were designed by Adam as part of the decoration of the room.

In addition to family portraits the rooms contain paintings by Jakob van Ruysdael, Van Dyck, Hogarth and other famous artists. The second Sir Rowland kept detailed accounts, which have been preserved. His Chippendale accounts are shown to visitors.

Nostell Priory, Yorkshire: the Saloon.

The original Nostell Priory was a house of Austin Canons, founded in the twelfth century, and the friars continued there until the dissolution of the monasteries. The property then passed through several hands and was bought in 1654 by Rowland Winn, a London City alderman with estates in Lincolnshire. It continued in the possession of his family until 1953, when it was given to the Trust, with its contents, by the trustees of the estate and the present Lord St Oswald (Rowland Winn).

Treasurer's House, York: the drawing-room.

Treasurer's House, York

YORKSHIRE

at the north-east corner of the Minster

The Romans had a building on the site, but there is no evidence to show exactly what it was, and Treasurer's House, as an official residence for the Treasurer of the See of York, starts with William the Conqueror and ends with Henry VIII. William appointed a canon of Bayeux to be Archbishop of York and the new archbishop built houses for various officers of the diocese, including the Treasurer. In 1547 the last Treasurer handed over his dignities and the key, saying that as the diocese had been plundered of its treasure it had no further need of a Treasurer.

Since then the house, which has been much altered, has changed hands many times, and a variety of people of interest have owned or been connected with it—Protector Somerset, Lord Fairfax (the Civil War general), Mathew Robinson (the father of the bluestocking Elizabeth Montagu) and Lawrence Sterne, who was a frequent visitor when the house belonged to his uncle.

In 1896 it was in use as three dwellings. Then a new owner (Mr Frank Green of Nunthorpe Hall, who gave the house to the Trust thirty-four years later) undertook extensive alterations. He opened up windows which had been bricked up, and within the hall removed a seventeenth-century upper floor.

Above ground, the house as it stands today is largely the house as it was rebuilt in 1620. Beneath is part of the undercroft of the house of the time of Edward I, the eleventh-century house having, probably, been destroyed by the fire that wrecked most of the town in 1137. The interior decoration ranges over the seventeenth and eighteenth centuries and includes some interesting

Tarn Hows, near Coniston, Lancashire.

Wessenden Moor, Yorkshire, seen from Wessenden Head.

fireplaces and painted ceilings. The furniture and paintings are to match, as they include seventeenth-century portraits, eighteenth-century landscapes, Jacobean tables and George II mirrors.

Wessenden Moor

YORKSHIRE

about eight miles south-west of Huddersfield, south of Marsden

The illustration on this page shows the view from Wessenden Head looking northwards across the Trust's Marsden Moor property. This amounts to nearly 5,700 acres of open moorland, the southern part being in the Peak District National Park. It stretches from Buckstones Moss, astride A 62, to Wessenden Moor, north of A 635, and includes Holme and Binn Moors. Given in 1955 by the Treasury, who had accepted it in payment of death duty.

Coniston

LANCASHIRE

Tarn Hows (photograph on page 260) lies in the Trust's Monk Coniston estate, which runs from Coniston northwards on both sides of A593 to Little Langdale. Part of the Monk Coniston estate was left to the Trust in her will by Mrs W. Heelis. Mrs Heelis (Beatrix Potter) was an ardent and generous supporter of the Trust. Her gifts and bequests—in addition to Hill Top, the farmhouse at Sawrey where she wrote the *Peter Rabbit* books—amounted to over four thousand acres and farm and cottage buildings.

The other illustration taken from this area is *Low Arnside Farm* (photograph on page 263). Today's tenants are law-abiding farmers; but in the early nineteenth century it was the home of Lanty Shee. He set up an illicit still in the stables and reputedly did a useful trade until arrested and jailed in 1833.

Opposite: Hawkshead, Lancashire: the Court House.
Low Arnside Farm, near Coniston, Lancashire.

Hawkshead Court House

LANCASHIRE

about three miles east of Coniston and five miles south of Ambleside

The Court House dates mainly from the fifteenth century, though parts may be older. Furness Abbey held the Manor of Hawkshead during the Middle Ages and the Court House is all that remains of the manorial buildings. It was given to the Trust in 1932 by Mr H. S. Cowper, whose grandfather had bought it in 1860.

The Trust owns several cottages in the village of Hawkshead and land in the neighbourhood including, about two miles to the north-east, Blelham Bog, which is let to the Nature Conservancy, and 260 acres overlooking Blelham Tarn.

Formby, Lancashire: sand dunes to the west of the town, with marram grass.

Formby

LANCASHIRE

The nearest unspoiled coastline to Liverpool and other large towns in Lancashire is the stretch of coast just west of Formby, about ten miles from the centre of Liverpool. In 1967 the Trust bought four hundred acres of the sand dunes and foreshore with the proceeds of a local appeal, made as part of Enterprise Neptune, the Trust's appeal for coastal preservation.

Speke Hall, Lancashire.

Speke Hall

LANCASHIRE

eight miles south-east of Liverpool, just north of the Mersey

Like another most interesting black-and-white house preserved by the Trust (*Little Moreton Hall* in Cheshire), Speke grew as additions were made to suit the needs and preferences of succeeding generations of one family. The first Sir William Norreys made a start by building the hall soon after 1490. His grandson rendered this more comfortable by adding the screens, about

Rufford Old Hall, Lancashire: the Great Hall.

1520. As his family grew he built the Great Parlour in the West block, and the East block for his domestic staff. His son and grandson both made further additions, but after 1626 there were no more extensions. Between them they made the interior extremely handsome. The hall has a large Elizabethan fireplace with a massive carved oak mantel-beam. Its walls are panelled and contain carved reliefs. The Great Parlour is finished throughout in oak and has an Elizabethan ceiling modelled with a design of fruits and flowers.

Their eighteenth-century descendants allowed irresponsible tenants to neglect the house and serious damage was done to parts of the interior. But it was rescued in 1797 by Richard Watt, a Liverpool man who had made a fortune in Jamaica. He bought the house and spent much care and discrimination as well as money on its restoration. Through provisions in the will of his descendant, Miss Adelaide Watt, it was acquired by the National Trust in 1944. The Trust has leased it to Liverpool Corporation.

Rufford Old Hall

LANCASHIRE

five miles north of Ormskirk

At Rufford one sees a composite building. On the one hand there is the *Great Hall* of the half-timbered fifteenth-century house, on the other the brick-built west wing of Charles II's time, and joining them the section which was reconstructed in the 1820's. The fifteenth-century hall, with its massive movable screen, had few rivals in its own day for the elaborate and pleasing detail of its interior and it has been preserved practically unaltered. Indeed the bulk of the timbering is five hundred years old. When it was found in the late 1950's that despite the use of modern preservatives some parts needed replacement, the new was carefully matched to the old, the craftsmen trimming the timber with hand tools such as the original builders would have used.

In recent years the 1821 wing and part of the Carolean wing have been made a village museum housing tools, domestic furniture and other relics of village life in south-west Lancashire in earlier centuries. This collection was made by the late Philip Ashcroft, who gave it to the Trust.

When the late Lord Hesketh gave the hall to the Trust in 1936, his family had been at Rufford since the thirteenth century and responsible for the building of both the hall and the later additions.

Alderley Edge

CHESHIRE

on the south-east edge of Alderley Edge, four and a half miles north-west of Macclesfield

Two hundred acres on a sandstone escarpment with fine views across the Cheshire plain, the Edge (page 268) was the site of a Neolithic settlement and of prehistoric copper mining. A mile and a half to the south, at Nether Alderley, the Trust owns Alderley Old Mill, and holds covenants over the house that was formerly the Eagle and Child Inn. The fifteenth-century water-mill was in use till 1939, and in 1967 repairs were started with a view to its working again.

Alderley Edge, Cheshire: a view of the Cheshire plain.

Little Moreton Hall, Cheshire, seen from within the courtyard.

Little Moreton Hall

CHESHIRE

four miles south-west of Congleton

A most apt description of Moreton is given by James Lees-Milne in the Trust's guide-book to the house: 'Moreton appears like some great doll's house about to collapse into the waters of the moat, in which its chequered surface is quietly reflected.'

It was not planned like that, indeed it was never planned as one whole but grew at intervals during the sixteenth century as successive Moretons contributed the accommodation they thought desirable. It seems that the hall itself and the lower parts of the gatehouse were built about 1520; a porch and a parlour were added around 1560. Then twenty years later, feeling the urge to follow fashion and have a long gallery, the owners decided that the only place for it was above the gatehouse range. So there it sits, the whole structure looking a bit top heavy but with the aid of brick

Lyme Park, Cheshire: the inner courtyard.

buttresses still secure. Since that date virtually no changes or additions have been made.

The presence of the moat makes it clear that the Tudor Moretons were building where their medieval ancestors had established a secure lodging. Inside, the hall and gallery and other rooms are decorated with carving and plasterwork and contain some interesting pieces of furniture.

For a time during the nineteenth century the hall was used as a farmhouse. But its last two Moreton owners, Miss Elizabeth Moreton, who died in 1912, and her cousin Bishop Abraham, who with his son gave the hall to the Trust in 1938, ensured its preservation.

Lyme Park

CHESHIRE

six and a half miles south-east of Stockport

The house was built originally in about 1560 and the Long Gallery and the Drawing Room with its exceptionally fine Elizabethan woodwork are still there to proclaim the fact. But without ever being pulled down it has been

Lyme Park, Cheshire: the south front.

completely—and very grandly—transformed inside and out. Alterations have been made at various times, but principally about 1720. Then it was that Sir Peter Legh got the distinguished Venetian architect Giacomo Leoni to Lyme: he remodelled the *south front* into what James Lees-Milne describes in the Lyme guide-book as 'one of the boldest achievements of English Palladian architecture to survive'. The box-like structure behind the portico was not in Leoni's design. It was added in 1816. Leoni also refashioned the *inner courtyard* and much of the interior of the house.

Inside, as well as the fine woodwork in the Elizabethan rooms, there is some remarkable pear-wood carving in the saloon. It consists of six eight-foot panels of fruit, flowers, musical instruments and cherubs. This beautiful work is strongly reminiscent of Grinling Gibbons and it is possible, though by no means certain, that it is by him.

The park at Lyme runs to thirteen hundred acres and rises to 850 feet on a Cheshire spur of the Pennines. It still has a herd of deer, and has been a deer-park since medieval times. It used also to be famous for Lyme mastiffs, exceptionally large beasts, some of them the size of a small pony. The Sir Piers Legh who fought at the battle of Agincourt is said to have taken one to the campaign, and in the shield of arms of his descendant, Lord Newton, two mastiffs act as supporters.

The Leghs first came into possession of Lyme through the marriage of Sir Piers Legh to the daughter of the then owner in 1388. This Sir Piers had served with his father-in-law at Crécy. The family remained continuously in occupation for nearly six hundred years. In 1946 Richard Legh—the third Lord Newton—gave the property to the Trust and left there on loan the principal tapestries and furniture. The house has been leased to Stockport Corporation.

Styal

CHESHIRE

about ten miles south of Manchester, a mile and a half north-west of Wilmslow

Quarry Bank Mill, illustrated on page 274, was built in 1784 and shortly afterwards millworkers' cottages were added to form a complete industrial community. It is on a beautiful wooded stretch of the River Bollin and was given with the cottages and 250 acres of the valley in 1939 by Mr A. C. Greg. It is no longer a textile mill, but part is let.

Styal woods are illustrated on page 273.

Styal, Cheshire: Styal woods.

Tatton Park, Cheshire: the Library.

Styal, Cheshire: Quarry Bank Mill.

Tatton Park, Cheshire, from the south-west.

Tatton Park

CHESHIRE

two miles north of Knutsford

Tatton offers an unusually varied choice of interest. The imposing stone-built mansion is surrounded by sixty acres of variegated gardens and set in a two-thousand-acre park with a large lake. The principal rooms contain the collections of paintings, furniture and silver made by the Egerton family over the last 450 years. In the huge room which he had built to house them are displayed the curiosities and big game hunting trophies which the last Lord Egerton brought back from his travels—and with them a motor-car that he bought in 1900 (a Benz) which bears Cheshire's first registration number, M.1.

The house is beautifully sited, looking over the terraced garden to the park and meres, and is described in the guide-book as 'of a severely classical design with little external ornamentation'. It was started by one architect and completed by another (Samuel Wyatt and his nephew Lewis Wyatt) between the years 1790 and 1810. Inside, the principal rooms are of a size and proportions to match the imposing exterior. The books in the *Library* (page 274) were collected mainly in the eighteenth century or earlier. But the furniture is early nineteenth-century, some of it made for the room. The two Canalettos in the Drawing Room were commissioned from the artist by Samuel Egerton while he was living in Venice about 1729.

The gardens, too, are the work of successive generations of the family. The orangery, which was designed about 1810 by one of the architects of the house, contains orange trees in tubs and various exotic plants. The tall glasshouse containing New Zealand tree-ferns dates from the middle of last century. The Japanese garden, laid out round a Shinto temple said to have been brought from Japan, was started in 1910. There are also a rose garden and an arboretum.

The Trust was given the house by the last Lord Egerton in his will and acquired the park from the Treasury, which had accepted it in part payment of death duties. Both are leased to the Cheshire County Council.

Bodnant

DENBIGHSHIRE

four miles south of Conway

The gardens at Bodnant were begun in 1875 against backgrounds of large native trees, many of which were then eighty years old, and in a setting which enhances immeasurably the beauty of the gardens as they are seen today. They are on a south-westerly slope looking down to the River Conway and across to Snowdon. On the upper part of the slope are *terraced gardens* and lawns; lower down, in the valley formed by a tributary of the river, there is a less formal layout known as the Wild Garden. The whole extends now to about seventy acres. There is a great variety of plantings, the guide-book making special mention of formal rose and flower borders, conifers, rhododendrons, azaleas, magnolias, camellias, primulas and gentians. Among the rhododendrons are a great many of the Chinese species sent over by Dr E. H. Wilson in the early 1900's and by other collectors. Hybridization of rhododendrons has been carried out at Bodnant for a long time. Hybrids have also been brought from other gardens.

The gardens were begun by Mr Henry Pochin, and when he died in 1895

Bodnant, Denbighshire: view from the terraced gardens.

his daughter, the first Lady Aberconway, continued his work. Her son, the second Lord Aberconway, took over while still a young man. He gave the gardens to the Trust in 1949 and his son, the present Lord Aberconway, continues their development on behalf of the Trust. Like his father before him Lord Aberconway is President of the Royal Horticultural Society. In their work at Bodnant the Aberconways have had the support of two head gardeners of great knowledge and skill, the late Mr F. C. Puddle and his son, the present head gardener, Mr Charles Puddle, M.B.E.

Aberglaslyn Pass

CAERNARVONSHIRE

south of Beddgelert

The Trust owns a one-and-a-half-mile stretch running south from Beddgelert along both sides of the pass and covering about five hundred acres. From Pont Aberglaslyn there is an exceptionally fine view of the Snowdon range. The property was acquired by purchase and by gifts from several donors between 1935 and 1958.

Braich-y-Pwll

CAERNARVONSHIRE

near Aberdaron in the south-west tip of the county

This is the westernmost point of Wales, or at least of the mainland. Bardsey Island is about two miles to the south-west. It was at Braich-y-Pwll that medieval pilgrims embarked for Bardsey. The Trust was given 120 acres here, including Mynydd Gwyddel and part of Mynydd Manwr. Illustration on page 280.

Conway Suspension Bridge

CAERNARVONSHIRE

The bridge (page 283) was built by Telford in 1826 and is preserved as one of the outstanding monuments of the Industrial Revolution. (Telford's Menai Bridge antedates it by a few months but has been altered since its building.)

Conway Suspension Bridge was handed over to the Trust in 1966 with the balance of accumulated tolls by Conway Borough Council, and this endowment is being supplemented by a public appeal.

Aberglaslyn Pass, Caernarvonshire.

In Conway, the Trust also owns Aberconwy, one of the surviving medieval houses, now let as an antique shop, at the junction of Castle and High Streets.

Another medieval building, Tu Hwnt I'r Bont, is at Llanwrst about twelve miles from Conway on the Betws-y-Coed road. Once a courthouse, it is now let as a shop and tearoom.

Porth Neigwl, Caernarvonshire: a view from the hill above Plas-yn-Rhiw on the west side of the bay.

Braich-y-Pwll, Caernarvonshire, the westernmost point of Wales.

Porth Neigwl

CAERNARVONSHIRE

in the Lleyn Peninsula between Abersoch and Aberdaron

In the Lleyn Peninsula, between Aberdaron and Llanbedrog, the Trust's Plas-yn-Rhiw estate of 370 acres is largely coastal land; but it includes also viewpoints at Penmynydd, Mynydd Cilan, Mynydd-y-Graig and on Foel Felin Wynt (Windmill Hill), a well-known landmark near Mynytho, on which stand the walls of a windmill that was last in use about the turn of this century.

This property has been acquired and given to the Trust at intervals since 1950 by the Misses Lorna and M. Honora Keating and their late sister, Miss Eileen Keating. The manor-house, Plas-yn-Rhiw, part Georgian, part Tudor and part earlier, was derelict, having been uninhabited for fifteen years. The Misses Keating restored it, together with the traditional Welsh cottage, Sarn Rhiw, and replanted the garden with subtropical shrubs.

Penrhyn Castle

CAERNARVONSHIRE

one mile east of Bangor

Although there has been a fortified building on the site at least since the fifteenth century, the present castle (page 283) is less than 150 years old. It was built at a time when there was a vogue for a 'Norman' style, and in 1827 Thomas Hopper was commissioned to be the architect of a vast building in neo-Norman style. He had already built two castles in this style in Ireland and entered into his task with immense thoroughness, designing the furniture as well as the interior decoration. The castle is splendidly sited on a ridge at the end of the Menai Strait, with views of Beaumaris Bay, Great Orme's Head, Anglesey and Snowdonia. The rounded arches say 'Norman', but for the detail of the outside and the lavish decoration of the interior Hopper seems to have drawn inspiration also from oriental styles. In all he produced one of the most remarkable architectural ventures of the nineteenth century, and very little indeed has been changed since he finished it.

The castle is built in Mona marble from Anglesey. The furniture, some of elaborately carved wood and some made of slate from the local quarries, is massive (the dining-room table, for example, seats sixty-four), so that it is not dwarfed by the size of the rooms. The lavish decoration includes plasterwork as well as wood, stone and slate carving and stained glass designed by Thomas Willement, designer of much of the glass in the Houses of Parliament. Queen Victoria visited Penrhyn in 1859, and the heavily carved oak bed in which she slept remains in the State Bedroom.

In addition to its original furniture Penrhyn now contains other collections with a diversity of interest. In the Dining Room there is a collection of pictures which includes works by Velasquez and Van Dyck. In upstairs rooms there are eight hundred dolls from all parts of the world and a collection of stuffed animals. In the stables there is a collection of locomotives and quarry rolling stock.

The Pennant family acquired the Penrhyn property, part by marriage and part by purchase, in the 1760's. They developed the slate quarries into an important business. The castle and the estate of over forty thousand acres in Caernarvonshire and Denbigh were accepted by the Treasury in part payment of death duties in 1951 and transferred to the Trust. The principal contents of the castle belong to Lady Janet Douglas-Pennant.

Ysbyty Estate

CAERNARVONSHIRE

The pictures of *Tryfan* and *Glyder Fawr* on page 284 were taken on a section of the Trust's Ysbyty estate which lies south-east of Bangor, astride A 5 near Capel Curig. Tryfan and Glyder Fawr are to the south of the road. This section of the estate extends to nearly sixteen thousand acres and embraces some of the finest scenery in Snowdonia, including the peaks illustrated, Carnedd Dafydd, the north-west slopes of Carnedd Llewelyn and the head of Nant Ffrancon pass.

Another large section of the Ysbyty estate (twenty-six thousand acres) lies south of Betws-y-Coed, part in Caernarvonshire and part in Denbighshire. It includes the village of Ysbyty Ifan, where there was a hospice of the

Conway, Caernarvonshire: the suspension bridge in August 1967, after removal of the catwalk.

Penrhyn Castle, Caernarvonshire: the staircase.

Knights of St John, and, mainly to the west of the village, some beautiful hills, valleys and moorland with Llyn Conwy, a lake nearly 1,500 feet above sea level.

The whole Ysbyty estate amounts to over forty thousand acres and is the largest owned by the Trust. It was given in 1951 by the Treasury, who had accepted it in payment of death duty.

Opposite: Tryfan, Caernarvonshire, from Helyg.
Glyder Fawr, Caernarvonshire: Glyder Fawr and Castell-y-Gwynt from Glyder Fach.

Powis Castle

MONTGOMERYSHIRE

on the south edge of Welshpool

Powis (page 286) began life strictly as a castle, a thirteenth-century stronghold on the English border of Montgomeryshire commanding the upper end of the Severn valley. Some of that building remains; but a great deal has been added and parts have been altered. It has been in continuous occupation as a dwelling-house, and succeeding generations have made the alterations and additions which were considered comfortable or beautiful in their own day. Thus the sixteenth century added a long gallery, a remarkably fine one with excellent plasterwork. The seventeenth century put in the staircase hall which was decorated a little later with murals by Lanscrom. The formal terraced gardens—four terraces nearly two hundred yards long—were designed to the formal taste of the early eighteenth century and have not been since altered to suit any more romantic idea of layout.

The principal rooms contain paintings, tapestry and a variety of interesting furniture accumulated by successive owners of the castle.

The earliest owners were the Princes of Powis. They allied themselves to the English in the thirteenth century and in 1283 became Barons de la Pole. Their line died out in the sixteenth century and Sir Edward Herbert bought the castle. He was a relative of Lord Herbert of Chirbury, whose papers are preserved at Powis. In 1784 a Herbert heiress married Edward Clive (son of Clive of India), and he later became the first Earl of Powis (of the third creation). The fourth earl gave the castle to the Trust in 1952. Most of the contents, including relics of Clive of India which his son brought to the castle, were accepted by the Treasury in payment of death duty and are on loan to the Trust.

Powis Castle, Montgomeryshire: the east front.

Mussenden Temple, County Londonderry, looking over the mouth of Lough Foyle.

Mussenden Temple

COUNTY LONDONDERRY

When it was built Mussenden Temple was a summer-house or a clifftop library, an adjunct to Downhill Castle, which is now in ruins. It was built about 1783 by the Earl of Bristol, who was Bishop of Derry, and named by him for his cousin, Mrs Mussenden. It overlooks the mouth of Lough Foyle and commands views of the Atlantic and the Antrim coastline. The inscription round the entablature is a quotation from Lucretius which has been rendered into English as

'Tis pleasant, safely to behold from shore,
The rolling ship, and hear the tempest roar.

The Temple was given to the Trust in 1949.

Another surviving adjunct of Downhill Castle, Bishops Gate, a gate with lodge which provides the entrance to Mussenden Temple, also belongs to the Trust. It was given by the Ulster Land Fund in 1962.

Springhill, County Londonderry.

Springhill

COUNTY LONDONDERRY

near Moneymore on the Moneymore–Coagh road

Springhill was built towards the end of the seventeenth century and was originally a fortified dwelling. It was the type of house designed to suit the needs of those who had come to Ulster shortly after the Plantation of James I and had been supporters of Oliver Cromwell. A hundred years later the defensive barriers and fencework which surrounded it were removed to give the house its present accessibility and to open up the views from the house. But the long, low outbuildings for the servants and the buildings that were laundry, brew-house, slaughter-house and turf-shed remain. Additions were made to the dwelling-house during the eighteenth century and again in 1850.

The Trust was left the property in 1957 under the will of William Lenox Conyngham, a descendant of the Colonel Conyngham who acquired it in the seventeenth century.

White Park Bay

COUNTY ANTRIM

on the north coast a mile and a half west of Ballintoy

White Park Bay is a beautiful and almost unspoiled bay facing the north Atlantic. The beach is of the finest white sand and extends about a mile, with several cliff streams cutting across it. In the hilly grassland which fringes the bay, archaeological finds indicate that there was a Neolithic settlement here.

The Trust owns about 180 acres in the bay bought in 1938 through the efforts of the Youth Hostels Association and the Pilgrim Trust.

White Park Bay, County Antrim.

Castleward

COUNTY DOWN

seven miles north-east of Downpatrick

Though Castleward cannot escape being viewed as an architectural oddity, it can also claim with assurance that it is a highly successful one. The first Lord Bangor and his wife, when they came to build, could not agree on an architectural style. So he had one half built in a classical style which conforms to mid-Georgian taste and she did the other in the 'modern Gothick'. The style she chose may well have startled her neighbours because although it had had its following in England for some time (Walpole's Strawberry Hill was built in the 1750's), it was new to Ireland when she chose it in about 1770. It is believed that one obliging architect coped with both their commissions, but unfortunately nobody knows who he was. Some alterations were made in the early nineteenth century, but it is clear that the architect did his work well, and having given the house its two distinct faces contrived, within, to provide different rooms in the two different styles. Thus there is a classical hall with a pillared doorway giving access to the Gothic saloon.

The house is set in a lovely park and gardens. There are giant oaks and beeches, and a mild climate has also favoured many foreign growths.

The property was acquired by the National Trust in 1950 through the Ulster Land Fund.

Mount Stewart Gardens

COUNTY DOWN

five miles south-east of Newtownards

The layout of Mount Stewart Gardens on the Ards Peninsula embraces both formal terraces and informal lakeside plantings, covering altogether about eighty acres.

In their present form the gardens are the creation of Edith, Lady Londonderry, who began them in 1921. As she wrote many years later, in her introduction to the guide-book to the gardens: 'I soon discovered that the climate

Castleward, County Down: the classical front.

Mount Stewart Gardens, County Down: the Temple of the Winds.

Mount Stewart Gardens, County Down: the lake.

was congenial to many half-hardy shrubs and especially to the more tender rhododendron species usually termed greenhouse subjects; acacias, which we call mimosa trees, grow out of doors, Banksian roses and Lapagerias, a rose-red wax-like greenhouse climber. . . . Groves of eucalyptus trees and Cordylines, palm trees and many kinds of bamboos add to the sub-tropical effect of these gardens, as well as the massive ilex trees and enormous tree heaths which give an Italian appearance to the scene.'

All the work of making the garden, including the stonework in the Italian garden, was done by local men.

The gardens were transferred to the Trust by Lady Londonderry and Lady Mairi Bury through the Ulster Land Fund in 1956.

The *Temple of the Winds* is a charming eighteenth-century building about half a mile from the entrance to the gardens, standing above the lough shore. Its salon has a handsome ceiling and inlaid floor. Its architect is unknown, but was reputedly 'Athenian' Stuart (James Stuart), who designed the Temple of the Winds in another Trust garden, at *Shugborough* in Staffordshire. It was given to the Trust by Lady Mairi Bury in 1962, when the Ulster Land Fund gave an endowment.

Rowallane, County Down: viburnum in the gardens.

Rowallane

COUNTY DOWN

eleven miles south-east of Belfast

The gardens at Rowallane, which consist of a walled garden and informal plantings with woodland, rock and stream, cover about fifty acres and are about sixty years old. They provide splendid displays of colour in the spring and autumn and are of particular interest to specialists for their magnificent collection of rare trees, shrubs, plants and bulbs.

They are the creation of the late Mr Hugh Armytage Moore, who inherited Rowallane in 1903. He began then to plan the garden in a waste land of whins and outcrops of rock.

The gardens were given to the Trust by the Ulster Land Fund, with an endowment.

Ardress

COUNTY ARMAGH

four miles west of Portadown

To begin with Ardress was a simple seventeenth-century manor-house, built in 1660 to replace an earlier building which had been destroyed during the Civil War. Then, about 1770, two wings were built on and the interior altered to suit the taste of that time. These additions were made so skilfully and sympathetically that the two building styles were joined to make a pleasing, graceful country house. The man who achieved this transformation was the architect George Ensor, who practised for some time in Dublin, where he was Clerk of Works to the Surveyor General. He came to Ardress when, in 1760, he married the heiress to the property. In the design and decoration of the interior of Ardress he was assisted by Michael Stapleton, a most talented and successful Irish stuccoist whose work in Dublin included the plaster decorations in what is now the residence of the President. Many of his original drawings are housed in the National Library in Dublin. Guided by these the Trust has been able to restore the decorative plasterwork in the principal rooms at Ardress to the water-colour tints he indicated.

George Ensor was followed at Ardress by his son, another George Ensor, who did not follow his father's profession but in the intervals of managing the estate wrote on political and religious subjects, and there are a number of his books in the house. Other members of the Ensor family continued at Ardress until 1960 (completing a connection of two hundred years), when it was acquired by the National Trust through the Ulster Land Fund.

Derrymore House

COUNTY ARMAGH

one and a half miles north-west of Newry

Derrymore House is a rare survival of the small, thatched country mansion which was popular with the lesser Irish gentry in the eighteenth century. Although there is no certainty as to the date, it seems to have been built for Isaac Corry just after 1776. He was member for the borough of Newry at

Ardress, County Armagh.

Derrymore House, County Armagh.

Florence Court, County Fermanagh.

Florence Court, County Fermanagh: the entrance hall.

that time and legal records show that his family had come into possession of Derrymore property a short while before. He was a supporter of the Union of Ireland and Great Britain, and a lifelong friend of Castlereagh. Castlereagh was a visitor to Derrymore, and it is a tradition that the Act of Union was drafted there in the room now called the Treaty Room.

The house changed hands several times during the nineteenth century and some additions were made. In 1952 the then owner, whose family had not lived in the house, gave it to the Trust. The nineteenth-century additions were demolished and the house regained its original appearance.

Florence Court

COUNTY FERMANAGH

seven miles south-west of Enniskillen

Florence Court provides the visitor with much grandeur outside and ornamentation within. It has also provided students and historians with a fine architectural 'Whodunit?'

There is no record of the date of building nor of whom the architect may have been, nor of the craftsmen who created the outstandingly fine plasterwork in the rooms. There has been much comparison of scanty and sometimes contradictory contemporary writings; much comparison of the designs used in the decoration with designs in Dublin houses which can be dated with certainty. As the outcome of all this the Georgian Society take the view, merely, that 1764 was the date of completion.

Whoever was responsible achieved an east front (his main frontage) of great grandeur. It runs 260 feet, the centre block in three storeys with flanking pavilions joined to it by arched openings. There is plenty of detailed ornamentation. Inside, all is solid Georgian craftsmanship for staircase, bookshelves and doorcases, and the principal rooms have walls and ceilings decorated with delightful and intricate plasterwork designs.

The family which was responsible for this remarkable house had first settled in Ireland at Inniskillen in the person of Sir William Cole, a Devonshire knight who had fought for Queen Elizabeth in the Low Countries. His great-grandson was the first of the family to build at Florence Court and it was possibly the latter's son who built the present house. The family continued at Florence Court, becoming Earls of Enniskillen in 1789. They gave the house to the Trust in 1953. There was a serious fire in 1955 but fortunately the damage was repairable.

Castlecoole, County Fermanagh.

Castlecoole

COUNTY FERMANAGH

south-east of Enniskillen

Castlecoole is a house that was designed and made, inside and out, all at one time, and has not been subjected by succeeding generations to improvements, additions, alterations or any kind of second thoughts. For all this we can be immensely grateful, as it was designed in a grand, late eighteenth-century manner by a most distinguished architect (James Wyatt) for a patron who had the site, the taste, the determination and the money for such an undertaking—Armar Lowry-Corry, M.P. for County Tyrone, who had inherited estates in Tyrone as well as his mother's Castlecoole property. Later he was created Earl of Belmore.

Wyatt's design has great grace and simplicity, and some of the best London craftsmen of the time (1788–99 was the decade during which the house was

Castlecoole, County Fermanagh: the landing at the top of the staircase.

building) were brought over to carry out the beautiful interior decoration. Indeed some of the furniture also was made on the spot, as in the later stages joiners who had been making the splendid doors, bookcases and shutters were set to making appropriate furniture. Lord Belmore acted as his own contractor and his accounts for the building work have survived. The Portland stone for the fabric of the house he had landed at Ballyshannon, then taken by bullock cart ten miles to Lough Erne and finally water-borne again to Enniskillen. It is not known whether the park which provides such a fine setting for the house was laid out by Lord Belmore or by his son. But fairly certainly its splendid beeches and oaks were already well-grown trees when he planned his house.

Keys

NORTHERN COUNTIES, NORTH WALES, ISLE OF MAN

1 Aberconwy (Conway Suspension Bridge)
2 Aberdaron Headland (Braich-y-Pwll)
3 Aberglaslyn Pass
4 Alderley Edge
5 Allen Banks, The
6 Arnside Knott
7 Beadnell Bay
8 Beningbrough Hall
9 Bodnant
Braich-y-Pwll: *see* Aberdaron Headland
10 Braithwaite Hall
11 Bridestones Moor
12 Burton Wood
13 Cadair Ifan Goch
14 Cae Glan-y-Mor
15 Caldy Hill
16 Calf of Man
17 Cartmel Priory Gatehouse
18 Cautley
19 Cemaes
20 Cloud, The
21 Coedydd Maentwrog (Ffestiniog Woodlands)
Conway Suspension Bridge: *see* Aberconwy
22 Cregennan
23 Dalton Castle
24 Derlwyn
25 Derwent Estate
26 Dinas Gynfor
27 Dinas Oleu
28 Dolobran
29 Dolymelynllyn
30 Dunstanburgh Castle and Links (Newton Links)
31 Dunthwaite
32 East Riddlesden Hall
33 East Scar Top Farm
34 Ebchester
35 Eddisbury Park Field
36 Farne Islands
37 Formby
38 Gamallt
39 Glyn Ceiriog
40 Hadrian's Wall (The Roman Wall)
41 Hafod Lwyfog
42 Hag Wood
43 Harlech Cliff
44 Harrock Wood
45 Hebden Dale
46 Helsby Hill
47 Hudswell Woods
48 Lady's Well
49 Lindisfarne Castle
50 Little Moreton Hall
51 Llangollen (Velvet Hill)
52 Llechwedd Wood
53 Lyme Park
54 Maggoty's Wood
55 Maister House
56 Malham Tarn
57 Marsden Moor (Wessenden Moor)
58 Medlock Vale
59 Middle House Farm
60 Mobberley Manor
61 Moorhouse Woods
62 Morfa Bychan
63 Moulton Hall
64 Mount Grace Priory
65 Mow Cop
66 Musgrave Fell
67 Mynydd Cilan
68 Mynydd-y-Graig
69 Nether Alderley
70 Nostell Priory
71 Nunnington Hall
72 Ogwen
73 Ormesby Hall
74 Penrhyn Castle
75 Penshaw Monument
76 Pen-y-Mynydd
77 Plas-yn-Rhiw (Porth Neigwl)
Porth Neigwl: *see* Plas-yn-Rhiw
78 Powis Castle
79 Rhiw Goch
80 Ribchester Fort
The Roman Wall: *see* Hadrian's Wall
81 Ros Castle
82 Rufford Old Hall
83 St Aidan's and Shoreston Dunes
84 Saltwick Nab
85 Sandburrows
86 Scarth Wood Moor
87 Segontium
88 Sharow Cross
89 Silverdale
90 Sizergh Castle
91 Speke Hall
92 Stainforth Bridge
93 Stubbins
94 Styal
95 Tatton Park
96 Temple Sowerby Manor
97 Thurstaston Common
98 Treasurer's House, York
99 Tu Hwnt I'r Bont
100 Wallington
101 Washington Old Hall
Wessenden Moor: *see* Marsden Moor
102 Wetheral Woods
103 Wylam (George Stephenson's Cottage)
104 Ynysgain
105 Ynys towyn
106 Ysbyty

LAKE DISTRICT

1 Ambleside (Dora's Field)
2 Borrowdale
3 Buttermere Valley
4 Castlerigg Stone Circle
5 Coniston
6 Derwentwater
Dora's Field: *see* Ambleside
7 Duddon Valley
8 Ennerdale
9 Eskdale
10 Grasmere
11 Hartsop
12 Hawkshead Court House
13 Hobcarton Crag
14 Keld Chapel
15 Langdales
16 Nibthwaite Woods
17 Peel Island
18 Sawrey
19 Scafell
20 Stockdale Moor
21 Troutbeck
22 Ullswater
23 Wasdale
24 Windermere
25 Wordsworth House

NORTHERN IRELAND

1 Ardress
2 Ballymacormick Point
3 Ballymoyer
4 Carrick-a-Rede Cliff-land
5 Carrick-a-Rede Island
6 Castlecoole
7 Castleward
8 Collin Glen
9 Coney Island
10 Cushendun
11 Derrymore House
12 Dundrum
13 Florence Court
14 Giant's Causeway
15 Gray's Printing Press
16 Kearney
17 Killynether
18 Lighthouse Island
19 Lisnabreeny
20 Minnowburn Beeches
21 Mount Stewart Gardens
22 Mussenden Temple
23 North Antrim Cliff Path
24 Rough Fort
25 Rowallane
26 Springhill
27 Strangford Lough
28 Templetown Mausoleum
29 White Park Bay

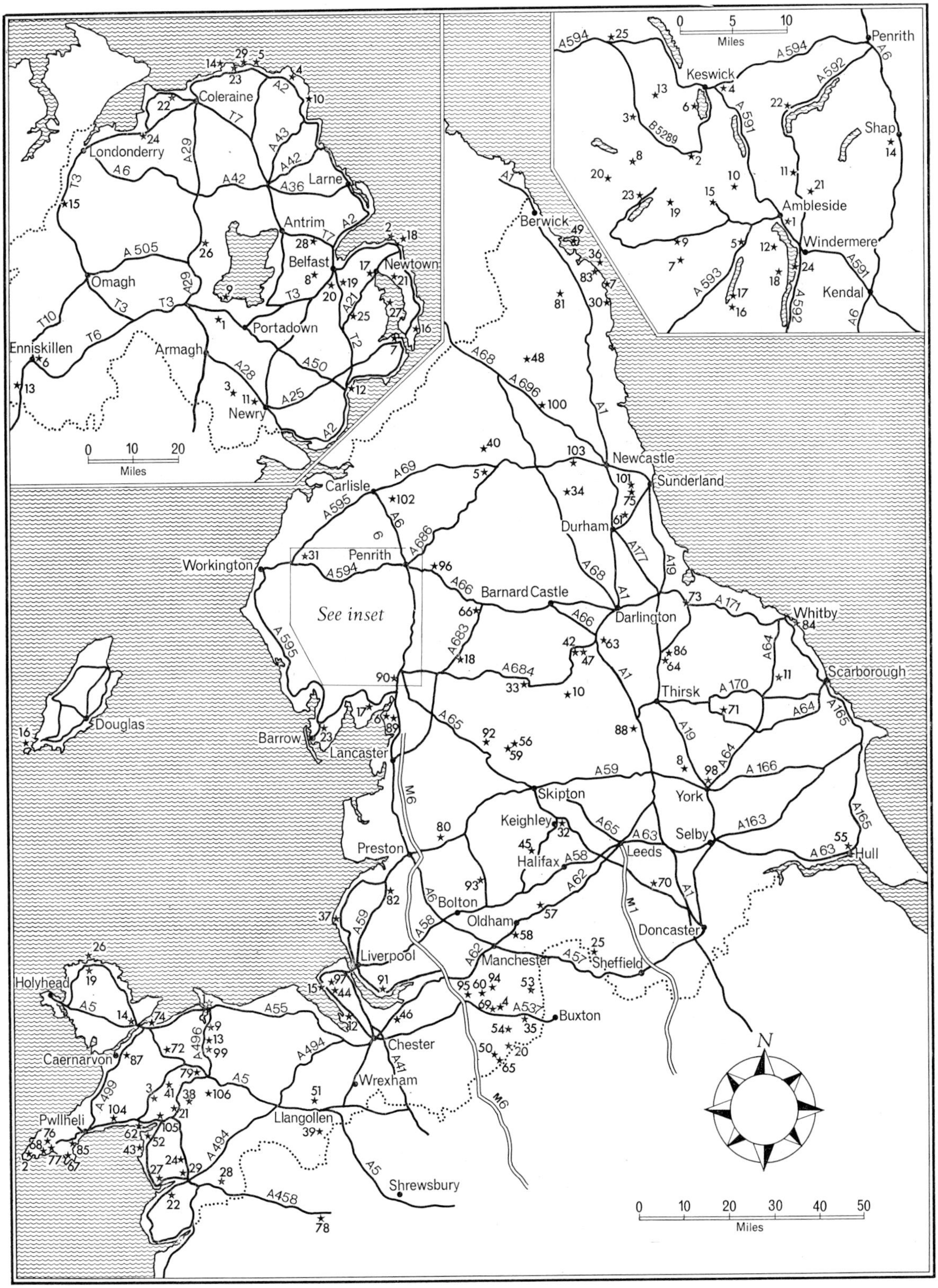

Coleraine
Londonderry
Larne
Antrim
Belfast
Newtown
Omagh
Portadown
Enniskillen
Armagh
Newry
0 10 20
Miles
Penrith
Keswick
Shap
Ambleside
Windermere
Kendal
0 5 10
Miles
Berwick
Newcastle
Sunderland
Carlisle
Durham
Workington
Penrith
Barnard Castle
Darlington
Whitby
See inset
Scarborough
Thirsk
Douglas
Barrow
Lancaster
York
Skipton
Keighley
Halifax
Leeds
Selby
Hull
Preston
Bolton
Oldham
Doncaster
Manchester
Sheffield
Liverpool
Holyhead
Buxton
Chester
Caernarvon
Wrexham
Llangollen
Pwllheli
Shrewsbury
N
0 10 20 30 40 50
Miles

Appendix

Properties not illustrated

Properties which are not illustrated and are not referred to in the notes that accompany the illustrations are noted below. In addition to the properties which it owns there, the Trust holds Restrictive Covenants (see note in Introduction) over 25,220 acres in these counties, and over a number of farmhouses and cottages, several other buildings and part of Middleton Colliery Railway built in 1758.

NORTHUMBERLAND

The Allen Banks, three miles west of Haydon Bridge; 190 acres of hill and woodland where the Allen joins the Tyne. Given by members of the Bowes-Lyon family between 1942 and 1961.

Beadnell Lime Kilns, 2½ miles south of Seahouses. A group of eighteenth-century kilns.

Dunstanburgh Castle, nine miles north-east of Alnwick, five hundred acres of foreshore and the ruins of the fourteenth-century castle now under guardianship of the Ministry of Works.

Lady's Well. At Holystone, seven miles west of Rothbury. Traditionally associated with St Ninian.

Ros Castle, twelve miles north-west of Alnwick. A hilltop with views given in 1936 as part of a memorial to Viscount Grey of Fallodon.

St Aidans and Shorestone Dunes, two miles south-east of Bamburgh. Sixty acres of sand dunes with views of the Farne Islands.

Wylam-on-Tyne. Eight miles west of Newcastle. George Stephenson's cottage. The eighteenth-century stone cottage where the inventor was born. Not open.

COUNTY DURHAM

At Ebchester, twelve miles south-west of Newcastle, ten acres of woodland on the bank of the Derwent, some of it given by the Ebchester Rowing Club.

On the Wear, three miles north-east of Durham, Moorhouse Woods, sixty acres of woodland replanted after 1945.

CUMBERLAND

In addition to property noted under the heading of the Lake District the Trust has in Cumberland some woods on the bank of the River Eden, about twenty acres of Wetheral Woods five miles east of Carlisle.

LAKE DISTRICT

More than seventy thousand acres of the Lake District are now in Trust ownership. Illustrations on previous pages show the variety of these properties and the texts accompanying the illustrations give notes on the Trust's holdings in the neighbourhood of Buttermere, Derwentwater, Ullswater, Langdale, Coniston, Hawkshead and Sawrey. Other properties are:

Near Ambleside, in addition to Dora's Field illustrated on page 251, two hundred acres of farm and fell 1½ miles south-east of Ambleside with views of Windermere, Coniston Old Man and Langdale Fells; 190 acres of wood and grassland a mile south of Ambleside on the shore of Windermere; Wray Castle, two miles south of Ambleside on the west side of Windermere, a nineteenth-century castle with sixty-four acres—grounds open, but not the house; and in Ambleside itself, on a bridge over the Stock Ghyll, Bridge House, probably an eighteenth-century garden house, now used by the Trust as an Information Centre.

In the Duddon Valley, several farms including large properties rising to Grey Friars (2,536 feet), Hardknott Pass and Bow Fell (2,960 feet). Of these farms, three were gifts from the Rev. H. H. Symonds and one was given as a memorial to him.

Dunthwaite, two miles west of the north end of Bassenthwaite, farm and woodland bordering the Derwent for 1½ miles.

Ennerdale. Farms on the north and north-west of Ennerdale Water, and to the east 3,600 acres of fell on both sides of the River Liza.

Eskdale. Farms at the head of the valley, including land on which Eskdale Youth Hostel stands, and Butterilket Farm of 3,300 acres on the left bank of the Esk, which runs up to the summit of Bow Fell (2,960 feet), where it marches with one of the Trust's Duddon Valley farms (Blackhall). Also Burnmoor Tarn (fifty-seven acres) by the path from Eskdale to Wasdale.

Grasmere. Several small properties in and near the village including Butterlip How, the viewpoint just behind the village which Wordsworth recommended in his *Guide to the Lakes*.

Hobcarton Crag, four miles west of Derwentwater, twenty-seven acres of the face of the crag.

Stockdale Moor, four miles south of Ennerdale, 2,500 acres. Cairns.

Troutbeck, three miles south-east of Ambleside, a farmhouse in the village built about 1626 and in occupation of one family until 1944. Contains their furniture, books and papers. About three miles south of Troutbeck, Troutbeck Park Farm (1,900 acres), acquired mainly under the will of Mrs Heelis (Beatrix Potter). A famous Lake District sheep farm.

Wasdale. Several large farms including land at the head of the lake and fell land reaching up towards Scafell, and towards Blacksail Pass; half a mile of lake shore and thirty-five acres of woodland at the foot of Wastwater; and fourteen hundred acres to the west between Netherwasdale village and Santon Bridge.

Windermere. Land on the lake shore at Claife on the west shore; woodland between Ferry Nab and Wray Castle; at Fell Foot on the east shore at its south end; at Queen Adelaide's Hill on the east shore; at Cockshott Point on the outskirts of Bowness. Also land at Allen Knott and Latter Heath about two miles north of Windermere station, on the outskirts of Windermere adjoining the viewpoint of Orrest Head; at Post Knott above Bowness. A viewpoint at Bordriggs Brow half a mile south of Bowness. Storrs Temple, an early nineteenth-century folly; no access.

WESTMORLAND

In addition to property noted under the heading of the Lake District the Trust has the following properties in Westmorland:

Temple Sowerby Manor, six miles east of Penrith. Part sixteenth century part eighteenth century. Not open.

Musgrave Fell, two miles north of Brough, manorial rights over eleven hundred acres of grassland and limestone outcrop. Interesting habitat for plants.

Keld Chapel, a mile south-west of Shap, a small pre-Reformation building.

Arnside, about a mile south of Arnside four miles north-west of Carnforth: The Knott, a hundred-acre open space overlooking Morecambe Bay.

In Coniston Water, Fir Island and Peel Island, and Nibthwaite Woods on the lake shore. Also four hundred acres of woodland and fell on the east of the lake; a bequest from Mr W. T. Hawkshead-Talbot and a gift from Col. J. T. Bretherton-Hawkshead-Talbot.

Great Mell Fell, south of Troutbeck. A 1,700-foot hill. Accepted by the Treasury in lieu of death duty and given to the Trust.

High Rigg, west of Grange, fifty acres, part of Riggside Farm. Bought with a bequest from Mrs A. W. G. Bowes and donations from Miss Grace Tavener and others.

Nicholas Wood, south of Grasmere village, ten woodland acres. Given by Mr E. R. Bindloss in memory of his son Richard.

Newlands, south-west of Keswick: High Snab farm, ninety acres. Bought from Lake District funds.

YORKSHIRE

Ormesby Hall, three miles south-east of Middlesbrough. Mid-eighteenth-century house with contemporary plasterwork. Bequeathed by Colonel J. W. B. Pennyman. Acquired 1962.

Nunnington Hall, 4½ miles south-east of Helmsley. A manor-house, mainly late seventeenth century.

Braithwaite Hall, 1½ miles south-west of Middleham, the seventeenth-century hall which is now a farmhouse, and 750 acres of farm and moorland.

Maister House, Hull. Mid-eighteenth century house with superb staircase hall. Given by Georgian Society for East Yorkshire.

Moulton Hall, five miles east of Richmond. Mid seventeenth century. Fine carved wood staircase. Open by prior arrangement.

Mount Grace Priory. Ruins of fourteenth-century priory under guardianship of Ministry of Works.

Cautley, five miles north-east of Sedbergh, Cross Keys Inn. Early seventeenth century with later alterations. By the donor's wish, an unlicensed inn.

In Wensleydale, a mile south-east of Bainbridge, East Scar Top Farm. 280 acres. Views of the dale.

Near Hudswell, ninety acres on the south bank of the Swale, close to Richmond, and Hag Wood, forty acres of woodland half a mile north-west of Hudswell.

Scarth Wood Moor, 250 acres of moorland about eight miles north-east of Northallerton.

Malham Tarn, six miles north-east of Settle. The Tarn House and two thousand acres between Ribblesdale and Wharfedale including the tarn (150 acres). Part let to the Field Studies Council. Also the adjoining Middle House and Low Trenhouse farms.

Stainforth Bridge, a seventeenth-century bridge over the Ribble, 2½ miles north of Settle on the old packhorse route from York to Lancaster.

At Sharrow, half a mile east of Ripon station, the stump of a cross marking the limit of the abbey sanctuary.

A mile east of Whitby at Saltwick Nab, a small piece of cliff-land.

Twelve miles south of Whitby, on Bridestones Moor, 870 acres of moorland. The Bridestones are curious masses of rock left by erosion of softer surrounding rock.

Hebden Dale. The Trust has three pieces of property north of Hebden Bridge, about five miles north-east of Todmorden. Two hundred acres of woods and the Hardcastle Crags on the north of Hebden water; forty acres of woodland on its west bank and farm and woodland to the south of it.

Derwent Estate, thirteen miles west and north-west of Sheffield, a six-thousand-acre estate in Yorkshire and Derbyshire in the Peak District National Park. Moorland rising to 1,775 feet. Given by the Treasury, which had accepted it in payment of death duty.

LANCASHIRE

Cartmel. The Priory Gatehouse, built about 1330. Now used as an artist's studio.

Dalton Castle. A fourteenth-century tower in the main street of Dalton-in-Furness.

Medlock Vale, fifteen acres on the banks of the Medlock 1½ miles north-west of Ashton-under-Lyne. Described in the Trust's list of properties as 'a rural oasis in an industrial area'.

Ribchester Fort. The Museum of Roman Antiquities and the foundations of two Roman granaries.

Silverdale, four miles north-west of Carnforth, land at Castlebarrow overlooking Morecambe Bay and ninety-seven acres of wooded hill east of Castlebarrow Head.

Stubbins, five miles north of Bury, 430 acres of small farms preserved as an agricultural zone.

CHESHIRE

Congleton. The Cloud, three miles to the east, and Mow Cop, five miles to the south of Congleton, both just over a thousand feet, give excellent views over the Cheshire plain. The first camp-meeting of the Primitive Methodists was held on Mow Cop in 1807. Mow Cop Castle is an eighteenth-century imitation ruin.

Helsby Hill half a mile south of Helsby, land at the top with views of the Mersey and the Welsh mountains.

Near Macclesfield, Eddisbury Park Field, a meadow by the Buxton road a mile east of Macclesfield and three miles south-west of the town. Near Gawsworth, Maggoty's Wood, a small woodland where Maggoty Green, an eccentric eighteenth-century dancing-master and dramatist, was buried.

Mobberley Manor, three miles north of Knutsford, given with twenty acres to protect the approach to the church. Not open.

The Wirral. At different times since 1916 five small properties in the Wirral have been given to the Trust: a viewpoint at Caldy Hill; 175 acres with views on Thurstaston Common; woodland at Burton Wood; and wood and meadow at Harrock Wood.

Glyn Ceiriog, eight miles north-west of Oswestry, meadowland and a mile of the Glyn Valley tramway, now a public walk.

Llangollen, Velvet Hill. Above the road from Llangollen to the Horseshoe Pass, seventy acres with fine views.

CAERNARVONSHIRE

Segontium. On the south-east outskirts of Caernarvon, the remains of a Roman fort. Under guardianship of the Ministry of Works.

A viewpoint on Cadair Ifan Goch, three miles north of Llanrwst on the east of the Conway valley.

At Hafod Lwyfog, five miles north-east of Beddgelert, 320 acres overlooking Lyn Gwynant.

Rhiw Goch, on the road from Betws-y-Coed to Dolwyddelan (A 496) two miles from Dolwyddelan, 160 acres with views of Lledr Valley.

Ynysgain. Two hundred acres of coastland foreshore and farm a mile west of Criccieth, including the mouth of the Afon Dwyfor.

Morfa Bychan, $1\frac{1}{4}$ miles south-west of Portmadoc, seashore, sand dunes and a golf-course.

Gamallt, three miles north-east of Ffestiniog, three hundred acres of moorland and part of two lakes. Access on foot by 11-mile track from Bala road.

Ynys Towyn, on the south-east side of Portmadoc, two acres with magnificent views.

Abersoch Sandburrows. Nineteen acres of the sandhills between the Llanbedrog road and the sea.

Aberglaslyn Pass, Bryn-y-Felin land. Twenty-one acres of wooded bank. Old copper mine workings. Bought from the Snowdonia Fund.

Porth Ysgo. A beach and waterfall (twenty acres). Given by the Misses Lorna and Mary Honora Keating in memory of their sister Eileen.

ANGLESEY

On the Menai Straits between Telford's bridge and Stephenson's railway bridge, Cae-Glan-y-Mor, seven acres given to preserve this view over the straits.

Cemaes on the east side of Cemaes Bay, fifty acres of farm and cliff-land.

Dinas Gynfor, $4\frac{1}{2}$ acres of cliff on the northernmost point of Wales.

Cemlyn, two miles west of Cemaes Bay, three hundred and twenty acres covering two miles of coast. A bird sanctuary. Bought through Enterprise Neptune with the help of Anglesey County Council.

Dinas Oleu, above Barmouth at its south end; 4½ acres of cliff-land overlooking Cardigan Bay given by Mrs F. Talbot in 1895. The first property acquired by the Trust.

Harlech Cliff. A piece of land with footpath to the sea a mile south of Harlech on the Barmouth road; and some land with views at Llechwedd wood just north of Harlech.

Cregennan, a mile east of Arthog (on A 493), seven hundred acres of farm and mountain land with two lakes. Given in 1959 by Major C. L. Wynne-Jones in memory of his two sons killed in the 1939–45 war.

Dolobran and Braich-Melyn, nine miles east of Dolgellau north of A 458, two mountain farms, good examples of early Welsh farmhouse architecture. Given by Squadron-Leader J. D. K. Lloyd and his brother as a memorial to men of Bomber Command who lost their lives in the 1939–45 war.

Dolmelynllyn, five miles by road north-west of Dolgellau. A twelve-thousand-acre estate with farms and two hotels. Rises to the spectacular waterfall on the Gamlan, Rhaiadr Ddu.

Derlwyn, 114 acres of rough moorland and part of a small lake six miles north-west of Dolgellau.

Coedydd Maentwrog (Ffestiniog Woodlands), south-west of Ffestiniog, two hundred acres on the wooded side of the valley of Afon Dwyryd near Maentwrog. Bought in 1965 with the help of the North Wales Naturalists' Trust.

NORTHERN IRELAND

Giant's Causeway, County Antrim, nine miles from Portrush. The unique rock formation given with cliff-land by the Ulster Land Fund and Sir Anthony Macnaghten, Bt, in 1961.

North Antrim Cliff Path, a ten-mile right of way from the Giant's Causeway to Ballintoy. Bought in 1963 with money given to the Ulster Coastline Appeal. The route covers the rocky peninsula on which are the ruins of Dunseverick Castle. Also White Park Bay, which is illustrated on page 289.

Carrick-a-Rede island and thirty acres of cliff-land west of Ballycastle, County Antrim. Sixty-foot rope bridge to the island.

Cushendun, County Antrim, sixty acres of the bay on the east coast of Antrim at the foot of Glendun, twenty-three miles north of Ballymena.

Templetown Mausoleum, Templepatrick, between Antrim and Newtownabbey. Built 1783 by Robert Adam in memory of the Hon. Arthur Upton.

Strangford Lough, County Down. The Trust has leased from various owners sixty-three miles of the foreshore, and the Strangford Lough Wild Life Conservation Scheme embraces all of the lough. Shooting is controlled and refuges have been established for bird-watching. There is access to the foreshore and visitors should take care not to disturb birds, using viewpoints, hides and car parks where provided.

Dundrum, two miles north-west of Newcastle, County Down; Murlough Nature Reserve, 475 acres of sand dunes and heathland of botanical, zoological and archæological interest. A nature reserve. Entry by permit only, but access to beach at all times. Bought by the Ulster Land Fund and given to the Trust in 1967.

Knockmelder, east of Portaferry, County Down. Eight acres of beach and adjacent land adjoining Trust land at Kearney. Accessible to the public. Bought from Enterprise Neptune funds.

Kearney, County Down, three miles east of Portaferry, forty acres of foreshore and village land with thirteen houses.

Lighthouse Island, Copeland Islands, a forty-three-acre island three miles off the mouth of Belfast Lough. Managed by the Copeland Island Bird Observatory.

Lisnabreeny, two miles south of Belfast near Newtownbreda, 156 acres with a waterfall and view over Belfast and Strangford Loughs.

Ballymacormick Point on the south side of the entrance to Belfast Lough north-east of Bangor, forty acres of rough land on the shore.

Coney Island, an eight-acre wooded island at the southern end of Lough Neagh. Recent excavations revealed a Neolithic settlement.

Ballymoyer, eight miles west of Newry. Fifty acres of woodland north and south of Ballymoyer House. Leased to the Ministry of Agriculture.

Minnowburn Beeches, 3½ miles south of Belfast at Shaws Bridge on the Lagan, 128 acres on the banks of the Lagan and Minnowburn rivers.

Killynether, a mile south-west of Newtownards, a house and forty acres, mostly woodland. House not open.

Collin Glen, a mile south-west of the Falls Road boundary of Belfast (B 38), thirty-nine acres giving access to the foot of Collin Mountain.

Rough Fort, County Londonderry, a mile west of Lunarady: an unexcavated rath or ring fort and an acre of trees.

In Strabane, County Tyrone, Gray's Printing Press. Here the printer of the American Declaration of Independence is said to have learned his trade.

REPUBLIC OF IRELAND

Kanturk Castle, County Cork, is let to the National Trust for Ireland and is under guardianship of the National Monuments branch of the (Eire) Office of Works.

ISLE OF MAN

Calf of Man. The six-hundred-acre island is a nature reserve to which there is controlled public access. Leased to the Isle of Man National Trust.

Culzean Castle, Ayrshire: Robert Adam's staircase.

5

THE NATIONAL TRUST FOR SCOTLAND

St Kilda, Western Isles: gannets off St Kilda.

St Kilda

WESTERN ISLES

There are two sides to the Trust's preservation work in the St Kilda island group—on the one hand the preservation of the wild life of the islands, and on the other the study of the way of life established there during the long period of occupation before 1930.

The Trust organizes periodic expeditions to the group, which has been leased to the Nature Conservancy.

The picture below shows a *cleitt*, one of several different styles of construction of which specimens are being preserved. The cleitt was a combined store and drying chamber. The turf roof is thick and keeps out rain; the drystone walls let through enough wind for drying purposes. A cleitt might have contained food, fuel, nets and clothes.

St Kilda, Western Isles: a cleitt.

Key

SCOTLAND

1 Abertarff House, Inverness
2 Bachelors' Club, Tarbolton
3 Balmacara
4 Balmerino Abbey
5 Bannockburn Monument
6 Barrie's Birthplace, Kirriemuir
7 Ben Lawers
8 Binns, The
9 Blackhill, Stonebyres
10 Boath Doocot
11 Brodick Castle, Isle of Arran
12 Bruce's Stone, New Galloway
13 Carlyle's Birthplace
14 Charlotte Square, Edinburgh
15 Corrieshalloch Gorge
16 Craigievar Castle
17 Crail
18 Crathes Castle
19 Culloden
20 Culross
21 Culzean Castle
22 Cunninghame Graham Memorial
23 Dollar Glen
24 Dunkeld
25 Fair Isle, Zetland
26 Falkland Palace
27 Folk Museum, Glamis (Kirkwynd Cottages)
28 Gladstone's Land
29 Glencoe and Dalness
30 Glenfinnan Monument
31 Goat Fell and Glen Rosa, Isle of Arran
32 Grey Mare's Tail
33 Hamilton House, Prestonpans
34 Hermitage, The
35 Hill of Tarvit
36 Hugh Miller's Cottage
37 Inveresk Gardens
38 Inverewe
39 Kintail
Kirkwynd Cottages, Glamis: *see* Folk Museum, Glamis
40 Lamb's House, Leith
41 Leith Hall
42 Linlithgow, houses on High Street
43 Menstrie Castle
44 Mote of Mark
45 Pass of Killiecrankie
46 Phantassie Doocot, East Linton
47 Pitmedden
48 Pittenweem
49 Plewlands House
50 Preston Mill, East Linton
51 Provan Hall, Glasgow
52 Provost Ross's House, Aberdeen
53 St Kilda
54 Souter Johnnie's Cottage, Kirkoswald
55 Strome Ferry
56 Threave Gardening School
57 Torridon Estate
58 Turret House, Kelso
59 Weaver's Cottage, Kilbarchan

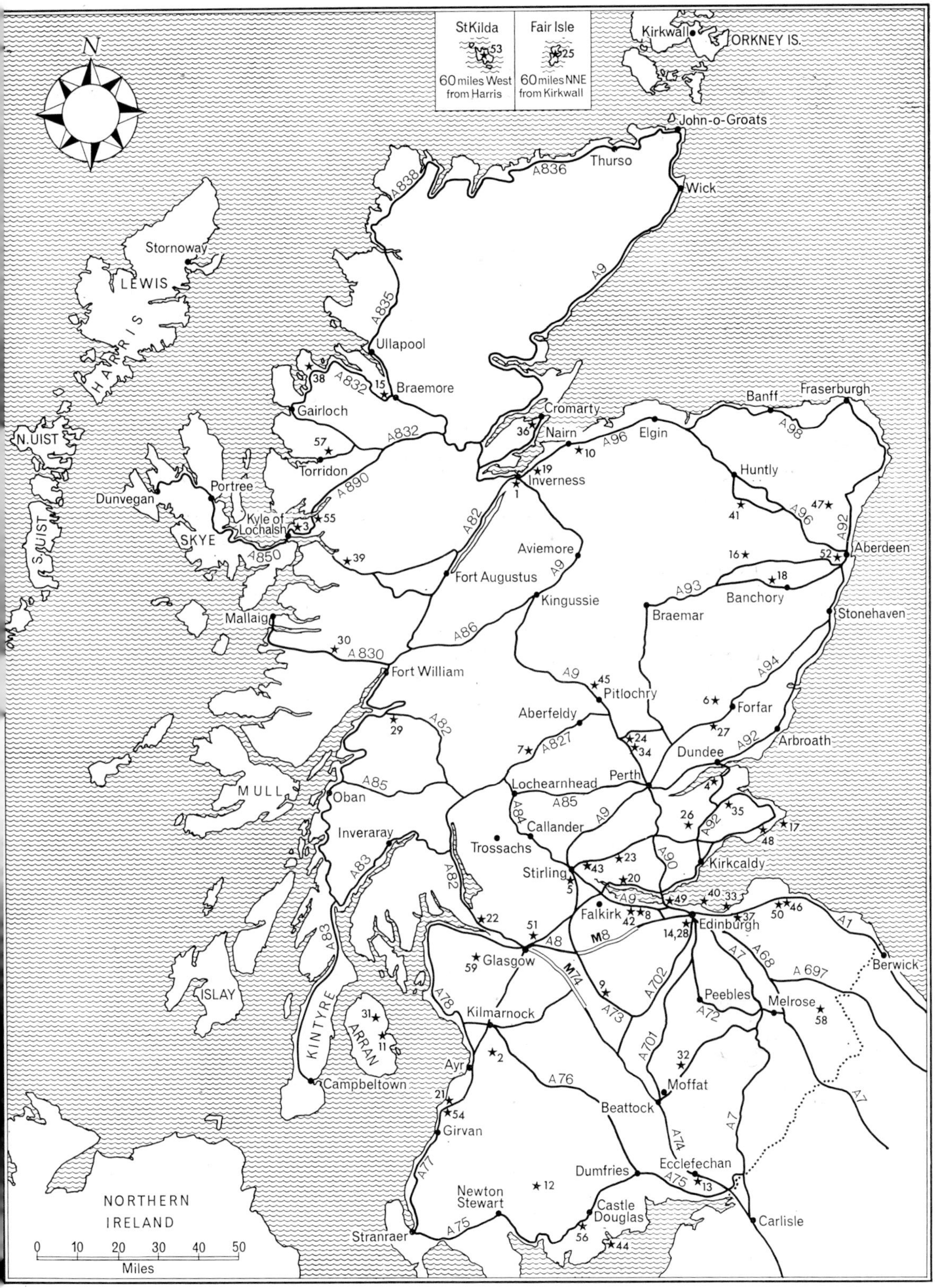

N
St Kilda
53
60 miles West from Harris
Fair Isle
25
60 miles NNE from Kirkwall
Kirkwall
ORKNEY IS.
John-o-Groats
Thurso
A836
A838
Wick
A9
Stornoway
LEWIS
HARRIS
A835
Ullapool
38
A832
15
Braemore
Gairloch
Cromarty
36
Nairn
A96
Elgin
Banff
Fraserburgh
A98
N. UIST
57
A832
10
Torridon
19
Inverness
1
Huntly
Dunvegan
Portree
A890
41
A96
47
Kyle of Lochalsh
3
55
S. UIST
SKYE
A850
A82
A92
39
Aviemore
16
52
Aberdeen
Fort Augustus
A9
A93
18
Banchory
Kingussie
Braemar
Stonehaven
Mallaig
A86
30
A830
Fort William
A9
45
A94
Pitlochry
6
Forfar
Aberfeldy
29
A82
27
24
34
Arbroath
7
A827
Dundee
A92
A85
Perth
MULL
Oban
Lochearnhead
4
A85
A84
35
A92
26
17
48
Callander
A9
Inveraray
Trossachs
A90
A83
43
23
Kirkcaldy
Stirling
5
20
A82
49
40
33
A9
50
46
Falkirk
42
8
37
22
51
14,28
Edinburgh
A1
A8
M8
A7
A68
A83
Glasgow
59
M74
A697
Berwick
9
A702
A78
A73
Peebles
Melrose
ISLAY
31
A72
58
KINTYRE
ARRAN
11
Kilmarnock
A701
2
32
Ayr
A76
Moffat
Campbeltown
21
54
Beattock
A7
Girvan
A74
A7
Ecclefechan
Dumfries
A75
13
A77
12
Newton Stewart
Castle Douglas
NORTHERN IRELAND
Carlisle
A75
56
44
Stranraer
0 10 20 30 40 50
Miles

Brodick Castle

ISLE OF ARRAN

The delights of Brodick Castle on the Isle of Arran are many and varied. It has a beautiful setting between the bay and the hills and an incomparable garden; its principal rooms contain a wealth of fine furniture, paintings, china and porcelain; and it has a long, eventful history.

The Vikings appreciated the merits of the site and had a fortress there. Robert the Bruce stayed here in 1306 before returning to the reconquest of Scotland. In the fifteenth century the castle was sacked three times, twice by the English. In Covenanting times it changed hands on several occasions. In the Civil War it was held for Charles II until after the battle of Worcester. During the Commonwealth the medieval castle was enlarged, but it was not again to be the scene of violence. Instead the castle was embellished during the eighteenth and nineteenth centuries with the fine collections which it now contains, and during the 1840's was given a new wing. This addition was an ingenious and successful piece of designing by James Gillespie Graham, the architect of a number of Scotland's country houses and of the Tolbooth Spire in Edinburgh. He contrived to make his new wing harmonize very satisfactorily with the exterior of the older building and, at the same time, to provide the more spacious rooms needed as settings for fine furniture and works of art.

These enlargements and the accumulation of the contents of the castle were the work of the Hamilton family. Their connection with Brodick began early in the sixteenth century by a marriage with the sister of King James III, and it continued till 1958. They garnered an important contribution to the collections in the castle from the great English collector William Beckford of Fonthill. Beckford's daughter married the tenth Duke of Hamilton in 1810. When her father died she inherited some of his magnificent collection of European and oriental porcelain, Flemish ivories, pastoral paintings by Watteau and other treasures.

The gardens, for all that there have been gardens at Brodick at least since the eighteenth century, owe their present great distinction and interest to the late Duchess of Montrose (daughter of the twelfth Duke of Hamilton), who began the creation of the *woodland garden* soon after the 1914–18 war. She brought the vision and skill of a creative artist to the task, and her garden blooms from early spring to late autumn. She took full advantage

Brodick Castle, Isle of Arran: the woodland garden.

of the climate of Arran, which is astonishingly mild and helpful to the gardener, to introduce a variety of shrubs and plants from overseas.

The Trust acquired the castle and grounds in 1958 from the Treasury, who had accepted them in payment of death duty. Endowment towards their upkeep was furnished by public subscription. At the same time Lady Jean Fforde (daughter of Mary, Duchess of Montrose, the creator of the gardens) gave to the Trust eight thousand acres of mountainous country on the island. A note on this property will be found on page 318.

The Isle of Arran: Goatfell, with Brodick Castle below.

Goatfell and Glen Rosa

ISLE OF ARRAN

The Trust's Arran property, which extends to eight thousand acres, includes Glen Rosa, Cir Mhor (2,618 feet) and Goatfell (2,866 feet). Here is fine rock-climbing and ridge-walking. Also, which is encouragement to less adventurous spirits, the Trust's Guide to its Brodick and Arran Hills property concludes with the reflection: 'Despite the rugged nature of the Arran

Brodick Castle, Isle of Arran: the drawing-room.

Hills they are remarkably safe, being low enough to be climbed quickly but high enough to give that authentic feeling of the wild which is one of the great rewards of hill country.'

Given a clear day these hills command sweeping and impressive views to Ireland, to the Lake District and to the western seaboard of Scotland. Their bird population reads like a catalogue of predators: peregrine falcon, merlin, hen-harrier, buzzard, sparrow-hawk, kestrel and, for good measure, not only the short-eared owl, a daytime hunter, but also the golden eagle. The golden eagle was for a time extinct in Arran but is now re-established.

This property was given to the Trust in 1958 by Lady Jean Fforde at the time when *Brodick Castle* and the garden which her mother had created there were also acquired.

Hugh Miller's Cottage

CROMARTY

The seventeenth-century thatched cottage in which Hugh Miller was born is one of the buildings which are preserved by the Trust rather for their association with some famous Scotsman than for their architectural interest. (*Carlyle's Birthplace* and *Barrie's* also come into this category, as does the *Bachelors' Club* at Tarbolton.)

Miller, who was born in the cottage in October 1802, was a man of great versatility. He was a stonemason by trade. He was for a time accountant in the Commercial Bank of Cromarty. As a man of letters, he contributed to Mackay Wilson's *Tales of the Borders.* He also gained wide recognition as a geologist. The cottage now houses a small museum.

The cottage was given to the Trust by the Cromarty Town Council in 1938.

Inverewe

WESTER ROSS

The garden of Inverewe in Wester Ross was begun just over a hundred years ago, not on the site of an earlier garden, nor in an area where exotic plants already flourished. Quite to the contrary: Mrs Mairi T. Sawyer wrote of the place her father, Osgood Mackenzie, chose that it was almost devoid of vegetation; that the only soil was acid black peat and that the exposed position caught nearly every gale that blows. But in conclusion she wrote: 'To counter the more vicious of the elements there is the benevolent warm flow of air emanating from the Gulf Stream.'

So, supported by the Gulf Stream and an annual rainfall of sixty inches, and armed with both a love of trees and flowers and a knowledge of the coast (his father and grandfather had been Lairds of Gairloch), Osgood Mackenzie began in 1862 to make the garden which today delights visitors from all over the world with its profusion of exotic plants.

Frost is not entirely unknown at Inverewe—indeed the Fahrenheit thermometers showed twenty-five degrees below freezing-point in early 1947

Inverewe,
Ross and Cromarty:
view of
Ben Airrdh Char
from the
walled garden.

Hugh Miller's
Cottage,
Ross and Cromarty:
birthplace of the
geologist.

The Peaks of Kintail: Loch Duich in the foreground, Ross and Cromarty.

and during the winter of 1954–5—but it is unusual, and Mrs Sawyer was able to claim that her father could grow 'as many and as good plants at Inverewe in the open air as is possible at Kew under glass'.

Establishing them called for windbreaks, the physical importation of soil, and time. Mackenzie planted Corsican pine and Scots fir as his windbreak with a variety of other trees in support. His daughter has recorded that: 'To Corsican pine he awarded first prize for rapidity of growth on bad soil and exposed sites and confessed that among the trees, many of the foreigners were far and away hardier than most Scottish natives.'

After about fifteen years Mackenzie felt he was making real progress and introduced eucalyptus and Monterey pine. Some of these trees have now grown to a great size, and twining on them are creepers introduced from many parts of the world. The general layout of the garden is informal, winding paths leading from section to section. The names of some of the sections are self-explanatory, thus: 'Grove of Big Trees' and 'Azaleas', but others, like 'Peace Plot' and 'Bambooselem', need explanation. 'Peace Plot' is a post-

1914–18 war planting of the more tender rhododendrons. 'Bambooselem' covers not only bamboos but also massed hydrangeas and a twenty-eight-foot-high *Magnolia stellata.*

The Trust's guide to Inverewe, edited by D. J. Macqueen Cowan, former assistant keeper of the Royal Botanic Garden in Edinburgh, includes a list of what he describes as 'the more noteworthy plants and flowers to be found in the garden'. This list totals no less than 320 items.

Mrs Sawyer, who for many years helped her father at Inverewe and after his death in 1922 continued the work which he had set in hand, gave the garden to the Trust, with endowment for upkeep, in 1952. This endowment was added to by the Pilgrim Trust and an anonymous donor.

Kintail, Balmacara, the Falls of Glomach

WESTER ROSS

The Trust has three large properties in Wester Ross, Kintail of fifteen thousand acres, Balmacara of eight thousand and the Falls of Glomach of two thousand. They preserve a magnificent stretch of West Highland scenery embracing the Five Sisters of Kintail, which rise abruptly from the lochside to three thousand feet, most of the Kyle-Plockton peninsula, and the 370-foot Falls of Glomach.

Kintail is a perfect countryside for climbers and for hill walkers, and the Trust's property is freely open to them at all times of the year. The walker here is rewarded not only by magnificent views but in early summer also by a wealth of bird life—from meadow pipits to the golden eagle. The Falls of Glomach, the highest in Britain, are remote and difficult of approach and live up to their name—Glomach being in Gaelic 'forbidding'. The water sweeps down a high wild glen before making its abrupt drop, to be splintered on a rock projection three hundred feet below and fall again to the bottom pool. Balmacara is a well wooded property and shows some exceptionally fine Douglas firs. Balmacara House has been leased to the education authority for special schools.

The Kintail estate was given to the Trust in 1944 by the late Mr P. J. H. Unna; the Balmacara estate was bequeathed in 1946 by the late Lady Hamilton; the Falls of Glomach were given in 1941 by Mrs B. C. M. Douglas of Killilan and Captain the Hon. Gerald Portman of Inverinate.

The Torridon Estate and Alligin Shuas

ROSS AND CROMARTY

The fourteen-thousand-acre Torridon estate includes some of the finest mountain scenery in Scotland. The north-western boundary of the estate runs along the summit ridge of Beinn Eighe (3,309 feet); to the south is the great mass of Liathach (3,546 feet), its seven tops linked by narrow ridges nearly five miles long; and to the west the mountain of Beinn Alligin (3,232 feet). In addition to their scenic beauty the mountains hold great interest for geologists.

There is a diversity of wild life on the estate, including red deer, pine marten, wild cat, golden eagle, peregrine falcon and seals.

The estate, less the mansion-house and adjacent woods, was given to the Trust in 1967 by the Treasury, who had accepted it in payment of death duty following the death of the fourth Earl of Lovelace. During his last few years the earl had been in consultation with the Trust and others with a view to arranging for public access to the Torridon Mountains.

The Trust now also owns Alligin Shuas, two thousand acres which adjoin the western extremity of the Torridon estate and were formerly part of it. This was given, by their three sons in Montreal, in memory of Sir Charles and Lady Edith Gordon. Sir Charles was owner of the whole Torridon estate from 1927 to 1947.

Abertarff House, Inverness

INVERNESS-SHIRE

Abertarff House (page 327) is one of the oldest houses in the burgh of Inverness, dating from the sixteenth century.

The Trust received it as a gift from the National Commercial Bank of Scotland in 1963, and during the next three years restored it and improved the interior to modern standards. The restoration work was given a Civic Trust award. The house has been let to An Comunn Gaidhealach (The Highland Association), and is used as its northern headquarters.

Torridon, Ross and Cromarty, looking across Upper Loch Torridon to the Torridon mountains.

Plockton Village, Loch Carron and the hills of Applecross, Ross and Cromarty.

Culloden, Inverness-shire: Old Leanach Farmhouse.

Culloden

INVERNESS-SHIRE

In the 1930's it was feared that commercial development would encroach on the battlefield and its surroundings. This fear prompted the late Mr Alexander Munro of Leanach Farm to give two pieces of the battlefield to

Abertarff House, Inverness.

the Trust. Gifts from others (including the late Hector Forbes of Culloden) have followed, and the Trust now has in its care the graves of the Clans, the Memorial Cairn, the Well of the Dead, the Cumberland Stone and *Old Leanach Farmhouse.*

Old Leanach Farmhouse, illustrated on page 326, a silent witness of the battle, is now used as an information centre for visitors to the battlefield.

Glenfinnan Monument near Fort William, Inverness-shire, looking down Loch Shiel.

Glenfinnan Monument

INVERNESS-SHIRE

A tall tower topped by a statue of a kilted highlander stands within a grassy enclosure at the head of Loch Shiel. On the walls of the enclosure are inscriptions in Gaelic, Latin and English recording that the monument was erected in 1815 by Alexander Macdonald of Glenadale on the spot where Prince Charles Edward raised his standard on 19th August 1745.

Entrance to Glencoe, Argyllshire, showing Bidean Nam Bean.

This Alexander was a grandson of the Alexander Macdonald of Glenadale at whose house the prince stayed on the night before the raising of the standard.

The statue, which is the work of the sculptor Greenshields, is not a statue of the prince himself but a figure representative of the men who followed him. There is a staircase inside the tower which gives access to the top platform.

The monument was given to the Trust in 1938 by Sir Walter Blount, the Trustees of Glenadale Estates and the Roman Catholic diocese of Argyll and the Isles.

The preservation of the monument represents an important side of the Trust's work, namely the preservation of places with historic associations. In this same category other Trust properties are the *Pass of Killiecrankie*, *Bannockburn Monument* and *Culloden*.

Glencoe, Argyllshire, looking south across Loch Leven towards the north end of Glencoe.

Glencoe and Dalness

ARGYLLSHIRE

In Glencoe and Dalness the Trust owns 12,800 acres of rugged mountain country. Included in the property are Buachaille Etive Mor and *Bidean Nam Bean*, which is the highest peak in Argyll (3,766 feet). There is access for walkers and climbers, and the Trust opens an information centre in Glencoe village from May to mid October. The property was bought in 1935 and 1937 to prevent commercial exploitation, the money for the purchase being provided by the combined efforts of the Scottish Mountaineering,

Alpine and other climbing clubs, the Pilgrim Trust and a public subscription.

These Glencoe and Dalness properties make up a rough triangle, each side about six miles long, between the River Etive above Dalness and the River Coe above Clachaig. The Trust has published a useful guide to the area, which has a particularly interesting and helpful section on the hill walking for which the area provides the most glorious scope.

The scene of the massacre in 1692 is not on the Trust property.

The Grey Mare's Tail

DUMFRIESSHIRE

The Grey Mare's Tail, which is the Tail Burn flowing from Loch Skeen just before it enters Moffat Water, is a two-hundred-foot waterfall (page 332). Here the Trust acquired in 1962 a property of rather more than two thousand acres. It harbours rare flowers and, occasionally, some wild goats.

Craigievar Castle

ABERDEENSHIRE

twenty-six miles west of Aberdeen, five miles north of Lumphanan

In the scholarly yet racy guide to Craigievar (pages 334–5) which Dr Douglas Simpson wrote for the Trust he describes it as 'the most cultured, scholarly and refined' of all Scotland's many castles, and 'a masterpiece of old-time Scottish architecture'. Less learned visitors find it easy to agree with these superlatives.

It was finished in 1626 and remains virtually unaltered. It is impressively sited high up on a hillside. The lower walls are solid and plain and above there is a rich array of corbelling, turrets and cupolas. For the most part the design and decoration of the exterior come from native origins but there are also, as the balustrade on one of the towers, elements brought in from abroad. The

The Grey Mare's Tail, Birkhill, Dumfriesshire.

Leith Hall, Aberdeenshire.

interior, though largely medieval in its plan, has superb plasterwork, of the style used to decorate Elizabethan houses.

The castle was built by William Forbes, who had made a fortune as a merchant in trade with Danzig. He was a graduate of Edinburgh University and a man of culture. It is not known who assisted him in the design and building of Craigievar, but it is thought probable that he employed a master mason named I. Bel who is known to have worked in Aberdeenshire at the relevant time.

In 1963, following a public appeal, the Trust bought the castle from the trustees of the late Lord Sempill. A start was also made on building up an endowment fund, for which donations are still sought, for its permanent preservation.

Craigievar Castle, Aberdeenshire.

Craigievar Castle, Aberdeenshire: the Great Hall.

Leith Hall

ABERDEENSHIRE

seven miles south of Huntly on A 979

Leith Hall (page 333) is built round a courtyard. It was not designed as a whole but reached its present size and plan by stages as succeeding generations of the Leith family made their additions. The oldest parts are in the north wing and date from 1650. Much of the building was done during the eighteenth century. When James Leith began the Hall which was to be their home for the next three hundred years, the Leith family had been landholders in Aberdeenshire since the fourteenth century. The Hall contains many family and Jacobite relics.

The name of Hay was added to that of Leith when in 1789 General Alexander Leith inherited the Rannes estates from his great-uncle Andrew Hay. Andrew Hay had been an ardent Jacobite, 'out' in the '45 rising, and was excluded from the Act of Indemnity. He persisted in seeking a pardon and eventually this was granted. It is on view in the Hall; reputedly the only Jacobite pardon extant. Many of the family soldiered with distinction, notably Sir James Leith Hay, who commanded the 5th Division in the Peninsular War and was buried (in 1816) in Westminster Abbey. Charles Leith Hay, last male representative of the main line of the family, was killed in 1939 while serving as an officer in the Royal Artillery. Leith Hall, with twelve hundred acres of farm and woodland, was given to the Trust by his mother, the Hon. Mrs Leith Hay of Rannes, in 1945.

Pitmedden

ABERDEENSHIRE

Pitmedden Garden near Udny was designed in 1675. At that time the fashion was still for a formal garden, even if it were a large one with a variety of plants. As Miles Hadfield writes in an appendix to the Trust's guide-book to Pitmedden, 'the simple knot had been elaborated into the freely designed baroque parterre'.

Pitmedden Garden,
near Udny, Aberdeenshire.
Below : An aerial
view.

Alexander Seton, an eminent lawyer by profession, had studied the gardens at Holyrood House and other great houses. When he came to build a mansion-house on the site of the old castle of Pitmedden—his family had acquired the estate in 1603—he made his own plan for the garden. His descendants continued in possession of the estate till 1894, when it was bought at auction by Alexander Keith. The garden had not been maintained and had declined to the status of a kitchen garden. Alexander's son, Major James Keith, made improvements and in 1952 gave it to the Trust with sixty-five acres of the estate and an endowment. Since then it has been brought into being again as the garden of parterres and heraldic patterns which Alexander Seton made there.

This reconstruction has required much ingenuity as well as labour. No detailed plan of Seton's garden survived, as many papers were destroyed in a fire at Pitmedden in 1818; but strategically placed, surviving yew trees provided a guide to layout and Seton's garden pavilions were there to be repaired. Miles of box hedge have been replanted: literally miles, as planting in one year alone (1956) amounted to two miles. Colour is provided by thirty thousand annuals, raised under glass at Pitmedden. Of the four parterres one is now devoted to Alexander Seton and his family and the others are modelled on those of the garden at Holyrood House as shown by James Gordon of Rothiemay, since it is believed that Seton consulted their designer.

Crathes Castle

KINCARDINESHIRE

fourteen miles west of Aberdeen, on the north bank of the Dee

Crathes Castle—apart from the east wing which was added on during the eighteenth century as an enlargement to the building—was built between 1546 and 1596. It has been lived in continuously ever since, and retains not only its original interior decoration but also some of its original furniture.

It was built by the Burnett family, who had held land here on the River Dee at least since 1323. Shown in the castle today is the jewelled ivory horn reputedly given by King Robert the Bruce to Alexander Burnett in that year, with lands at Crathes and a duty to serve as coroner of the Royal Forest of Drum. It was his descendants who built the sixteenth-century castle, made the eighteenth-century additions to the building, and laid out the fine, formal eighteenth-century garden which has been maintained and

Crathes Castle, Kincardineshire.

improved and remains one of the attractions of Crathes. Though mindful of their family home, they were not always a stay-at-home family, and at different times provided Basle with a professor of philosophy and Salisbury with a bishop. During the eighteenth century a William Burnett was successively governor of New York and of New Jersey, Massachusetts and New Hampshire, and it is after him that the Burnett Society in America is named. In 1951 the late Sir James Burnett of Leys gave Crathes to the Trust with an endowment.

The castle is a four-storey building with six-foot-thick walls, but is far from being plain and forbidding, since it is topped with square and rounded turrets and has dormer windows and gargoyles.

Crathes Castle, Kincardineshire: tempera painted ceiling, one of the Nine Nobles.

Inside, apart from the interest of an interior which has been preserved as its sixteenth-century creators made it, there is the very special interest of the *tempera painted ceilings.* These were part of the original decoration and the painting is among the most beautiful in Scotland. With the tempera technique (which entails using egg-yolk as a binding agent for chalk colours) the medieval craftsman was able to achieve unusually bright colours. These remain, but the paintings present other problems of preservation, those at Crathes having been subject to a certain amount of flaking. But the Trust (which has similar paintings to care for in the chapel of *Falkland Palace*, in *Gladstones Land* in Edinburgh and at *Culross*) became engaged on a programme of research and experiment which has led to the establishment of a centre for restoration of tempera and other works at *Stenhouse Mansion*, Edinburgh, which it is hoped will establish a satisfactory method of treatment.

Of the three painted ceilings at Crathes one carries a miscellaneous assembly of figures; but the others each have an ambitious theme, vigorously executed. One shows the Nine Nobles—the stock pagan, Old Testament and Christian heroes of the troubadours' repertoire—each with a eulogistic rhyme. The other is the Chamber of the Nine Muses, where in addition to the figures of the four muses the painter has added figures for five virtues to make up his set of nine.

The gardens were given their formal plan at the beginning of the eighteenth century. Lime avenues were planted leading to the river, and yew hedges, now grown to twelve feet, were established to mark the division of the garden into rectangular sections. The various divisions of the garden have now been planted with a very great variety of shrubs and plants, some native and others from North and South America, Africa, India and New Zealand.

Kirkwynd Cottages, Glamis

ANGUS

This row of seventeenth-century cottages with stone-slabbed roofs (page 343) was restored by the Trust in 1957 and converted into a museum. They now house the very fine Angus Folk Collection.

Barrie's Birthplace, Kirriemuir

ANGUS

No. 9 Brechin Road (page 343), is a modest two-storey house in a corner of the town known as the Tenements. James Barrie was born in it in 1860 and lived there until he was eight. In the small communal wash-house behind the house he staged his first play—reputedly a drama with a finale in which the actors struggled to push one another into the boiler.

Ben Lawers, Perthshire, seen from a point west of Killin, looking north-east.

Opposite: Kirkwynd Cottages, Glamis.
Barrie's Birthplace, Kirriemuir, Angus.

Barrie wrote much of his home town—which he named Thrums after the loose threads used by the handloom weavers there to mend broken threads in their looms. His father was a handloom weaver, and at the time of Barrie's birth worked a loom in a downstairs room in the house. As the family grew, he moved it to a loom shop. Barrie always held a great love for Kirriemuir, revisited it in the years of his success, and in accordance with his wishes was buried in the cemetery there.

The house and wash-house have been restored and personal possessions and mementoes of the playwright and his family have been collected there.

The house was given to the Trust in 1937 by Mr D. Alves of Caernarvon. He had bought it in that year on hearing rumours that it was to be shipped to America as a Barrie museum and the wash-house taken to London and re-erected in Kensington Gardens.

Killin, Perthshire: the bridge over the River Dochart, Ben Lawers in the background.

Ben Lawers

PERTHSHIRE

On the southern slopes of Ben Lawers (page 342) and the nearby Ben Ghlas and Coire Odhar the Trust now has an eight-thousand-acre property. Ben Lawers rises to 3,984 feet—the highest mountain in Perthshire—and many rare alpine plants grow there. From the summit there are views of both the Atlantic and the North Sea. A Nature Trail has been established on Ben Lawers and an information hut is maintained at a car park there during the summer months. Coire Odhar is popular for winter sports. The property was bought in 1950 from the Trust's Mountainous Country Fund —a fund formed by Mr P. J. H. Unna.

The Trust has published an extremely interesting and informative book on Ben Lawers containing expert accounts of its history, plant and animal life and the skiing areas in the range. In his notes on its plant ecology Dr Duncan Poore of the Nature Conservancy describes Ben Lawers as far famed for the richness of its alpine flora and rightly called 'the botanists' Mecca'. To this the Trust's introduction to the book adds a rider that one of the main objects in acquiring Ben Lawers was to ensure the preservation of the rare alpine flora and urging visitors not to uproot and 'collect' these flowers as specimens.

Mr Unna, who died in a climbing accident near Dalmally in 1950, was a president of the Scottish Mountaineering Club in the 1930's. His generosity and his active interest have enabled the Trust to acquire or to accept *Glencoe and Dalness*, *Kintail*, Ben Lawers and *Torridon.*

Dunkeld

PERTHSHIRE

The Trust has achieved an excellent work of preservation and restoration at Dunkeld (page 347). In the early 1950's almost all the charming *little houses* between Atholl Street and the cathedral, dating from the rebuilding of the town after the battle of Dunkeld (1689), were half derelict and being considered for demolition. Between 1954 and 1966 the Trust restored twenty of these houses and the Perth County Council another twenty. The charm of the exteriors has been retained while the interiors have been improved to modern standards. The Trust was enabled to carry out this work by receiving most of the property as a gift from the Atholl Estates and by the response to a public appeal for funds to pay for its restoration. See also the Little Houses, Fife, page 355.

The Hermitage

PERTHSHIRE

The Hermitage, near Dunkeld (page 351), also once called Ossian's Hall, was the centre-piece of an eighteenth-century garden and sited to command a dramatic view of the waterfall below. It was built by the third Duke of Atholl in 1758 and decorated inside in 1783 with paintings of Hospitality, supported by Justice, and Fortitude and Harmony, attended by Temperance and Prudence. It suffered damage from vandalism during the nineteenth century but was restored, in simplified form, by the Trust in 1952 as the centre-piece of a delightful walk through the woods along the River Braan. Together with fifty acres of the woodland it was given to the Trust in 1943, in accordance with the wishes of the eighth Duke, by his widow.

Pass of Killiecrankie

PERTHSHIRE

The Pass of Killiecrankie (page 348–9) ranks for preservation as well for its beauty as for its historical association. The viewpoint towards the head of the Pass has long been admired by visitors, among them Queen Victoria, who came here in 1844.

The site of the battle of 27th July 1689 was the hillside above the main road a mile north of the Pass. But it was through the Pass that King William's men advanced to engage the Jacobite army led by 'Bonnie Dundee', and through it that many of them later fled in retreat.

The Trust property of fifty acres here was given in 1947 by Mrs Edith Foster.

Dunkeld, Perthshire: little houses.

Pass of Killiecrankie, Perthshire: the railway viaduct over the River Garry.

Pass of Killiecrankie, Perthshire: the River Garry.

Bannockburn, Stirling: statue of the Bruce.

Bannockburn Monument

STIRLINGSHIRE

The battle area has for the most part been built on. But about sixty acres around the Borestone were bought for preservation in 1930 and later given to the Trust. The purchase in 1930 was made from a public subscription which was raised by a national committee led by the Earl of Elgin, head of

The Hermitage, near Dunkeld, Perthshire.

the Bruce family. According to tradition the Borestone site was Bruce's command post before the battle, and takes its name from a large stone block with a socket in which it is said that he placed his standard. Only fragments remain.

On the 24th June 1964, the 650th anniversary of the battle, Her Majesty the Queen unveiled the statue of King Robert the Bruce which now stands on the site.

The statue, a bronze by C. d'O. Pilkington Jackson, was presented to the Trust by the King Robert the Bruce Memorial Fund Committee which had commissioned it.

An information centre, operated by the Trust in association with the Royal Burgh of Stirling, has been established beside the main road.

Falkland Palace, Fife: seventeenth-century Dutch bed in the King's Room; workmanship comparable to that of furnishing of Stuart royal bedrooms.

Falkland Palace

FIFE

Although no sovereign has lived at Falkland since Charles II and the Palace has been in the custody of hereditary keepers, it is still the property of the sovereign. In 1952 the present hereditary keeper (Major Michael Crichton-Stuart) appointed the National Trust for Scotland to be deputy keeper and

Falkland Palace, Fife: the Chapel Royal.

made over to the Trust an endowment for future maintenance of palace and gardens.

There were earlier buildings on the site but the Palace, which has been in part restored during the last eighty years, was built in the mid-fifteenth century and enlarged and improved about 1540. It was a hunting palace of many of the Stuarts, including James V and Mary Queen of Scots. James V made the sixteenth-century improvements in the palace in part, it seems, to welcome his French bride. He also had a tennis court built, the only real-tennis court in Scotland.

Charles II in 1650, on practically his last visit to Falkland, gave new colours to the troops selected to guard him. This is now considered to have been the christening of the Scots Guards. The regiment has retained a connection with Falkland. In 1958 it mounted guard when, on the occasion of the quincentenary of the royal burgh, the Queen visited there.

Misfortune occurred in 1653 when the East Range of the palace was burned, apparently by accident not design, during the occupation of the town and palace by Cromwellian troops.

During the eighteenth century and until 1855 maintenance of the fabric was neglected and the palace became ruinous. The hereditary keeper of that date, on the advice of Sir Walter Scott, began to restore it as a 'romantic ruin'. But in 1877 John Crichton-Stuart, third Marquess of Bute, became

The Giles, Pittenweem, Fife, restored under the Trust's Little Houses scheme.

Nos. 5 and 6 Rumford, Crail, Fife, restored under the Trust's Little Houses scheme.

hereditary keeper and set about the full restoration of the Gatehouse. His policy has been maintained, and today not only the Gatehouse has been restored but also the finely decorated *Chapel Royal*, and the *King's Room*, in the East Range, has been redecorated and refurnished. Since 1945 the Palace Garden has been re-created.

Beside the Palace Gatehouse is St Andrew's House, once occupied by a member of the royal household. This was restored and given to the Trust in 1952 by Major Michael Crichton-Stuart.

Little Houses, Pittenweem and Crail

FIFE

In 1960 the Trust formed a Little Houses Restoration Fund. This is being used to preserve the charm and individuality which many Scots burghs derive from their domestic architecture. Old houses of interest are bought, reconstructed to modern living standards and sold under safeguards—the proceeds of the sale being then available for another reconstruction. The illustrations on page 354 show what had once been two small seventeenth-century houses in an advanced state of disrepair now restored and made into one family-size house that complies with modern standards of comfort, and a block of seventeenth-century houses after reconstruction. Similar restorations have been carried out or are in progress in six other towns including *Dunkeld* (see page 345) and *Culross*.

The Binns

WEST LOTHIAN

three and a half miles east of Linlithgow on A 904

The site has been inhabited, traditionally, since Pictish times, but the house of the Binns (page 356) now is substantially early seventeenth-century, with some additional rooms acquired in the middle of the eighteenth century, and battlements early in the nineteenth century. The battlements were substituted

The Binns,
West Lothian.

A moulded plaster ceiling in the Binns.

for crow-stepping and pointed turrets. Four of the main rooms have very fine ornate *plaster ceilings* that date from 1612 to 1630. It has not been established whether this beautiful work was carried out by Italians or by Italian-trained Scots, though there is good evidence that the latter were concerned in it.

In 1944, when Eleanor Dalyell of the Binns gave it to the Trust, the house had been the home of the Dalyells for more than three hundred years. Included in the contents of the building, which formed part of her gift, are a number of interesting family portraits. Among those portrayed is the builder of the house, Thomas Dalyell. He had accompanied James VI to London in 1603 and there made such a fortune that on his return to Scotland nine years later, he was able to buy the Binns and enlarge and transform the house. Also, there is his son, the famous General Tam Dalyell of the Binns. It was in 1681, while he was commander-in-chief of the forces in Scotland, that the regiment which became known as the Royal Scots Greys was formed and held its first musters at the Binns. Succeeding generations of the family have given loyal and gallant service in the armed forces of the Crown, and Sir John Graham Dalyell, author of works on a variety of subjects, was knighted in 1836 for his services to literature and science.

Phantassie Doocot, East Linton

EAST LOTHIAN

Phantassie Doocot, as the illustration on page 359 shows, is a highly picturesque building. Its round walls, which are four feet thick at the base, project upwards to a horseshoe embracing the roof and giving the 'doos' a sheltered southern exposure. It has been suggested that the builder got his idea for the design from southern France. It has nesting-places for five hundred birds. The date of its building is not known, but many 'dowcots', as they were then known, were built during the sixteenth century, as an Act of 1503 required lords and lairds to make such provision for food supply. By 1617 so many had been built that they had become an embarrassment to the authorities. So, the latter announced that because of 'the frequent building of doucottis by all manner of personnes', the privilege would be restricted to those owning a specified amount of land.

Hamilton House, Prestonpans, East Lothian.

Hamilton House, Prestonpans

EAST LOTHIAN

Hamilton House was scheduled for demolition in 1937 under a road-widening scheme, but was later reprieved and acquired by the Trust.

It was built in 1628 by John Hamilton, who is referred to as a prosperous Edinburgh burgess. It has had two tastes of military life, having been used as a barracks while there was the threat of a Napoleonic invasion, and earlier (by repute), occupied by Prince Charles Edward's troops after the battle of Prestonpans.

Edinburgh,
Charlotte Square.

Phantassie Doocot,
East Linton,
East Lothian.

Preston Mill, East Linton

EAST LOTHIAN

Preston Mill on the River Tyne is a delightfully picturesque group of buildings and it is a subject much favoured by artists. It is also a working mill, being (it is believed) the oldest water-mill in Scotland which is still in operation. The machinery was renovated for the Trust a few years ago by Messrs Joseph Rank Ltd. In addition to the mill building itself, the photograph on page 361 shows the grain-drying kiln. This is the building with the conical roof, which looks as though it might, perhaps, be an oast house. It is connected to the mill by a stairway. The grain is dried by underfloor heating, and the cowl at the top of the roof turns with the wind to clear the smoke. Its projecting rudder is known locally as the Long Arm of Friendship.

The mill was given to the Trust in 1950 by the trustees of the late Mr John Gray and money for restoration work raised through a public appeal.

Nos. 5–7 Charlotte Square, Edinburgh

MIDLOTHIAN

These houses (page 359) are on the north side of a square designed by Robert Adam in 1792 and, so far at least as the north side is concerned, completed almost exactly as he intended. It is easy for layman and expert alike to endorse Sir Basil Spence's verdict on one of the finest squares in Europe: 'It is here that we find civic architecture at its best, created by a master.'

Nos. 5, 6 and 7 were accepted by the Treasury in part payment of death duty on the estate of the fifth Marquess of Bute and given to the Trust in 1966.

No. 5, of which the National Trust for Scotland has been tenant since 1950, is the headquarters of the Trust. Nos. 6 and 7 have been let—No. 6 to a group of distinguished Scots who are collectively the Bute Trustees and have renamed it Bute House. They intend to furnish it as the official residence of the Secretary of State for Scotland.

Preston Mill, East Linton, East Lothian.

Turret House, Kelso, Roxburghshire.

Turret House, Kelso

ROXBURGHSHIRE

Turret House, though altered and enlarged during the eighteenth and nineteenth centuries, was probably built in the seventeenth to contain two or perhaps three sets of apartments.

It was restored by the Trust in 1965 with the co-operation of St Andrew's Episcopal Church, Kelso, to whom it is now leased as a church hall.

Provan Hall, Glasgow

LANARKSHIRE

Provan Hall, near Stepps (page 364), built in the fifteenth century, is probably the most perfectly preserved pre-Reformation mansion-house in Scotland.

It was given to the Trust in 1935 by a group of people who also had the building restored.

Bachelors' Club, Tarbolton

AYRSHIRE

Among Trust properties associated with famous Scotsmen there are two associated with Robert Burns—*Souter Johnnie's Cottage* in Kirkoswald and the Bachelors' Club in Tarbolton. The club was formed about 1780, and for their meetings Burns and his friends used the small stone house dating from the seventeenth century which is illustrated on page 364. It is said that Burns became a Freemason here. The Trust acquired the property in 1938. It now contains a small museum.

Culzean Castle

AYRSHIRE

ten miles south-west of Ayr

The Trust's guide-book to Culzean (page 365) refers to the castle's 'romantic shell and Georgian interior'. That is a classic example of the understatement which tersely points towards the whole glorious truth.

Culzean stands on the site of a medieval castle. It would be hard to find

Provan Hall, near Stepps, Glasgow, Lanarkshire.

Bachelors' Club, Tarbolton, Ayrshire.

Culzean Castle, Ayrshire.

a more romantic natural setting or more beautiful man-made approaches. The transformation of the old castle and the design and decoration of its 'Georgian interior' was no routine exercise by eighteenth-century craftsmen, but the work of Robert Adam himself.

About 1770, just before the work of transformation began, Culzean belonged to the ninth Earl of Cassillis, whose family (the Kennedys) had played their part in many warlike encounters since medieval times. The ninth Earl's interests lay in peaceful pursuits. He was active in improving standards of farming on his estate, and made some additions to the old castle. His brother, who succeeded him in 1775, employed Adam first to reconstruct the old castle internally, then to build a brew-house and later to demolish the seaward side of the castle and build it anew. Adam's brew-house was replaced a hundred years later by the present west wing, which accords satisfactorily with the older parts of the building.

While at work on the castle itself Adam also designed the archway and viaduct at the approach to the castle, and farm buildings in the grounds.

In designing the exterior of Culzean, Adam was concerned to provide his patron not with a strong place capable of withstanding siege, but a

Culzean Castle, Ayrshire: the Round Drawing Room.

romantic, castle-like building of a style then in vogue. He brought to this task both the memory of his youthful study of Scottish traditional styles and all that he had seen of castles in Italy.

For the interior he designed a grand central staircase with elaborate gilt balusters and large columns. This links all the great apartments on the first two storeys.

In the 'Eating Room' (since converted to being the Library), the *Round Drawing Room* and the Long Drawing Room, he exercised to the full his genius for decoration. Ceilings, fireplaces and mirrors and other fittings are to his design.

In the grounds of the castle, the walled garden was established in the 1780's. This is devoted partly to roses and subtropical plants and partly to flowers, peaches and other fruits. The rest of the grounds were laid out during the earlier part of the eighteenth century. A profusion of flowers border the Avenues; there is a Camellia House and other ornamental garden buildings.

Culzean remained in the possession of the Kennedy family during the nineteenth century, the twelfth Earl of Cassillis being created Marquess of Ailsa in 1831. His great-grandson (the third Marquess of Ailsa) carried out the Victorian changes in the castle and improved the gardens, establishing rare trees and shrubs there. In 1945 the fifth Marquess gave the castle and 565 acres to the Trust.

In 1946 a flat in the castle was put at the disposal of the late ex-President Dwight D. Eisenhower as a token of Scotland's thanks for his services as Supreme Commander of the Allied Forces in the Second World War.

Souter Johnnie's Cottage, Kirkoswald, Ayrshire: figures of Souter Johnnie and the innkeeper's wife.

Souter Johnnie's Cottage, Kirkoswald

AYRSHIRE

The thatched house now known as Souter Johnnie's Cottage (page 367) was built in 1785 by John Davidson, the village cobbler of Kirkoswald, and he lived in it for the next twenty years. Burns knew Davidson well and took him as prototype for Souter Johnnie in *Tam O'Shanter.*

The house has been furnished with contemporary furniture, including things used by the Souter's family and a cobbler's chair that was almost certainly his, and with Burns relics.

In the garden are life-size *stone figures* of Souter Johnnie and other characters from *Tam O'Shanter* which were carved in 1802 and exhibited in various parts of Scotland and England before being brought to the cottage in 1924.

Appendix

Properties not illustrated

Properties which are not illustrated and are not referred to in the notes that accompany the illustrations are noted below.

Restrictive Agreements

In addition to property owned, the Trust for Scotland has Restrictive Agreements over lands in Kirkcudbright and other counties, and over several houses of architectural importance. (See note in Introduction.)

Properties under the guardianship of the Ministry of Works

Arrangements have been made for several properties to be placed in the guardianship of the Ministry of Works. These are:

The Stones of Clava near Culloden Moor in Inverness-shire. Stone circles dating from about 1600 B.C.

In Culross the 'Palace', which was built around 1600 and has decorative painted interior woodwork.

Castle Campbell near Alloa in Clackmannanshire dates from late in the fifteenth century.

Scotstarvit Tower near Cupar, Fife, a fine seventeenth-century tower.

Threave Castle, Kirkcudbrightshire, a fourteenth-century Douglas stronghold on Threave Island in the River Dee.

Other properties are as follows

ROSS AND CROMARTY

Braemore, Wester Ross: Corrieshalloch Gorge, a spectacular mile-long gorge and the 150-foot Falls of Measach.

Inverewe. Inverewe Stage House was an abandoned army camp between Inverewe Garden and Poolewe village. It has now been turned by the Trust and Shell & B.P. (Scotland) Ltd into a caravan and camp site.

Strome Ferry, Wester Ross, ruins of the ancient Strome Castle which was destroyed in 1603.

Morvich Caravan Site, Wester Ross, by Loch Duich on A87. Small camping site (space for 20 caravans) opened 1966.

Fair Isle, Zetland. The most isolated inhabited island in Britain was acquired by the Trust in 1954, with the help of a grant from the Dulverton Trust. Housing and other improvements have been made with a view to retaining the existing population and encouraging new families to settle. A bird observatory was founded here in 1948 by Mr George Waterston. About three hundred species have been noted and there are breeding colonies of great and arctic skuas. Access (twice weekly in summer) by mailboat from Shetland. A hostel for bird-watchers accommodates 14. Apply to warden.

NAIRN

Auldearn, Boath Doocot. Seventeenth-century dovecote on the site of an ancient castle.

ARGYLL

At Burg, Mull, two thousand acres of farmland in south-west Mull.

DUMFRIES

In Ecclefechan, Carlyle's birthplace, the Arched House built by his father and uncle (master masons both) in 1791. It now houses some of Carlyle's letters and belongings. Given by the Carlyle's House Memorial Trust in 1935 at the same time as they gave to the National Trust the house in which he lived in London.

ABERDEEN

In Aberdeen, Shiprow, Provost Ross's House. Built 1593 and the oldest house in Aberdeen. Now the north of Scotland headquarters of the British Council.

PERTHSHIRE

Dunkeld. Stanley Hill, an artificial mound of 1730 given to the Trust in 1958, provides a wooded background to the 'little houses' (page 347).

Craigower and Linn of Tummel. The Trust has two small properties close to Pitlochry in Perthshire. At Craigower, though only thirteen hundred feet up, there is a viewpoint which commands wide views over country typical of the Perthshire highlands. Eleven acres here were given to the Trust in 1947. A mile or so from Craigower, near the Pitlochry–Blair Atholl road, are fifty acres of the banks of the Tummel and the Garry, given to the Trust in 1944. This property adjoins the Trust's property in the Pass of Killiecrankie.

The Linn of Tummel was formerly known as the Falls of Tummel. Development of hydro-electric schemes in the area has taken off some of the Tummel water so the falls can no longer claim to be spectacular, but the river and the woodlands provide a delightful walk.

Perth. Branklyn Garden, a small garden (two acres) with an outstanding collection of plants, particularly alpines. Bequeathed with endowment by Mr John G. Renton, who with his wife made it. The City of Perth is giving practical support in its maintenance.

Menstrie Castle was the birthplace of Sir William Alexander, James VI's Lieutenant for the Plantation of New Scotland, an object furthered by the creation of Nova Scotia baronetcies. The castle is not Trust property, but the latter has had rooms in the castle decorated as Commemoration Rooms. Coats of arms of 107 existing baronets are displayed.

CLACKMANNAN

At Dollar Glen, the paths and bridges which provide attractive walks to the castle were restored after a public appeal for funds in 1950.

FIFE

Balmerino Abbey. Ruins of a thirteenth-century Cistercian monastery.

Culross. In addition to the 'Palace' (under guardianship of the Ministry of Works) the Trust owns other property in Culross. The Study, the Ark and Bishop Leighton's House have been restored. The Study is open at advertised times. Other buildings are being restored as funds permit.

The ruins of St Mungo's Chapel (five miles east of Kincardine off A 985) built 1503 on the traditional site of the saint's birth, were presented to the Trust by the Earl of Elgin in 1947.

Near Cupar, Hill of Tarvit, a late seventeenth-century mansion-house given with its contents and a farming estate. Leased to the Marie Curie Memorial Foundation as a convalescent home.

Kirkcaldy, Sailors' Walk, a harbour-side group of seventeenth-century merchants' houses.

WEST LOTHIAN

Linlithgow, Nos. 44 and 48 High Street. Sixteenth–early seventeenth century. Not open.

South Queensferry, in the main street, Plewlands House. Built 1643. Threatened with demolition. Given to the Trust in 1953. Not open.

Edinburgh, Caiy Stone, a nine-foot-high monolith by Oxgangs Road, Fairmilehead, of which no history is known.

Edinburgh. Malleny, Balerno: early seventeenth-century three-storey stone-built house. Garden with herbaceous and shrub borders, yew trees and a doocot which is possibly eighteenth-century. House not open. Given by Mrs Gore-Browne Henderson, with endowment.

Gladstones's Land, No. 483 Lawnmarket, Edinburgh. Built 1620 and originally the home of an Edinburgh burgess, Thomas Gladstones. It has remarkable painted wooden ceilings. Leased to the Saltire Society and used also by the Trust as an information centre.

Stenhouse Mansion, off Stenhouse Road, Edinburgh. An early seventeenth-century merchant's house in which the Trust has now established a centre for the study and restoration of Scottish tempera paintings.

Leith. Lamb's House, Burgess Street. Five-storey merchant's residence and warehouse of about 1600. Now a day centre for Leith Old People's Welfare Council, which helped with its restoration.

Inveresk Lodge, Inveresk. Mainly early seventeenth century. House not open. Garden open.

LANARK

Three miles west of Lanark, Blackhill, Stonebyres, a viewpoint with a commanding view of the Clyde Valley.

DUMBARTON

Bucinch and Ceardoch, two of the thirty islands in Loch Lomond.

On Castlehill, Dumbarton, the cairn erected in 1937 in memory of R. B. Cunninghame Graham. Reputedly on the site of the castle where Robert the Bruce died.

RENFREW

Kilbarchan. Kilbarchan Weaver's Cottage, an eighteenth-century cottage that was used by a hand-loom weaver. Now houses an excellent collection of hand-loom weavers' equipment and types of workmanship.

Port Glasgow. Parklea Farm, a strip of land on the south bank of the Clyde leased to the town council as a recreation ground.

New Galloway, Bruce's Stone, a granite boulder on Moss Raploch where Bruce defeated the English in 1307.

At Rockcliffe, near Dalbeattie; Mote of Mark, the site of an ancient hill fort; on Rough Island a bird sanctuary; and fifty acres of rough coastline between Rockcliffe and Kippford.

At Castle Douglas, the gardens of Threave House, which are open to the public, are used for two-year gardening courses for youths from all over Britain. The house and thirteen-hundred-acre estate were given with endowment in 1948 by the late Major A. F. Gordon of Threave. There has also been established on the estate, on and near the River Dee, a roosting and feeding place for wildfowl. There is controlled access to this Threave Wildfowl Refuge.

ISLE OF GIGHA

On the Isle of Gigha, west of Kintyre, a collection of valuable plants, including rhododendron hybrids.

These are in the garden of Sir James Horlick, who presented them to the Trust in 1962, with an endowment. Under a propagation programme many of the plants are being established in the Trust's own gardens. The Gigha collection is open to visitors during the summer.

LITTLE HOUSES

Some of the work which the Trust has done at Dunkeld, at Crail and at Pittenweem, with the help of the Little Houses Restoration Fund, is the subject of illustrations and notes on pages 345–7 and 354–5. Elsewhere similar work has been completed or is in progress as funds permit. The Trust has summarized the position as showing work completed at Anstruther (The White House, two houses restored as a shop and a flat, St Ayles' Chapel adapted for use as a Fisheries Museum); at Cellardyke (No. 1 Dove Street and No. 1 Harbour Head); at Dysart (The Anchorage; also the Trust is acting as agent for the Commissioners for Crown Estates in the restoration of a group of cottages at the Shore, the first of which is complete); at St Monance, 4–5 West Shore; and at North Berwick, The Lodge, a group of buildings in Quality Street; while further work is in progress or has been planned at Anstruther, Crail, Dysart, Pittenweem and St Monance. At Crail, restoration of the Customs House as a dwelling has been completed.

Index